REV. O. G. RAGAN.

HISTORY OF LEWIS COUNTY, KENTUCKY

By

REV. O. G. RAGAN,

Pastor Grace Methodist Episcopal Church,
Newport. Kentucky

FIRST EDITION

Southern Historical Press, Inc.
Greenville, South Carolina

This volume was reproduced
from a personal copy located in
the Publishers private library

Please direct all correspondence and book orders to:
SOUTHERN HISTORICAL PRESS, Inc.
PO Box 1267
Greenville, SC   29602-1267

Originally printed: Cincinnati, OH. 1912
ISBN #978-1-63914-045-9
Printed in the United States of America

DEDICATION

Just as the original book was dedicated to the author's wife, so this reprinting is dedicated to Mrs. Lenna Ragan, widow of the late author, Reverend O. G. Ragan.

The members of The Lewis County Historical Society wish to express most sincere appreciation to Mrs. Ragan for her gracious consent to the reprinting of this rare book, so that the new generations of the present and future can have the opportunity to learn of their heritage and to take pride in the achievements of those who were here before them.

Lewis County Historical Society

Mrs. O. G. Ragan.

To

My Wife and Co-laborer

IN THIS COMPILATION THIS BOOK IS
AFFECTIONATELY DEDICATED.

O. G. R.

INTRODUCTION

DEAR READERS: We have gleaned the material for these pages from every known source, and have spent many days and months in arranging these facts that you might not only be pleased, but instructed. Now, as we present this volume to you, receive it and read it in the spirit in which it is written, and we will be happy.

We owe a debt of thanks to our many friends for the cheerful assistance rendered; and especially do we thank Messrs. J. S. Mavity, John H. McCann and J. B. Bradley for their personal interest and zeal for the successful publication and distribution of this book.

It is proper and right to say that the author is responsible for the historical facts; but for the biographical sketches others are responsible.

Very sincerely,

O. G. RAGAN.

PREFACE

THE richest heritage of any generation is the heroism and valor of a noble ancestry. The mind and the heart are the only secure places for such a glorious heritage. From lip to ear, or from printed page to eye, are the only methods by which such values are handed down. He who collects and puts in lasting form for us the items of such inheritance has done us service that exceeds all possible compensation.

The only apology offered by the author for the production of this book is a desire to render to the former and present citizens of Lewis County that enduring service of a connected history of their devoted fathers.

What is dearer to us than the traditions of our fathers? What is sweeter than the loving service of our mothers? To have a book telling us of the heroic deeds of our ancestors is a privilege few possess; but with such we are favored in the possession of this book. It tells us that these fertile fields were once peopled with trees and clinging vines that yielded to the swing of the axman's blade in the hand of our fathers. It tells us that the smiling meadows were once the wilderness home of the

7

treacherous Red Man, and were bought for us
at the price of blood and life. It tells us that
these laughing brooks and streams that now
sing their songs of wealth and plenty were once
the battle lines of our sires contesting with the
savage for a home in the wilds. These templed
hills of Lewis County that echo the call of the
happy plowman or the laughter of the merry
milkmaid had their first silence broken by the
crack of the rifle and the groan of the suffering
pioneer.

But lost in the midst of the gathering years
are the glories of those struggling heroes. Buried
in unmarked graves of sacred soil are the forms
of our immortal dead—forgotten their work;
unsung their praises; unthanked their service.

From the fast-fading memory of the oldest
inhabitants the author has gathered the folk-
lore and traditions that render the unwritten
records of Lewis County; and with much care
and toil, from documents and letters fading
with age, he has gathered the authentic history
and put it all in a form convenient and permanent.

So that now while the ivy, myrtle, and
clambering wild-rose drape with fadeless green
and recurring blossom the resting-places of our
loved and own, in the chimney seat or parlors
of our God-blest "Home, Sweet Home" we

shall read the records of their loving toil. Or while the winter snow blankets with the emblem of purity the narrow beds of the silent dead; or while the wintry winds chant the requiem of peace over those tired but resting servants of the past—with this book in hand we will revive our thoughts and increase our love as we read again and again the undying deeds of our noble sires; and we will drop our tears of gratitude and love to the memory of our precious mothers, those Madonnas of the Woods and Hills.

GEORGE WALTER BUNTON.

Covington, Ky., June 1, 1912.

Six-Mile View of Vanceburg.

CONTENTS

CHAPTER I

PAGE

EARLY SETTLEMENTS: SALT LICK, KINNICONNICK, QUICK'S RUN, CABIN CREEK, SYCAMORE, POPLAR FLAT, CONCORD, TOLLESBORO, VANCEBURG, CLARKSBURG, QUINCY, VALLEY, PETERSVILLE, GARRISON, AND BURTONVILLE.............. 15

CHAPTER II

COUNTY ORGANIZATION: ACT RELATING TO—FIRST COUNTY SEAT—FIRST COURT—REMOVAL OF COUNTY SEAT TO CLARKSBURG—RIVAL TOWNS —REMOVAL TO VANCEBURG — CONVENIENCES AND INCONVENIENCES ARISING THEREFROM— CHANGE OF COUNTY OFFICES—THE INFIRMARY —GROWTH OF VANCEBURG—WISE HEADS WHO BOUGHT PROPERTY AT THE RIGHT TIME—PRESENT CONDITION OF THE CITY—ITS HOPES FOR THE FUTURE.............................. 87

CHAPTER III

LEGISLATIVE ACTS IN FAVOR OF THE COUNTY...... 137

CHAPTER IV

SUCCESSION OF OFFICERS—LIST OF REPRESENTATIVES—POLITICS—ISSUES IN THE VARIOUS CAMPAIGNS—DELEGATES TO THE CONSTITUTIONAL CONVENTIONS................................. 240

CHAPTER V

COMMON SCHOOL SYSTEM—COMMISSIONER—SUPER-
INTENDENTS—BOARDS OF EDUCATION—TEACH-
ERS—GROWTH OF THE SCHOOL SYSTEM IN THE
COUNTY—DISTRICTS AND SCHOOLHOUSES...... 348

CHAPTER VI

WAR PERIODS: INDIANS—SOLDIERS OF 1812 AND
1861 — COMPANIES ORGANIZED — OFFICERS —
NUMBER OF ENLISTED MEN—THOSE KILLED IN
ACTION—G. A. R. POSTS—MONUMENTS....... 362

CHAPTER VII

PUBLIC ROAD SYSTEM: MACADAMIZED ROADS—
ORIGINATORS OF IN THE COUNTY—THE FIRST
BUILT—NUMBER NOW IN THE COUNTY, AND
LOCATION—COST OF CONSTRUCTION—COUNTY
SUBSCRIPTION—PRESENT ROAD SYSTEM....... 367

CHAPTER VIII

BIOGRAPHY OF IMPORTANT MEN: THE BAR—THE
PULPIT—THE FORUM—TEACHER—THE DOCTOR 375

CHAPTER IX

WEALTH OF THE COUNTY—POPULATION: CENSUS
OF 1810, 1820, 1830, 1840, 1850, 1860, 1870,
1880, 1890, 1900, 1910—AREA—OCCUPATIONS:
AGRICULTURE, HORTICULTURE, MINING, MAN-
UFACTURING — SOIL — CLIMATE — SOCIETY —
CHURCHES—SUNDAY SCHOOLS—SECRET SOCI-

PAGE

ETIES—WATER TRANSPORTATIONS—RAILROADS
—POLITICAL PARTIES—NEWSPAPERS—PUBLIC
DEBT—CAPITATION AND PROPERTY TAXES—
DIVISION OF COUNTY FUND—MAGISTERIAL DIS-
TRICTS AND VOTING PLACES—MAP.......... 464

CHAPTER X

ANECDOTES AND TRADITIONS—CLOSING REMARKS.. 490

HISTORY OF LEWIS COUNTY, KENTUCKY

CHAPTER I

EARLY SETTLEMENTS: SALT LICK, KINNICONNICK, QUICK'S RUN, CABIN CREEK, SYCAMORE, POPLAR FLAT, CONCORD, TOLLESBORO, VANCEBURG, CLARKSBURG, QUINCY, VALLEY, PETERSVILLE, GARRISON, AND BURTONVILLE.

THE HISTORY of Lewis County begins contemporaneously with that of the State of Kentucky, for within its borders Vanceburg was one of the landing places for emigrants who came from Pennsylvania down the Ohio to the famous hunting grounds of "Old Kainturckee." It is stated in Collins' History of this State that the first horses brought to Kentucky were landed from a flat boat at the mouth of Salt Lick Creek, and that there was a marked trail from the salt works at Vanceburg up the creek and on past Burtonville to the Cane Ridge Settlement in Bourbon County.

Lewis County was formed from Mason County in 1806. Its first county seat was at Poplar Flat, and the logs which formed it are still extant, and are now builded into a barn on the farm of John McCormick. The county was named in honor of Captain Merriweather Lewis, the great explorer, and was the forty-eighth in order of formation. It is situated in the northeastern portion of the State, and is bounded on the east by Greenup, on the south by Carter, Rowan, and Fleming; on the west by Fleming and Mason Counties; and on the north by the Ohio River to the extent of forty miles. Its surface is much diversified by hill and dale, and watered by many creeks whose sparkling depths, clear as crystal, are full of fish of many kinds.

Among the principal streams are Kinniconnick, Salt Lick, in the eastern portion of the county; and Sycamore, Crooked Creek, and Cabin Creek in the western; and Mud Lick, Buck Lick, and North Fork of Licking in the southern portion.

Products.—The valleys of the Ohio and the creeks are very productive of all the cereals and roots usual to the Western country. The eastern portion is of free-stone formation, and produces the best of stone for building purposes. It is also famous for tan-bark, hoop-poles, staves, and cross-ties. The southeastern portion is of limestone formation, and the uplands are generally very productive as well as the bottoms.

The timber of this section consists of oak, ash, hickory, walnut, maple, dogwood, and kindred growths, which at one time densely covered the virgin soil and was the natural bivouac of the Red Man and the bear. But mighty changes have taken place here also, and the forest and its untamable occupants have given place to the fields of golden grain, rich pasturage, and the beautiful homes of peaceful citizens.

Fruits.—The county is noted for its apples, peaches, pears, plums, and all the small fruits.

Exports.—Cattle, hogs, tobacco, corn, wheat, timber, lumber, cross-ties, and cooperage.

Mineral Waters.—There are many mineral springs in the county, the most noted of which are McCormick, Esculapia, and Glenn Springs, at the head of Salt Lick Creek. Esculapia was a famous watering place in 1840 and 1850 under the management of Gould & Company. Its buildings were allowed after this to fall into decay, and in 1860 were destroyed by fire. Within the last few years the place has been re-built and modernized, and under the management of Walker Bros. bids fair to become the most popular watering place along the Ohio River.

There are other wells and springs, the most important of which are the Salt Wells, near Vanceburg, and Kirk Springs, near Burtonville.

2

The salt wells have long since been abandoned, and the charcoal remains of the salt furnaces testify to their exact location and stand as a souvenir to daring deeds of the pioneer, while the Indian mounds on the hills just above as fully testify who were their wily foe and cunning adversary.

Minerals.—Of minerals near Vanceburg, we quote Collins' History, page 467:

"Near Vanceburg, in this county, is a large quarry of slate stone; and immediately at the water's edge at a common stage of the river, at the same place, is a quarry of white limestone rock, which produces remarkably white lime, and is said to contain from fifty to sixty per cent of magnesia. Free white or sand stone is found in great abundance on the Ohio, a few miles from Vanceburg, where there is also a large quarry of alum rock. On Salt Lick Creek, near Vanceburg, there is a copperas bed, from which the people of the county supply themselves with that article; and one mile distant there is an extensive blue clay bank, suitable for stone ware and fire brick. There are also in the neighborhood two salt wells, three hundred feet deep, which afford a large quantity of water, from which this part of the State was formerly supplied with salt."

There has also been a lot of zinc discovered

near the mouth of Quicks Run, and it is said a silver mine exists on the same creek. Also silver has been found on "Kinney" in the days gone by, and is supposed to have been mined and minted by one Waite, who came over from Adams County, Ohio.

Survey.—The first survey within the bounds of Lewis County was made in Forman's bottom by Captain Thos. Bullett, in June, 1773. The land was afterward sold to William Triplette, who came to it in 1776. (See "Collins' History," page 465.)

Surface.—Ours is a hill county, with narrow but fertile valleys. Along the river front the hills are much higher than those in the interior, and also the valley along the Ohio, in places, is wide, level, and fertile, with few swampy sections as is common along some parts of the river.

Going further back into the county you find the surface broken by high hills, but for the most part tillable. Along the principal streams you find the most level land, although there are broad plateaus of very rich soil on the uplands.

Our county is not made principally in hills or valleys, but there are parts of the country gently sloping plateaus of very rich soil. In fact, there is scarcely a part of our county but can be utilized in one way or another to the great advantage of our farmers, either in tillable soil or pasture lands.

In those sections of the county where is the really rough part, high cliffs and deep gorges break the earth's surface. Here, too, is found the most rugged scenery in great boulders, tall trees, and the ivy clinging to the precipitous cliffs in absolute profusion. Here is found the nest of the eagle and the den of the fox and mountain lion.

Towns. — The principal towns are Vanceburg, the county seat; Clarksburg, Tolesboro, Fire Brick, Quincy, Garrison, Concord, Sand Hill, Poplar Flat, Petersville, Burtonville, and Valley.

Manufacturies.—The manufacturing industry is chiefly confined to lumber mills at several points in the county; flour mill, a button factory, and can factory, hogshead heading mill, spoke factory, saw mill, and planing mill at Vanceburg.

There are still great possibilities in the quarrying and manufacturing of freestone blocks. There is a brick plant at Fire Brick of large capacity, and at Garrison is a heading mill and spoke mill.

Religion.—Chief among the denominations represented in the county are the Methodist and Southern Methodist, Disciples, Baptist, Presbyterian, and New Light Disciples Church.

Salt Lick.—As Salt Lick seems to be connected with the first route from the river back to the settlements, we would suppose that settlers would probably be attracted to it sooner than to other parts, and for this reason we will

Ox Team.

give the history of its early settlers first, as it has been related to us from the children of those who actually made the settlements. We refer to Elijah Thomas and Dudley Calvert, both dead. The following is as Mr. Calvert related it:

"The first cabin in the Salt Lick Valley, I think, was near the mouth of Dry Run, where the remains of the first salt furnaces are yet to be seen, about one mile from Vanceburg.

Where the next was I am not sure, but I think it was not far from the "fork," as it is called— say the farm owned by Mr. Bertram or the farm owned by Wm. E. Carrington. The first was made by John McDaniel, and the other by Isaac Halbert, the grandfather of Wm. C. Halbert, late of Vanceburg, now deceased. When we get on as far as the year 1800, there were several cabins in different parts of the valley, occupied by the Carringtons, Thomas, Shortridges, Campbells, Wilsons, Johnsons, Eshams, Cottinghams, Calverts, Melsons, Harpers, Fishers, Davis, and others.

"We now come to the year 1806, that gave birth to our dear old Lewis County. Landon Calvert was the first justice of the peace for Lewis County after the county was organized. A Baptist Church was organized and an edifice erected in the primitive style of the times. The graveyard on the pike, near Mr. Bertram's residence, is where the old house stood. It is now among the things of the past. There was also another church building near where the Meffords lived, and this will bring us up to the year 1808. At this time there was some trouble to get corn ground for bread. There was a grist mill on the creek about one and a half miles below the Esculapia Springs; but it was said that a hungry hen could eat as much as it would grind. This mill was owned by one Wilson. After this a grist and saw mill was built near Clarksburg by Rowland T. Parker, and a horse mill was started near Bethel Church by Wm. Cordingly. A horse mill was started by Mr. Swearingen, and a grist and saw mill on Cabin Creek by Swearingen, and one near what was known as Old Union Church.

"But I have left Salt Lick Valley. I will now come to the year 1812, when the first steamboat passed down the Ohio. She was called the 'Orleans.' This year, '1811,' there were great shocks of earthquakes that alarmed the people very much, and also strange sounds in the air, crashing like the falling of many large trees, sometimes like drums beating. And in the year 1812 we all know was the beginning of the war with Mexico. There was much stir and commotion about this time among the people in the valley. Half of the young men volunteered this and the next year.

"The only school house in the valley was near where the Grange Hall stood. The first teacher occupying the old house was Edward Viers, or Veers. The scholars who attended school then are about all passed away. In the days spoken of we were much troubled by wild beasts of the forest, such as wolves, bears, panthers, wildcats, etc., so that it was hard to raise hogs or sheep, and even cattle and colts."

Some of the citizens of Salt Lick to-day will be interested to know the names of those old pioneers of a hundred years ago.

Beginning at Esculapia Springs, which was at that time a forest, never having been touched by the ax, the first man to begin improving was John Powling, an Englishman. He built a few rough houses, lived there a while, then moved to Maysville. The first improvement below the springs was by Jesse Melson. He cleared four acres of land, and built a cabin and moved in. The next to build, or rather to improve, was John McDaniel, who bought out Jesse Melson, and lived in this homestead until he died. This now leaves Mr. McDaniel the uppermost inhabitant of the valley.

We now come to what was known as the Carmack farm. This was owned by William Wilson. This old settler had several sons who built cabins on his land, one of which was built on the site of the old Jones' tanyard, and two others above and below the old home place in the same vicinity. One of the boys owned and operated a grist mill.

The next home was built by a man named Parker, from Ohio, and was afterwards known as the Cropper farm. In later years it was bought by Carmack, and became a part of his farm.

Down the creek farther was what was known as the Martin farm, first settled by Fisher and Joseph Melson, and was afterwards owned by Spurgin Melson, who built a grist mill and saw mill, then sold out to Martin.

The next farm down the valley is the Pugh farm, first settled by Henry Armstrong and afterwards sold to Daniel Thomas, who sold in turn to William Esham, and then was bought by Pugh. Down the valley, farther still, was the home of John Tulley, who seems to have been a tenant. John Tulley was the grandfather of John D. Tulley, of Cabin Creek. This place, after Tulley's time, was sold to Michael Dean, who sold to William Harper, and he sold to Daniel Thomas, and Thomas sold to Joseph Frizzell, and he to William Strade.

Next in order is the farm on which the above-named Harper lived when he owned both farms. The next home was owned by James McPike, and when trouble began to arise about land claims, McPike pulled up and left.

Next in order is the Campbell farm, owned by by an old Revolutionary War veteran. He served under Washington and fought at Brandywine Creek. Now comes the Calvert farm, settled by Landon Calvert in 1800. The Israel

Thomas farm is next in order, laid out by by Bartholomew Thatcher, and subsequently bought by Israel Thomas. The Carrington farm was laid out by Samuel Shortridge, then sold to Jesse B. Carrington, who lived and died there.

First Deaths, Births, and Marriages.—The first death was an infant son of Israel Thomas. The next was Landon Calvert. He was the first man that died, and was buried in the cemetery back of the old Baptist Church, long since torn down, and no one can tell the spot. It has long been a resort for cattle and sheep. The first birth was that of Sarah Thomas, March 16, 1802. The first marriages were Israel Thomas and Catherine Thomas, William Campbell and Mary Tulley, Henry Halbert and Sallie McDaniel, Archibald Frizzell and Alice Hance. The last of the early marriages was in the spring of 1805. The first settlers who belonged to any Church were Baptists, except George Thomas, who was a Presbyterian. William Carrington's family was grown when he arrived in the valley. His son Jesse taught the first school. The house stood on the pike, north of where the second tollgate used to stand, near the Valley post-office. Carrington married Margaret Esham, eldest daughter of William Esham.

It was here the author of a few notes for a part of this article, Elijah Thomas, witnessed his first dance. It was in the year 1809 or 1810, and the fiddler was Randall Smallin. He said one of the dancers was dressed in buckskin moccasins and hunter's shirt and trousers, with red fringe.

We have had a history of the early settlers and their deaths, births, and marriages; now we will study the people for a while. The Carrington people were well represented in the valley. In that early day the McDaniel family consisted of eight children, four boys and four girls, all grown to manhood and womanhood, and were married at the old homestead, except the eldest daughter, who died in childhood. Two sons and two daughters moved to Arkansas, and the eldest and youngest sons and the third daughter moved to Missouri. Ambrose, the eldest son, stopped in Rock House Prairie, Buchanan County, and was murdered by the guerrillas in 1864. Nancy Celia settled in the same county. She was the first woman to settle in Buchanan County, and died there in 1865. The youngest son, William, settled in Caldwell County, and was murdered by a highwayman. The same year, the "Squire," as he was called, after the death of his wife, sold the old home farm and bought the Halbert farm,

and built a tanyard. Soon after this he died,
and was buried by the side of his wife, on the
point of the hill in the woods on the east side
of the creek, opposite his old farm.

Landon Calvert had five sons and three
daughters, and all grew to maturity and married. After the death of the father, the widow
with her family, except the eldest and youngest
daughters, moved to Arkansas. The youngest
son came back among his people and made a
permanent home with them.

KINNICONICK.—Next in order comes the
settlements of Kinniconick, which are of about
equal date with those of Salt Lick. The Bruces
were, perhaps, the most conspicuous among
the early settlers of what is known as lower
Kinny. Henry C. Bruce, a father, I believe, of
a worthy citizen of Vanceburg bearing the
same name, settled at the mouth of Spy Run
in the year 1812, and built a mill at that place;
and shortly afterwards George W. Bruce, Sr.,
and his brother Alexander, commenced their
memorable career. At one time they had seven
water mills running on Kinny, four of them
sawing lumber, and three grinding grain. At
an early date in the history of our county, John
Craig located near the mouth of McDowell's
Run. About the same time J. Moore, Thomas
Clark, Basil Duke, and Abner Brightman set-

FISHING CAMP ON "KINNY."

tled on the same creek, above the mouth of the run. Oliver Dewey built a small cabin at the mouth of Trace Fork, and lived at that place about the time Lewis County was struck off from Mason. A short time afterwards, in 1807, Aaron Stratton and Basil Burriss located Kentucky land warrants on the west side of the main creek, opposite the mouth of Trace Fork, and lived upon their premises respectively for a number of years. The next early improvements on the creek, above the last named, was by Balden Smith, at the mouth of Town Branch, about five miles from Vanceburg, and is now occupied by a man named Conrad.(?) Major McDaniel, an old citizen then living on Salt Lick Creek, located a Kentucky land warrant at an early date on the creek, near and opposite the mouth of Laurel Fork, and settled a tenant upon it by the name of Morgan. About this time Ambrose D. McDaniel, a son of the old major, made an improvement on the Laurel, and went into the stock-breeding business, and finally sold out to Thomas Stone, Sr., and emigrated Westward. About this time the Bloomfields, Eulitts, Staggs, Dyers, Staffords, and others also commenced their careers on Laurel Fork. Simultaneously with these movements were those settlements made on what is known as Upper Kinny, or the Big Elk Fork, by McEldowneys, Wallingfords, Jones, Burriss, Rankins, and others. With a few exceptions, all these old citizens of Kinniconick have been gone for a number of years, and some of them have now not a single descendant left in the county to tell the story of their lives.

QUICK'S RUN.—The general course of Quick's Run is nearly east or a little north of east. This stream, for more than half its length, is only separated from the Ohio River by a ridge with many low gaps. Collins says, in his "History of Kentucky," that a line of forts was built on the Ohio River, in 1784, and fortified possession was taken of Kentucky, and was never after relinquished. So now, in the absence of any other historical information, we conclude that the old Block House Fort was built near the mouth of Quick's Run about this time, and that John G. McDowell was placed in command and was still in command when the Red Man gave up his beloved hunting ground for ever. Caldwell's "History of Adams County, Ohio," tells of two children being tomahawked and killed by the Indians near the mouth of Quick's Run. They were John and Obadiah Stout, children of Obadiah, Sr.

George Calvin, a noted Indian fighter, was then an inmate of the old Block House Fort, and gave aid to the settlers against any band of lurking Indians, and his services were marked, and his hatred for the Red Man was very bitter. Mr. John H. McCann tells us he was shown a spot, several years ago, by Samuel Ails, now deceased, that Calvin pointed out to him where he, Calvin, had killed an Indian. It happened about this way: In an early day it was the custom, when you turned your horses out to graze, to fasten a bell to the leader's neck so they would be easily found. On this particular morning the horse was wanted for some purpose, and search was made for it, but it could not be found. Finally the sharp ear of Calvin detected the sound of the bell far back in the forest on the side of the river hill. He became suspicious at once. Slipping away into the forest with his trusty rifle in hand, he crossed the ridge on the Quick's Run side, coming up behind the spot from which the sound of the bell was coming. He had a suspicion it was an ambuscade of one or more Indians, using the belled animal as a decoy. Moving silently and carefully through the forest, ever on the alert for Indian sign, he was finally rewarded. Looking just ahead of him, he saw an Indian standing watching the approach of the men from the valley. His intention was too plain to be mistaken. Calvin, raising his rifle, took deliberate aim and fired. The Indian leaped into the air with an

3

agonizing yell, and fell at the foot of the tree, a crumpled heap. Mr. Calvin died many years ago, and is buried near the old church at Martin, on Quick's Run, in an unmarked grave.

James Martin was another occupant of this fort, and while there, in 1793, his wife gave birth to a daughter. She was named Sarah, and afterwards became the wife of John Stalcup and the mother of B. C. Stalcup. Mr. B. C. Stalcup is still living near the mouth of the creek on a part of the old homestead, and is past eighty years of age.

Perry Martin, a relative of old James Martin, is still living at this date, and has reached the advanced age of ninety-four years. He was a soldier of the Civil War.

James Martin, after serving at the station for a year or two, moved from there and took up a large tract of land on the waters of Quick's Run, about two miles from the station on a stream that has ever after been called Martin's Fork. He remained here the rest of his life, and was buried on the farm. He has numerous descendants in the county. Mr. James Stricklett is the owner of the old farm at the present.

Jacob Stricklett was another occupant of this fort. He married Martha Cox, a widow, whose husband had been killed by the Indians. They were married in Adams County, Ohio, in

1798, and soon after settled near where Mr.
Thomas Irvin now lives, at the mouth of
Martin's Fork. He reared a numerous family,
and many of his descendants are living in the
county still. William G. Stricklett is a grand-
son, and Mr. Thomas Stricklett and son, of
Vanceburg, are all descendants of his. He died
many years ago, and is buried in the old burying
place near Martin.

Mr. Turner Davis came to what is now
Lewis County in 1796, and proved up on a
large tract of land extending from Martin's
Fork, up Quick's Run, including what has been
known in later years as the Henry Pell farm.
He had a large family, and settled them on land
around him. The old homestead is still standing, and, no doubt, is one of the oldest houses
in the county. John Doyal married one of his
daughters, Christena, in 1796, and settled on a
farm up the creek about one-half mile, on what
was known for years as the Doyal Branch. Mr.
Doyal was of Irish descent. He was born in
Maryland in 1762, and fought in the Revolutionary War. He came to Kentucky soon after,
and fought the Indians for several years. He
was one of the spies, in 1792, that ranged up and
down the Ohio River from Limestone (Maysville) to the mouth of Big Sandy River. (See
"Collins' History of Kentucky.") When Lewis

County was organized, in 1806, he was appointed justice of the peace, and occupied that office for several years. You will find his name prominent among the first officers of the county in its organization. He was a volunteer in the War of 1812, and served one year. The most of his life was spent in the service of his country. He died December 8, 1845, and was buried on his farm, and his grave is marked only by a grove of pine trees that are keeping vigil over the old warrior and pioneer's resting place. He left a large number of descendants: David M. Doyal, of Carrs; William T., of Martin, are his grandsons; and Mrs. Susie Ruggles, of Martin, is a grandaughter.

Another daughter of Turner Davis married Turner Nelson, and settled at the mouth of Nevel Branch. David, a son, settled on what is known as the William Pool farm, but did not remain there long, selling out to Mr. Shephard and moving farther West. The mother of the Hon. S. G. Hillis, deceased, was a daughter of this Mr. Shephard, and was born there in 1800, and married William Hillis, the father of S. G. Hillis.

Another daughter married Mose Arrns, and settled on what has been known for years as the Henry Pell farm. They had several children. One daughter, Sarah, born in 1800, married Henry Pell, and came into possession of the old farm. The whereabouts of the other descendants is unknown.

Mr. Pell was the father of several children, but most of them went West, and none now live in Lewis County.

The Ails family were early settlers on Quick's Run Creek. Benjamin Ails had a claim of several thousand acres of land near the mouth of the creek. They also had one or two water mills. Numbers of their descendants are still living in this county.

The Voires family were also early settlers, and many of the descendants are living on this creek and in the county.

The Thomas family were also early settlers on this creek. Plummer Thomas, who represented this and Greenup County in 1809 in the State Legislature, lived on the farm now owned by William Doyal.

John Carter, father of Thomas Carter, of Vanceburg, deceased, and of several other sons and daughters, settled on the farm now owned by Mose McVaney.

John and Elijah Cox settled on Martin's Fork in an early day, John on the farm where William Lawson now lives, and Elijah on the farm now owned by William Stricklett. They both built water mills in the forties, but have

long since died. The Millers ran these mills
until 1855, when a great cholera epidemic broke
out in Martin's Fork, and a large number of
the Bevens, Burrises, Kenards, and others, died
with this dreadful disease.

John Irvin, grandfather of Thomas M. Irvin,
Esq., of Martin, and Mrs. Elijah Graham, Mrs.
George Queen, Mr. Robert N. Irvin, of Manchester, Ohio, bought the farm now owned by
Elijah Graham and T. M. Irvin, of a Mr. Pitts,
in 1827. Also a water mill and a distillery.
Mr. Irvin discontinued the distillery, but operated the water mill for years, grinding both
wheat and corn. He took several boat loads of
flour to New Orleans. The mill has long since
gone down. Mr. Irvin's first wife, Margaret,
died March 13, 1839. Mr. Irvin died December 15, 1864.

John Greenhow emigrated from Yorkshire,
England, to the United States, and moved to
Lewis County and settled on Quick's Run. He
bought the old John Doyal farm. Several
children were born, who are among the best
citizens of our county. Mr. John Greenhow still
owns the old farm. Mr. Richard Greenhow, of
Vanceburg, is one of his sons. Mr. Greenhow
and his wife died several years ago, and their
lives were not in vain.

Nevel, a tributary of Quick's Run, was

named in honor of its first settler, who built a
home on this creek in an early day. Whatever
became of him is not known.

Thomas Essex was the next settler, and he
sold out to Edward B. McCann, in 1852. Mr.
McCann raised a large family, a part of which
is now dead. Edward and his wife, Elizabeth,
have long been dead. W: W. McCann, the
youngest son, still owns the old homestead.
William McCann was born in Pennsylvania in
1788 of Irish parents. His father's name was
John, and his mother's maiden name was Nancy
Culbreath. They came to Kentucky in a flatboat in 1792. The party was attacked by
Indians near the mouth of the Scioto River,
and some of the party were killed. They landed
at Limestone (Maysville), and went from there
out to Miller's Station, in Bourbon County;
and after the danger of Indians was passed, they
settled on a farm in what is now Nicholas
County, not far from Carlisle. Big John
McCann, as he was called, raised three boys—
William, James, and John. James went to Indiana in an early day, and his descendants live
now in Boone County, Indiana, and near Indi-
anapolis. John married and remained in Nicholas County. William came to Lewis County
and married Jane McKinzie, daughter of Alexander McKinzie, in 1812. In 1820 he bought

a farm of Samuel Cox, near the headwaters of Quick's Run. He and his wife raised a family of eight children—four boys and four girls. John, the oldest son, went to Illinois in 1839, where he died, leaving one son. Alexander was married twice, and raised a large family, and was a soldier in the Civil War. He is now dead. The third son, Edward, married Elizabeth Burris, a daughter of Abel Burris, one of the pioneer families of the county. Thomas, the fourth son, left a family of three children. One daughter, Ella, occupies the old homestead. Mary Ann, the oldest daughter, and also another daughter, Amanda, who never married. Nancy married a man by the name of Bolinger. They had no children. Ailsie married Morgan Cadwalader and had one son, and they live near Martin's on Quick's Run. William, his wife, and all of their children have long been dead. He was in the War of 1812, and witnessed the killing of Tecumseh, the great Indian chief.

Thomas Pool settled on the headwaters of Quick's Run in the early part of the last century. He served in the War of 1812, and was with Commodore Perry when he captured the English Fleet, Captain Barclay in command, and sent that great message to General Harrison, "We have met the enemy and they are ours." They landed then and helped General Johnson defeat

Tecumseh and the English, at the battle of the Thames, on October 5, 1813. Thomas Pool was truly a great and good man. He married a daughter of Alexander McKinzie, and was a brother-in-law to William McCann. He raised a family of several children, all of whom are dead. He has some grandchildren in the West. He died about 1853, and is buried in the old graveyard at Salem Church.

Shaw, Frank G., was born in New York in 1801, and moved to Decatur County, Ohio, with his parents. In an early day he moved from there to Ripley, Ohio, and learned the tanner's trade at Maysville, Ky. He moved from Ripley, O., to Vanceburg, Ky., in 1845, and went into the drygoods business in a little corner store, just below the old Cane's building. The next year he moved into the old Cane's building, on Front Street. He built a tanyard near Esculapia Springs, in 1846, and sold it to Jesse R. Grant, father of U. S. Grant, and bought a tanyard of the Grimes brothers, on Quick's Run, about two miles above the village of Martin, and took possession of it in 1847. He operated this tanyard two years, and then turned it over to his sons and moved back to Ripley, O., and bought a tanyard there, and operated it until 1865. He died at Washington C. H., O., in 1874. He married Harriet M.

Harden, and to this union were born seven
children. R. H. Shaw died four years ago on the
old farm near Muses Chapel, and is buried at
that place. Allan lived in Illinois, and died in
1911. E. A. lives on Salt Lick, was in the Civil
War, and is a jolly good fellow. Frank, Green,
and Alfred, we think, are all dead.

THE VILLAGE OF MARTIN.—G. L. Queen
and Thomas M. Irvin, general store and post-
officer; B. F. Jackson, grist mill and steam saw
milling; Thomas Jackson, blacksmithing; James
Stricklett, farmer and dealer in railroad cross-
ties and fence posts; C. E. Stout, physician and
surgeon; one Odd Fellows Lodge; one Independent Order of Red Men; Henry and Shumate,
farmers and blacksmiths; Elijah Graham, farmer
and poultry raiser. The town contains one
Christian Church, a fine building, and the
Church is in a flourishing condition; one fine
public school building, finished in 1911. Claude
and Forest Queen, farmers and dealers in fine
stock. William Kissick, retired farmer; John T.
Beven, L. M. Beven, Moses McVaney, Roland
Harvey, Morgan Cadwalader, S. B. Campbell, R.
O. Parish, W. W. McCann, George Greenhow,
Frank Greenhow, Robert Gilbert, John Doyal,
Arthur McCann, John L. Thoroughman are
farmers of marked ability and enterprise. Wil-
liam Lawson, mail carrier; a Methodist Episcopal

CHRISTIAN CHURCH AT MARTIN, ON QUICKS RUN.

Church, situated two miles above Martin, on Quicks Run, Rev. W. H. Morris, Pastor; W. H. Hughs, carpenter, and Eli Belyew, farmer.

JACKTOWN.—Craycraft and Henderson, dealers in drygoods and groceries, and post-office; Thomas Ruggles, blacksmith and general repair shop; Andrew Jackson, Thomas Burris, R. H. McCann, T. J. McKey, John McCall, Peter McCall, Thomas Manley, B. G. Kirkendall, Charles May, and John McCane are farmers of no mean ability of this community, and honored and respected citizens. William McCane, carpenter. There is one school house, District No. 25, near Jacktown.

AILS DISTRICT. — One schoolhouse, one Christian Church, Elder Hilderbrandt, Pastor. There is, running the length of Quicks Run, and then east up the river to Vanceburg, one turnpike road in very good condition.

CABIN CREEK.—Cabin Creek lies almost entirely in the limestone belt of Lewis County. Its course is very irregular, running, during its length of fifteen miles, towards nearly all points of the compass; but a straight line down from its source to its mouth would have a bearing of about N. 70° W. Its source is in a free-stone formation, and its upper waters is what is termed soft water. While the lower twelve miles, as it passes through the lime-stone, gradually loses its free-stone nature and changes to hard water. No section of Kentucky could boast of finer timber than grew along the hillsides and on the bottom lands of Cabin Creek. Sugar tree was the predominant growth, but black walnuts, blue ash, and black ash hickory, and red oak were abundant; and if the original black walnut trees were standing as they were in a state of nature, they would be worth on the market to-day, perhaps, half as much as the assessed valuation of the land. It was no uncommon thing to see one four feet in diameter and fifty or sixty feet without a limb. Such a tree, to-day, would pay for several acres of land; in fact, so plentiful was this timber, and so little did the early settlers value it, that not longer ago than twenty years a large per cent of the ordinary fence rails was of black walnut. Fully fifty per cent of the natural growth was sugar tree or hard maple, as it is usually called, and every farmer had his sugar camp opened each year as soon as the season would permit; and the sugar-making season was quite an active one.

Troughs were usually made of soft buckeye, which was admirably adapted to the purpose and seemed to grow in that locality for this purpose alone. The wood is soft and easily converted into troughs, but, lacking durability, great care was required in keeping them dry during the warm season. But alas for change! these primeval forests are mostly gone. The soil upon which they grew, when cleared, would produce large crops of any of the cereals, suited to the climate, such as corn, wheat, oats, potatoes, etc., and the sugar camp was made to give place to the cornfield. However, quite a number of the more thoughtful farmers on the creek have sugar tree orchards yet.

The timber growth on land usually indicates the quality of the soil, and while this is not at all times a safe guide, it may be taken as a very strong indication. Sugar tree, black walnut, blue ash, etc., may, at times, be found growing in inferior land, but it will be found characteristic of Lewis County, at least, that they never predominate on this soil.

The soil on Cabin Creek is a dark-brown loam, and is the most productive in the county. On many of the north slopes and in the bottoms it is frequently two feet deep. As an evidence of the fertility it may be as well to give an example. Mr. William Barkley had a bottom field measured by a surveyor, and then carefully measured the corn that grew on it one year, and found it produced a fraction more than one hundred bushels per acre.

About the year 1840 farmers began the cultivation of hemp, and found it to be a profitable crop. But few of them, however, engaged in its cultivation, owing to the fact that it involved a great deal of very hard labor; William Fenwick, John D. Tully, Chas. J. Tully, and John L. Bradley being the only men on the creek who made a regular business of it from year to year. The cultivation of tobacco was not begun to any great extent until about the year 1875, after the introduction of the white burley variety. From that time to the present tobacco raising has been the principal business of most of the farmers, obviously to the injury of the land. Tobacco raising has not proven a success to the farmers of Cabin Creek—they are poorer to-day, and their land is poorer than it would have been if they had never commenced its cultivation. Apparently twenty years' experience ought to convince them that it is best to abandon its cultivation altogether and go back again to stock and grain raising. The raising of tobacco, instead of adding to the wealth and prosperity of a community, is evidently an element of weakness to it, if long persisted in.

About the year 1854 or 1855 James H. Barkley introduced the short horn breed of cattle, and made a faithful effort to induce his neighbors to do the same thing; but the process was slow. Previously the stock of cattle was inferior, but gradually the scrubs were made to give place to superior stock; and principally through the persistent effort of Wm. Barkley, assisted a few years later by Harlan Teagar, Cabin Creek can boast to-day of as good cattle as are to be found anywhere. However, they were twenty-five years in doing what might have been done in ten.

Strange as it may seem, reform along all lines are slow in their operation. People seem inclined to hold on to old ideas and habits until forced by circumstances to let them go; and in no case is this peculiarity more rapidly carried out than in an effort to improve stock. Farmers, by the way, and very much to their own disadvantage, take hold of improvements more sluggishly than any other class of men. Even in this advanced age, when the demand is for the best of everything, many of them persist in handling inferior varieties of stock, vegetables, fruits, grains, etc. There is no paying market for an inferior article when the superior is obtainable, and the sooner the farming element of our country learns this truth the better it will be for them. "Produce a less quantity and a better quality," should be the motto of every farmer.

The geological character of Cabin Creek is peculiar in that its rocks seem to have been

4

formed, almost exclusively, of the remains of sea animals. The loose surface stones, especially, are the pure fossiliferous limestone. Every rock is a study for the geologist, and various kinds of petrified sea animals may be found along any of the tributaries of the creek, while in places, for instance in the vicinity of Cottageville, the geological specimens are plentiful and interesting, especially to any one who delights in tracing the origin of things along dim lines. He might ask, "How did these little creatures get so far away from their natural home?"—at least six hundred miles from the nearest sea water, and fully four hundred feet from the sea level. "What great upheavel of nature located them where they are? What mysterious power changed them from animal life to indestructible stone? Has our old world yet assumed its unchangeable makeup?" And many more questions of a like character might suggest themselves to the scientist—all of which we leave for him to answer. While timber growth is a strong indication of the quality of the soil upon which it stands, yet it is only an indication, but rocks may be taken as a proof, and all soil having fossiliferous limestone as its basic mineral principle is rich in the elements of plant food. The entire slopes of Cabin Creek, excepting a few of its upper tributaries, are abundantly supplied with this stone; in fact many of the hillsides facing the south have them so abundantly as to be somewhat in the way when plowing, but they are of a fine shape for fence building, and can be, and are, largely utilized for that purpose. Perhaps there is more stone fence on Cabin Creek than on any other creek in the county of its drainage. In the creek bed the stone lies in regular strata having a slight dip to the east.

These strata are from three to eight inches thick, and can be quarried at small cost, so that even fence necessary to be built on any of the farms on the creek can be put up at a cost not to exceed $1.25 per rod. This provision of nature renders the farmers independent of the owners of timber and the manufacturers of wire. This is true not only for the present, but will be true for thousands of years yet to come. In an early day, when driftwood was abundantly distributed along its banks, the creek would, at times, do much damage by washing away soil and fencing. By getting rid of the driftwood this has largely been checked, so that now but little damage is ever done by high water; however, since most of the hillsides have been cleared off, and quite a number of them have been set in blue grass, the shedding of the water into the

creek channel after a rain is much more rapid
than formerly, so that, at long intervals, the
creek yet does much damage. But if the land-
owners would quarry the rock from the creek
bed with which to build fence, instead of taking
them from the surface, where they are needed
as a fertilizer, the channel would be deepened
and all danger from high water would be ob-
viated. It will not be out of place to note in
this connection, that if Cabin Creek ran towards
the east, instead of running towards the west,
high waters in it would be much more common.
The creek and clouds would then be moving in
the same direction, and the smaller streams
would all be brought down together—of course
this assuming that a very large majority of our
storm clouds move eastward, which is the fact.
They come up from the west and shed their
waters first on the lower tributaries, and, owing
to the fact that the drainage is sudden and
rapid, the lower tributaries receive and discharge their waters before the upper waters
come down. It can be seen that if the creek
and cloud were moving in the same direction,
and the condition as to soil and other circumstances remained as they now are, tremendously
high water would frequently be the result.
Salt Lick runs towards the east, but lacks one
important condition in the chain of natural

causes that tend to make a creek subject to damaging floods, namely, a clay subsoil. When the territory is perfectly saturated with water, as it sometimes is, this logic fails, so that streams conditioned like Salt Lick are, under such circumstances, liable to get very high—usually in the winter months, and very rarely in the summer. Nature seems to have provided for these matters by causing streams, in this section at least, whose water-shed has a clay subsoil, against the general direction of storm clouds. Cabin Creek is bridged three times— once by the M. F. S. L. and V. Turnpike Road Co.—this is a substantial lattice bridge, built by Thos. Hinton, of Flemingsburg; once by the T. P. F. and C. Turnpike Co., and once by Cabin Creek Turnpike Co. These last two bridges are substantial structures, built by a Mr. Bryant, of Ohio.

Tributary to Cabin Creek are about twenty-two miles of macadamized road, operated under five different charters; and, having plenty of limestone for repairs, they are among the best roads in the county. Cabin Creek has one pike exactly five miles long, extending from the Tollesboro and Concord pike, down the creek to the Mason County line. This is one of the nicest buggy roads in Kentucky, being throughout its whole length very nearly level, and is kept in repair with gravel of the best limestone variety, which is abundantly distributed along the creek. This road can be kept in repair for $20 per mile, and if it was extended up the creek a distance of two miles, so as to top the Vanceburg and Tollesboro road at the bridge, the travel on it would be very largely increased and the pike would become a nice paying institution. Under the present toll system, with the extension mentioned, the toll receipts would reasonably amount to $500 per year, leaving a net profit to the owner of $400 per year.

Cabin Creek was so named on account of the great number of Indian huts found along its banks, and while the name is not at all euphonious, it has clung to it for over one hundred years, and will probably be its name when Gabriel comes to wake up those who sleep there. Cabin Creek post-office was established by the Government in the year 1798, and was the only post-office outside of a large radius for the first forty years of the county's existence. Afterward Orangeburg was given a post-office, then Poplar Flat, and later still Tollesboro, so that the old Cabin Creek post-office is one of the oldest offices in the county. The mail was carried on horseback from Maysville to the mouth of Big Sandy once a week. By the way, our worthy fellow-countyman T. B.

Harrison, when a boy, carried the mail on this route one year. It was a dangerous route in those days on account of high water, and required a boy of good nerve and sound judgment, both of which Mr. Harrison possessed to an extraordinary degree. His judgment, however, was better on the dangers lurking in a stream of high water than on a horse trade—to which George Featherkile can testify, if he is yet alive. This post-office has a feature in its history worthy of mention—it has never been a political office. During the twenty-four years of Republican administration it was kept almost all the time by a Democrat, and during the eight years of Mr. Cleveland's administration it has been kept all the time by a Republican. The postmaster at this place has uniformly been acceptable to the people, and they did not desire a change.

The first fifteen or sixteen dwellings built on the creek were built on almost precisely the same plan, varying only in size. They were built of logs and covered with clap-boards. All the lumber used in their construction was whip-sawed, there being at that time no other kind of lumber obtainable. They were usually 20 x 30 feet, and 1½ stories high; the lower part was divided by a partition, leaving the front room 20 x 20 feet, in which was a large fireplace, usually wide enough to admit a 5-foot backlog. The remaining 10 x 20 was divided into two small bedrooms, with a stairway between them. Along one side was an open porch, and at the end of the porch another log room, which was used as both kitchen and dining-room. In fact, up to the year 1837 every house on the creek was built on substantially the same plan. In about the year 1837 or 1838 William Norwood made quite an addition to his house, and put weather-boarding over the old part, and painted the whole structure. This was the first painted house on the creek, and remained so for about ten years, when Mr. Moses Given renovated and painted his house, where Mr. Daniel Farris now lives. Not one of these old dwellings is standing today that has not been done over and put in an unrecognizable shape. Quite a number have been torn down and a more modern structure put in their places. Several of them have been burned down by accident, and the remainder have been added to and modernized. Thus has passed away most of the old landmarks of Cabin Creek. Mr. John G. Fee and his followers made an effort to have the name changed from Cabin Creek to Glenville, but were unsuccessful. The people of the vicinity persisted in calling it "Feetown" in derision. Strangers, in passing up and down the creek, would many of them get the idea that there were two places instead of one. They would get confused as to its location and distance away very naturally, but for quite a number of years this condition of affairs must be explained to all strangers when passing through. But in 1886 Mr. Thos. J. Tully, who was postmaster at Creek, succeeded in getting the name changed from Cabin Creek to Cottageville, and by the latter name it is now quite well known throughout the country.

During these good old times we were speaking of corn huskings were very popular and were events of much enjoyment. The corn would be gathered and thrown in a long ridge. The hands needed no invitation until the evening of the husking. Plenty of whisky would be on hand, and a bountiful supper would be prepared. The huskers would, usually, bring their wives with them, or, if he had no wife, his sister, and if no sister, then some other fellow's sister. The suppers were never eaten until the husking was all over. The women had to work hard to prepare a supper for seventy-five to one hundred men, women, and children. It was generally eaten between 11 and 12 P. M. Usually two captains would be selected of competitive strength, whose duty it was to divide the huskers into two lots, as nearly equal as possible, and be captain over those of his own choosing.

The ridge of corn was then divided in the middle by laying a rail across it. All hands would then get on one side of the ridge so that the corn could be thrown on the other, and the race would begin. Of a moonlight night—and such nights were usually selected for the purpose —it was a most interesting sight to watch the white ears of corn flying across the pile like great flakes of snow. In a company of forty or fifty the stream of corn would be constant. As the pile of unhusked corn melted away the pile of husked corn grew larger, and as the whisky in the jug went down the spirits of the huskers went up; and as the rail in the center was approached the hilarity would increase. The finale came when the successful side had reached the center mark. Their captain would be lifted up by some of his men and tossed on the captain of the other side. Then would begin a trial of strength between the two, while their men would cheer and yell until the hills for miles would ring with their shouts. Usually the affair would terminate not in favor of the strongest, but in favor of the one who had been most temperate in handling the jug.

And now for the supper—meats of all kinds; butter, milk, and cream to overflowing; great stacks of apple and pumpkin pies; wheat and corn bread; tea and coffee—all eaten at one course and finished up with hot biscuits and butter, sweet milk, and maple molasses— enough to make one's mouth water to think of it, even at this late date.

Emigration from Cabin Creek to the Western States began to be frequent along in the forties. William Norwood and his son James went to Washington, Iowa. David and Melville Maple; John, James, and George Brown went to Wapella, Ill. James Tolle went to Missouri, and quite a number of others sought homes in the more level lands of the West. James Norwood married the oldest child of Captain Samuel Ireland, and a sister of Judge William Ireland, late of Ashland, Ky. During the fifties the spirit of emigration struck the younger generation, and quite an exodus took place. Daniel, Samuel, and Thomas Barkley, sons of Wm. Barkley, went to Wapella, Ill.; Harvey Gidding to Champaign County, Ill.; John L. Tully to Ohio; Benjamin and Moses Given and families to Fleming County, Ky.; and Thornton Farrow to Piatt County, Ill. Cabin Creek has, since its first settlement, been remarkable for the homogeneousness of its population. The entire population has been, and is yet, purely American.

In 1807 Ramsey and Young put up a water mill and built the first dam across the creek. This mill passed into the hands of several parties without any material change being made in it in the way of improvement. In about 1836 John D. Tully bought or traded for the property, and did considerable improvement during his two or three years of ownership; after which he sold it to Mr. Wm. Norwood, who changed it into a five-story flouring mill and put in a steam engine, the first one ever operated on the creek. James Norwood, in the year 18—, put up a sash saw mill, which was the first mill of the kind for miles around, and, together with the steam engine at the flouring mill, attracted a great deal of attention and became quite a place of resort for the people of the neighborhood. The flouring mill, however, was short-lived. Improved methods of converting wheat into flour forced it to stop, and, although several efforts were afterward made to change it and put it in shape for successful work, it was never a paying institution. Minor and John Barrett did considerable work on it. They rubbed the rust off the old engine and put in a saw mill to be operated by steam, which might have paid, at that time, had it not been for the introduction of improved machinery, both in the way of steam power and saw mills, but steam engines underwent such an improvement about this time that such as were manufactured by Mr. James Jacobs in Maysville, Ky.—and this was a Jacob's engine—could not compete with the new engine, and were forced to idleness. New methods of converting logs into planks also came into general use and drove out the old, clumsy sash saw.

The Barretts, like their predecessors, lost money in the operation, notwithstanding they were good business men, industrious, frugal, and upright. When the great car of improvement comes along it crushes all who do not adopt its methods. Some men are fortunate in getting on the right side of these changes—make fortunes out of them—and then imagine that their own shrewdness has achieved the result; when, in truth, they have been only the passive recipients of favors, bestowed by circumstances with which they had nothing whatever to do. Others happen to get on the wrong side, and are crushed under the massive wheels of improvement.

The Barretts sold out to Mr. Andrew Blount, from Nicholas County, upon whose hands the old mill sank further and further into decay, and seemed a weight upon the shoulders of its owner. The property then passed into the hands of Asa McNeal, who had learned from the experience of his predecessors that the day for improving and operating such a mill was past, and that nothing could now be done with it more than to utilize the water power, already belonging to it, and use it as a grist mill. While Mr. McNeal operated the mill in such a way as to lose no money on it, it proved a very costly experience to his son, Johnson McNeal.

In November, 1861, Johnson, then a young man just in the prime of life, met with an accident that rendered him a cripple for life. He is living yet, and enjoying as good health as most men of his age, but has not been able to walk a step since the accident. When a boy he was of a quiet disposition, loving books and solitude much better than company, and this part of his nature has had much to do with lessening the burdens of his confinement for the space of thirty-five years. He is now fifty-six years old, and, while his hair is gray, his appearance, otherwise, is that of a man much younger. Books are his associates, and, having a good memory, he is, to-day, among the most intelligent men in the county. The accident from which he is suffering could so easily have been avoided that thoughtlessness alone is to be charged with it. It was not one of those calamities that come upon men sometimes in such a manner that no human ingenuity or forethought could have avoided it, but was the direct result of a want of care, not only on his part, but upon the part of those who were in the mill with him at the time. He was sitting on the lower one of a large pair of buhrstones, dressing it, and had raised the upper stone by means of a large wooden screw, fixed, permanently, for the purpose, and so arranged that when the stone was raised it could be swung around so as not to be over the lower stone. By this arrangement it was only necessary to raise the stone a few inches and then swing it around, leaving the lower stone free to be worked on, and obviating all danger. Instead of doing this, he, with the help of his brother James and the miller, Enos P. Fuller, had raised the upper stone, weighing, probably, one thousand lbs., sufficiently high for him to sit under it and work without swinging it around. The screw employed was of birch wood, about 4 or $4\frac{1}{2}$ inches in diameter, with a good, heavy spiral, and had, when new, been of sufficient strength to safely sustain such a weight; but it was very old, had probably been exposed to the action of the air for thirty years, and had in a large measure lost its strength. Without a moment's warning this ponderous stone stripped the threads from the screw and came down on young McNeal, crushing him in a frightful manner. By almost superhuman efforts, his brother and Mr. Fuller, using levers, lifted the stone and dragged him from under it, to all appearances dead; but, after suffering intensely, and struggling between life and death for three or four months, he so far recovered as to know that immediate death would not be the result, but that he was doomed to the life of a helpless invalid. And for thirty-five years he has been deprived of the use of his lower limbs; yet, in spite of this affliction, he seems to enjoy life as well as many others, owns a good farm, lies in bed and transacts his own business; reads, smokes his pipe, and takes life easy. The old mill finally passed from McNeal's hands, and became the property of J. B. Bradley; and, at last, in August, 1886, it crashed to the ground during a heavy storm, and thus disappeared from Cabin Creek one of its oldest landmarks, "Norwood's Old Mill."

From about 1850 to 1862 there were three water grist mills on the creek. To-day there is none. The steam engine has driven them to idleness, and hence to decay.

The public schools of Cabin Creek have probably kept pace with other schools of the county. Before the creek was bridged it seemed necessary to make the creek district boundary lines. Since the bridges have been built the reason for making the creek the verge of school districts instead of making it the center no longer exists. Prior to building the bridges, and while the creek was the district line, schoolhouses were built as nearly in the center as possible. This arrangement placed them away from the creek, and hence away from the pike and the denser population; and, although many efforts have been made to have the unlucky combination changed, and the schoolhouses brought out and placed on the pike, none has ever been successful. Our county school superintendents seem to have seen no way to make the change agreeable to all concerned, for, while it would be a great benefit to a large majority of the patrons, it would be a present injury to the minority, and minorities have their rights. The disadvantage and injury to the minority would be only temporary, for what they would lose by having the schoolhouse at a greater distance from them, they would more than gain by improved schoolhouses and renewed interest on the subject of education, and, no doubt, ten years after the change they would not wish to return to the old state of affairs. Any change that will encourage the cause of education generally should be made, even if there are a few objections.

Cottageville should have a schoolhouse by all means, but unless its citizens pull loose from

5

the school district on which they are located,
and build a school of their own, they are cut
off from all hope while the main creek remains
a divisional line.   This little village of fifteen
families, having a church house, two stores,
two grist mills, post-office, blacksmith shop, a
physician, and resident farmers, is incomplete
without a schoolhouse; and a change making
it the center of a school district, instead of placing it on the verge of two, would awaken a
new interest in the subject of schools, and the
whole neighborhood would feel the good influence.   For the benefit of this quiet little village, permit us to call the attention of those in
authority in these matters to this opportunity,
here offered, to do its people a lasting good, and,
at the same time, push forward the general cause
of better schools.

Lewis County has been organized as one of the
counties of the State for more than one hundred
years, and during this time it has been represented in the State Legislature thirty years by
citizens of Cabin Creek.   This is much over its pro
rata, and would indicate that lawmakers thrive
best in a limestone country having a clay subsoil.
Benjamin Given served one term; Joshua Given,
one term; Clayton Bane, one term; Thomas
Marshall, three terms; Uriah McKellup, one
term; John L. Fetch, one term; Rufus Emmons,

one term; A. J. Hendrickson, one term; Frank Hull, one term; Isaiah Grigsby, one term; Dr. Wm. Bowman, two terms; and A. D. Pollett, one term. There are only about forty-five square miles of territory tributary to Cabin Creek, which is just one-tenth the area of the county; yet this small territory has furnished one-third of the county's representatives. Coming to the office of county judge, we find but one accredited to Cabin Creek—Thomas Henderson, of Poplar Flat—and making a mathematical calculation, we find that nine county judges should have been sent up from this section. This excess of lawmakers, and extraordinary lack of county judges, coming from this particular part of the county, evidently teaches this lesson, that lawmakers, generally, must get some one else to explain the laws they have made.

Cabin Creek, like all other sections of the county, was violently divided in sentiment when the Civil War broke out. Quite a number of its citizens saw cause to oppose the coercion of the seceded States to the authority of the President-elect, and seemed to treat the matter as one which was yet a subject of argument. Men of good moral standing—intelligent and upright, patriotic in every sense of the word—who would not consider for a moment a proposition to disobey lawful authority—failed to

consider the fact that the time for argument
was over when the President-elect of the United
States was denied the right of authority over
a certain portion of its members. It must not
be considered that those who opposed coercion
were rebels, and desired a divided government.
True, this epithet was applied to many of them
during the excitement of actual war; but with
the return of peace came a return of greater
liberality, and society very soon came back to
its old conditions of good feeling. While the
strife lasted, however, the feeling of animosity
between those favoring the war and those opposing it was very bitter, and manifested itself
many times in unpleasant scenes. It is remarkable, and at the same time praiseworthy, to
note how rapidly this bad feeling passed away.
A very short time after the close of the war
differences vanished and neighbors were neighbors again.

Cabin Creek was fully up with other portions of the county in furnishing soldiers for the
Union Army. The 4th, 10th, 16th, and 54th
regiments were all represented. Most of these
escaped the dangers of war, returned to their old
homes, and probably one-fourth of them are
yet living in the same neighborhood from
which they enlisted. Fully one-fourth of them
failed to answer to the home roll-call, the re-

maining half have either emigrated to other parts of the country or crossed over the River of Death. Casualties and violence belong to the history of Cabin Creek, as well as to other portions of Lewis County. Every county in every State of the Union, unfortunately, has these things to contend with, and no history would be complete that omitted them. Histories should go in pairs—one should be written by a friend and one by an enemy. The friend, following the impulses of his love and sympathy, is inclined to enlarge upon everything praiseworthy, and to minimize everything of an opposite character. Thus he shows us the place and the people of whom he writes, not in their true light, but presents them with enlarged virtues; while their vices are either hidden entirely or so bound around with palliating apologies as to leave an impression on the mind of the reader far from correct. If we read only history written by a friend we lose much information to which we are, of right, entitled, and which belong to a full knowledge and understanding of the places and persons written of. History should be truth; and while it may be unpleasant to make record of crime, when speaking of home and home people, yet it must be remembered that the reader is entitled, not only to the truth, but to the whole truth, and nothing but the truth.

During the winter of 1856, probably in
January, Brigadier General Thomas Marshall
was shot and instantly killed by John Tyler.
The shooting took place in the yard of Mrs.
Gray, on the headwaters of Clear Creek, a
small stream emptying into Cabin Creek about
one-fourth of a mile below Ebenezer Church.
The circumstances surrounding the shooting
were of such a nature as to deprive Marshall
almost entirely of the sympathy of the neighborhood, and but little effort was made to capture
Tyler, who made his escape and was never
brought to trial. Marshall was impetuous and
overbearing, and especially to those who would
not readily yield to his authority. Tyler was a
stern, uncompromising man, easily insulted,
and revengeful, and both men were strangers
to fear. They had had a difficulty about the
measurement of some land, during which Marshall struck Tyler across the left temple with a
heavy cedar cane, the small limbs of which had
been left about a half inch long, and then
sharpened. The blow was a savage one. The
blood flowed from the wounds made by the
sharp knobs on the cane in torrents, and to add
to Tyler's rage, Marshall's men, of whom he
had three or four with him at the time, would
not let Tyler get hold of him, or the trouble
would have been settled on the spot. Tyler,

finding that he could do nothing with Marshall at that time, went immediately home and got his gun, and then went on the hunt of his adversary, and, as has been stated before, found him at the widow Gray's, just in the dusk of the evening. He took no advantage of Marshall, but immediately notified him that one of them must die that evening, and told Marshall to get ready. Marshall took him at his word, and went hastily into the house and got his rifle and came out with it presented towards Tyler. Tyler fired, and Marshall fell, mortally wounded. Just as he fell, he exclaimed, "My God, he has killed me," and never spoke afterward. Thomas Marshall was a man of but few kind impulses, and rendered assistance to the needy only to show his superiority. He was a man of considerable wealth, and consequently had influence; was chosen three times to represent his county in the Legislature, and was a boastful, but efficient, representative.

In October, 1859, George W. Bovard struck Jack Johnson on the head with a stone, from the effects of which he died in about twenty-four hours. This unfortunate occurrence took place at Brown's Run schoolhouse during the progress of a debate among the boys of the neighborhood. Johnson had been to the mouth of Cabin Creek on some business, and had been induced to drink of the whisky sold there. The mouth of Cabin Creek is in Mason County, about three miles from the crossing of the Lewis County line, and was known by the name of the Dead Fall for miles around; and, indeed, a more appropriate name could not have been found. It proved a dead fall to many a poor fellow, Jack Johnson among the number. He came to the schoolhouse on the evening referred to in a maudlin state of intoxication, and behaved in such a manner that Bovard, in a gentle way, undertook to quiet him. But Johnson became more boisterous than ever, and instead of quieting down, took offense at Bovard's remarks, and, drawing a long knife, made as though to cut him. A bystander told Bovard to get out of his way, that Johnson had a knife. Bovard backed away from him until obstructed by the schoolhouse, when he suddenly stooped down and picked up a rock, weighing about two pounds, and struck Johnson on the head, just over the left ear. Johnson fell unconscious, and died within twenty-four hours. Previous to this time Johnson had been in the employ of Mr. George Rowland as a farm hand. He was a member of the Christian Church, and had behaved himself in the most exemplary manner during his entire stay in the neighborhood. Bovard had an examining trial before Magistrates Jas. Boyd and David Ferris, and the evidence was so much in his favor that the case was dismissed. But some member of the grand jury had him indicted at the December term of court of 1859, and his case came up before the June term of the Circuit Court of the next year, Judge Elijah Phister presiding. When the case was called and the witnesses sworn, only two witnesses for the defense had testified when the judge peremptorily threw it out of court, pronouncing it a plain case of self-defense.

Until about 1850 Cabin Creek had never had a resident physician. Dr. W. D. Greer about this time came from New Hampshire and settled about half a mile above Cottageville, and commenced the practice of his profession. Shortly after he came to Cabin Creek his wife died, and he afterwards married Harriet Boyd. In 1861 they moved to Aberdeen, O., and again Cabin Creek was without a physician. Some time in the sixties Dr. Barnett practiced medicine a few years at Cottageville; also Dr. Barnes tried it a while immediately after Dr. Barnett. After this there was a space of probably ten years, during which time there was not a physician on the creek; then Dr. N. F. Jordan, of Bloomington, Ill., came and began practicing at Cottageville, and he remained a little over a year. A Dr. Winters succeeded him, and remained about six months. After him came Dr. Honaker, a former resident of Vanceburg, and remained about three years, and then moved to Pond Run, O. Dr. Morgan Pollitt came next, and remained about two years, and moved to Maysville, leaving his practice to Dr. Dumont, who had already invaded his territory. Dumont remained but a short while, and moved to Georgetown, Ky. Dr. Winder then, after purchasing a nice house and lot of T. J. Tully, and beginning like a man who intended to do something, moved his family and began the practice of medicine in 1893 at Cottageville. Since then he has built up a good-paying practice, gained the respect and esteem of the community, and has made himself so useful that he could not well be dispensed with. Dr. T. J. Rowland also practiced medicine at Cottageville a few years, probably about 1858-59, and Dr. Day at Poplar Flat, sometime during the seventies.

Ebenezer Presbyterian Church house was located about 1806, and is consequently one of the oldest church houses in the county. It was first built of logs, and the old log structure remained until 1850, when it was remodeled inside and out, Mr. Jas. Gidding doing the work. It seemed to be an idea of those olden times that church, schoolhouse, and grave ground should be located near each other—that the trio formed an inseparable combination; and in accord with this idea a schoolhouse was located within fifty yards of the church house, and the church house was located inside the graveyard. Some who are living on Cabin Creek to-day attended school for the first time in this old schoolhouse, but about 1847 it was torn away, and schoolhouses began to spring up in new places. Washington, Brown's Run, and Owl Hollow schoolhouses were built about the time Ebenezer schoolhouse was abandoned, and afterward these houses determined the location of school districts; for, in districting the county, according to the public-school system which was at this time being set in opposition, these houses were made, as nearly as possible, the centers of districts. Sometime in the fifties, D. H. Baldwin, of D. H. Baldwin & Co., of Cincinnati, O., taught singing school at Ebenezer Church. He could not sing on account of some defect in his voice, but was fully acquainted with the principles of music, and had good use of the violin, so that he was a successful teacher. Ebenezer being the only church house for miles around had much to do with shaping the religious sentiment of the neighborhood, so that the community was, and is yet, strongly Presbyterian. Dr. Grundy, of Maysville, was their preacher for many years. Rev. Hendrick, of Flemingsburg, has preached there, regularly, a portion of the time, and, occasionally, for the last fifty years. He seemed to have, by common consent of the members, a general supervision over the affairs of the Church, and is to-day regarded by them as their best adviser. Rev. Condit, of Washington, Mason County; Adams, Fate, Gould, Fields, and Brown, who is their pastor now, have all preached there. The last four were regularly installed as their pastors for the time being.

SYCAMORE.—Sycamore Creek has its head near Covedale, and runs in a northerly direction to the Ohio River. Like many of the other streams of Lewis County, it had along its course many of the early settlers. Chief among the historic spots along Sycamore is the site of the old water mill back of Concord, which was operated by Elijah Wade more than seventy years ago. He sold out to Jesse Marklin, who operated the mill until about 1884. Since then the old mill has fallen into decay. The machinery has been removed and the building used for a barn.

Among the early settlers were Rolley Feagans, Paul and Abraham Blew, Joseph Epson,

William Reed, John Vance, Henry Tolle, Charles Wood, Frank Feagans, and Henry Schwartz.

It is said that the noted and eccentric Lorenzo Dow, a Methodist preacher, once owned land and lived on this creek.

COVEDALE.—Covedale is situated on the watershed at the head of Sycamore Creek, and one branch of the east fork of Cabin Creek. The public buildings consist of a schoolhouse and a church, owned by the Christian denomination.

E. M. Marshall is postmaster and general merchant, and J. H. Reidinger, D. F. and S. V. Fry are tobacco merchants; and J. N. Hughes is a dealer in lumber. O. E. Secrest, Matthew Virgin, H. C. Myers, Bruce Vance, O. M. Reganstien, A. H. Graham, C. A. Taylor, and G. W. George are prosperous farmers.

CONCORD.—We are under obligations to W. R. Burns for the following history of Concord:

"In 1828 Chauncy B. Shepard, the representative from Lewis County, had a bill before the General Assembly which authorized the formation of a town or village on the land owned by John and Edward Stephenson in said county, and at the March term of the Lewis County Court, in 1830, on petition of said John and Edward Stephenson, said petition was granted and the name Concord given the village. It is situated on the Ohio River, immediately below the mouth of Sycamore Creek. The area was 46¼ acres, and the same was vested in the hands of Chauncy B. Shepard, George Boyd, Tavenor Moore, and William Watkins, as trustees.

"Samuel Stephenson was appointed clerk for said village. The village was laid off in lots, streets, alleys, and out-lots. The lots were sold on July 16, 1830, and Thomas Lindley was made treasurer, and Isaac Chandler, collector.

"To give all the names or history of those who were here in the earlier days would be impossible now; all are dead, perhaps, and their descendants gone.

"Samuel Stephenson was the first postmaster. He had a general store in these days. Only two or three mails each week were received, and these by overland route. In those days Mr. Stephenson and John Lovel, who was also in the general store business, bought their goods in Philadelphia and Baltimore, going and coming in wagons.

"Mr. Stephenson retired from business here and moved his family to his farm, a few miles from here, where he died some years later. Luther and Calvin Stephenson are his sons, who inherited his estate and are among our most thrifty farmers and respected citizens.

"There was at one time a large tannery here, operated by the Grimes family, who were related to Jesse R. Grant, who worked in the tannery for a time. It is said that General U. S. Grant did some work also in this tanyard. The large currier's stone used to dress hides on in this yard is now in front of the Burns' home.

"When the village was laid out, a large part of it, fronting on the river, was reserved for the purpose of the farmers, who put their logs, wood, and tanbark there to send away on flatboats, or to sell to the steamboats. Some times three or four wood yards were here supplying the boats with fuel, and a number of cords were sold daily. All this reserved ground has been carried away by the river, and what was once a wide street (100 feet) none remains. In 1874 several feet of land and several buildings were carried away by a slip in the bank; fortunately, no lives were lost.

"Flatboat building was at one time carried on extensively here, as many as eight or ten buildings at one time. Five or six steamboat hulls have been built here.

"Mr. John Lovel had the first saw mill here, and did a large business. Several houses now standing received their lumber from this mill. Uncle Patrick Bivan (colored) was the engineer. He lived near here on a little farm. (Died 1901.)

John Taylor succeeded Mr. Lovel in the milling business, and he was succeeded by Hon. R. B. Lovel and G. L. Purcell.

"At one time the fine Merchant Flouring Mill, built by Taylor & Brown, did a large business and made the best of flour; for a few years last past it has done no other than a small custom business in grinding and sawing lumber, there having been a saw mill attached to it.

"The old saw mill, first built and then rebuilt on the same ground, was wrecked in the flood of 1884, being then owned by G. L. Purcell. It has never been rebuilt since that time.

"There are three churches in the village— the Methodist Episcopal Church, South, built in 1848; the Freewill Baptist Church, built in 1888; and the old Union (brick) Church, built in 1830 and deeded to trustees to be used by all religious denominations in good standing, has been replaced by a building now owned by the Christian, or Disciples denomination.

"We have a good new schoolhouse, just completed, which is a credit to the village.

"In 1850 Concord had the first newspaper published in the county. It was called the Concord *Pioneer*, and later *Pioneer of Progress*. It was edited and published by E. Holderness. A few copies are still to be seen. We extract from the issue of September 6, 1850: 'A Gala Day at Concord.'—'A gala day at a celebration given by the Sons of Temperance of this place.' 'Professor Bell, of Maysville,' was orator of the day, and the 'Manchester Band' discoursed sweet music. 'Fifteen hundred to two thousand people were present.' The editor then lauds the citizens of Concord for their hospitality, etc. 'Sam. P. Armstrong' also made one of his fine speeches. 'Pacific Division' of the Sons was then one of the largest in the State, and it seems to have been spreading itself on this occasion.

"In the same issue, J. L. Boyd advertises as having just received a fine, large stock of goods and groceries, and adds, 'Call, and get more than you can carry away, for a little money.'

"'The Boyd House and Wharfboat, No. 1,' 'John R. Duke, Saddler,' 'Wm. Rea, Hotel and Wharfboat,' are among the advertisers.

"The *Pioneer* was a four-page, four-column, 14 x 20 sheet, published weekly, containing very good editorial matter, together with some prose and poetry as general reading matter. Its motto was: 'Justice, Truth, and Virtue.'

"At the regular election for village officers the following voters and candidates appeared:

"J. H. Hayslip, John Irvin, William Wade,

6

John Lovel, James H. Davis, D. B. Morgan, Edward Stephenson, M. Harvey, J. L. Boyd, James M. McMiller, John Greenlee, A. Levy, Thos. Tucker, Arthur Stephenson, Thos. Lindley, D. Sampson, William Greenlee, W. Barrett, C. B. Shepard, Samuel Stephenson. The candidates received the following vote: J. M. Hayslip, 13; Arthur Stephenson, 15; E. Berriman, 12; John Lovel, 13; David Sampson, 14; Samuel Stephenson, 11; J. L. Boyd, 8; J. H. Davis, 2.

"Wyatt Owens, R. M. Owens, R. D. Taylor, J. V. White, and William Sparks have been blacksmiths here at different times. The only one of these now living is Mr. White, who resides at Manchester, O. J. M. Freeman, Samuel White, and John Sparks, Sr., have been the wagon makers, of whom Mr. Sparks is still alive and living here, and Mr. White living at Manchester, O. Mr. Freeman died a few years ago. All these shops had a good run of business —wagons, plows, single and double-trees being shipped from here to the South. Many of the wagons—timber wheels—for the South, had only two wheels, 10 or 12 feet in diameter, with an iron screw through the axle to raise logs up from the ground while hauling. The tongue of these wagons was crooked so as to come down to the level of the team to be attached.

"In the early part of this century, Mrs.

Camming, a widow with seven sons, came to this county and located on the farm now known as the Bedford farm. They bought the land just below Stout's Run, at the foot of Brush Creek Island, down to Sycamore Creek. At the foot of this island they had a horse mill, and also a mill built on two flatboats with a water wheel between them, so that the current of the river ran the mill.

"The horse mill on the bank was later turned into a steam mill. At this mill lumber was sawed to build several flatboats and the steamboats 'John Hancock,' 'Clendel,' 'Lady Byron,' and 'Elk.' They also had a flour and saw mill just above the mouth of Sycamore Creek. At this mill George Dozier went crazy over trying to produce a perpetual motion machine. One of the buhrs used in this mill is now in front of Burns' residence in the village. William Cummins was the first man to command a steamboat between Cincinnati, O., and Charleston, W. Va. He married Eliza Myers, on February 1, 1827. His widow and two daughters, now in Newport, Ky., still survive him. He owned about three hundred acres of land, known as 'the Cummin's tract,' and about thirty slaves at one time.

"*Some Short Items of Interest About Concord.*—At Cummin's mill, near Sycamore, Jack

Stevenson built a 'horse-boat' to run from Maysville to the mouth of Great Kanawha.

"In 1859 Jack Parker killed Solomon Dillinger with a skiff oar.

"John Calvin was shot and killed in Parkers' Hollow in 1861.

"Wilson Phipps shot and killed Pleasant Stricklett in 1874.

"Aunt Polly Stevenson burned to death in a fire.

"John T. Wood gored to death by a bull in 1874.

"Some time in the '40's Ezekiel Berriman had a carding mill here, run by horse power.

"Buck Fegeans was killed in the saw mill here in 1855.

"Edward Stevenson was first magistrate; Larkin J. Proctor, first attorney; David Mumford, first hotel and bar-room; King D. McClain, first brickyard—all the brick houses now in Concord got the brick at this yard; Dr. Lindley, first physician; John Lovel, first cabinet maker; Samuel Stevenson, first merchant and postmaster; Martin Bliss, first tailor; Thomas Brown, first regular ferryman. Mr. Brown also built barges and flatboats. His two sons, Hon. Paris C. (dead) and August W. Brown, are now in business in Cincinnati.

"J. P. Hendrickson was the first cooper, and John Taylor had the first wharfboat.

"In ye olden time, and up to 1870, perhaps, large balls were given, where the brave lads and fair lassies would trip the light fantastic toe after the music of Roch. Robb and the Mitchell brothers until the wee sma' hours.

"In December, 1845, the steamboats "Delarck' and 'Martha' collided in front of Concord, and both boats were a total loss. A few weeks after, in January, 1846, the 'Raleigh' run into the 'Lawrence,' just below town, and both boats sank in very shallow water. Two of these boats were laden with flour.

"In the town to-day there is a lodge of Free Masons and a lodge of Independent Order of Odd Fellows; both have good halls for their meetings, and each have a large number of members.

"Concord and vicinity sent many brave boys to the war in 1861; some wore the blue and some—a few—wore the gray. Many returned to their homes after the war. Some were killed or died in the service. Dr. Cartmell, now of Maysville, Ky., was a physician here in 1830-40, and was a surgeon in the 16th Regiment Kentucky Volunteers, a company of which came from Lewis County. Cartmell was succeeded as physician in Concord by Dr. M. H. Burns, in 1847, who practiced his profession here until October, 1864, when he died suddenly of apoplexy. At the time of his death he held

the second highest office in the Grand Masonic
Lodge in the State. Dr. L. A. Grimes and
Dr. W. H. Campbell located here after the
death of Dr. Burns. Dr. Grimes is still living
here. Dr. Campbell moved to Vanceburg
several years ago. Dr. W. L. Day is also a
resident physician here, and at this time both
these physicians have a good practice. Hon.
R. B. Lovel, born and reared here, was at one
time a merchant and saw mill owner in the
village, and later sheriff of Lewis County for
two terms, and once State Senator, representing
Lewis and Mason Counties in the Kentucky
Legislature. Mr. Lovel is now in business in
Maysville and enjoys a flourishing trade.

"The following are the remaining business
men and places of Concord:

"W. H. Currin, hotel proprietor and organ
and piano dealer; A. A. Shenhurst and Son,
general merchants; McCone & Parker, general
merchandise; W. W. Secrest and Son, general
store and post-office; O. D. Carr, general store;
C. A. Taylor, grist mill; A. A. Taylor, grist mill;
John Sparks, blacksmith; McClain & Blyew,
dealers in logs, railroad ties, and posts; Burns,
wharfmaster; one two-room schoolhouse."

CHAPTER II

COUNTY ORGANIZATION: ACT RELATING TO—FIRST
COUNTY SEAT—FIRST COURT—REMOVAL OF COUNTY
SEAT TO CLARKSBURG—RIVAL TOWNS—REMOVAL
TO VANCEBURG—CONVENIENCES AND INCONVEN-
IENCES ARISING THEREFROM—CHANGE OF COUNTY
OFFICES—THE INFIRMARY—GROWTH OF VANCE-
BURG—WISE HEADS WHO BOUGHT PROPERTY AT
THE RIGHT TIME—PRESENT CONDITION OF THE
CITY—ITS HOPES FOR THE FUTURE.

ACT ORGANIZING LEWIS COUNTY:—Be it remembered that in pursuance of an Act of the
General Assembly of the Commonwealth of
Kentucky, passed on the second day of December in the year of our Lord one thousand
eight hundred and six, and in the fifteenth
year of the said Commonwealth; and an Act
supplementary thereto passed on the twenty-
seventh day of the same month, for the division
of the county of Mason and establishing a new
county called and known by the name of Lewis:

George Fearis, Aaron Stratton, Aaron Owings,
John G. McDowell, John Stephenson, Landon
Calvert, George Brown, Hugh Hannah, and
John Dyal met at the house of Oke Hendrickson
in the said county, on Monday, the twenty-

seventh day of April, one thousand eight hundred and seven, and each produced Commission from his Excellency, Christopher Greenup, Esquire, Governor of Kentucky, appointing them justices of the peace in and for the said County of Lewis, with all the rights and privileges thereto pertaining.

Whereupon Aaron Stratton, Esq., produced a certificate from under the hand of John G. McDowell, a justice of the peace for said county —who had himself been previously qualified as such before Benj. Bayles, Esq., a justice of the peace for the County of Mason—of his having taken as well the oath to support the Constitution of the United States as the oath prescribed by the Constitution of Kentucky. S. Plummer Thomas produced his commission as sheriff in the same court. "And therefore a County Court was begun and held for the said County of Lewis."

The first act of the court was to appoint Walker Reid as clerk for said court.

The following attorneys were also admitted to the Lewis County Bar:

Thos. Dougherty, Aaron Beatty, Wm. P. Fleming, John D. Stockton, Marshall Key, John Miller, and John G. Heath.

John G. Heath was appointed commonwealth attorney for the county.

THE ABOVE GROUP IS A FEW OF THE PAST AND PRESENT OFFICERS OF LEWIS COUNTY:

First Row, left to right: R. M. Parker, Magistrate, District No. 6; W. M. Fry, Magistrate, District No. 1, term expired 1909; Thomas Stone, Magistrate, District No. 4; U. C. Thoroughman, County Attorney; W. R. Henderson, County School Superintendent; O. P. Pollitt, County Clerk; O. F. Lee, Magistrate, District No. 5, resigned, now in Idaho; P. C. Henderson, Magistrate, District No. 7; T. F. Bagby, State Senator; E. A. Jones, Circuit Court Clerk, 1909; Ivan W. Saunders, County Surveyor.

Second Row: J. Q. Adams, County Surveyor, 1909, now County Normal School Teacher; L. N. Rayborn, Deputy Sheriff, District No. 4, 1909; M. M. Bertram, Sheriff of the County, 1909, now Police Judge of Vanceburg.

Third Row: A. R. Campbell, Magistrate, District No. 2; J. M. Lee, County Judge; G. P. Adams, Jailer, 1909.

Lewis County was made from a part of Mason, and was organized April 27, 1807. Its first county seat was at Poplar Flat, and its first court was held at the house of Oke Hendrickson by the following magistrates: Landen Calvert, George Fearis, Aaron Stratton, John G. McDowell, George Brown, Hugh Hannah, John Doyle, and John Stephenson. We have found the record of this court, and therefore give further on some of the causes considered by it.

The first sheriff was Plummer Thomas; county clerk, Walker Reid; county attorney, John Heath; coroner, Samuel Cox. The representatives of these families are still among the best citizens of the county. We note the family of the late Lewis Calvert, near Clarksburg; the Fearis family, at Fearis P. O., on East Fork of Cabin Creek; Mr. Robert Stratton, deceased, on Spy Run; Thomas and David Hannah, of Quick's Run; D. M. Doyle, of Carr's Landing; Thomas and Plummer Thomas, of Kinny, and Dick Thomas, of Kirk Springs; Zachariah Heath and his son Erastus Heath, formerly of Vanceburg; W. H. Cox, late of Concord, are all descendants from that list of first county officers, besides a generation of younger people more remotely connected with them who still reside in the county.

First Court, April, 1807.—Each of the justices showed his commission from Governor Christopher Greenup, as also did Plummer Thomas, as sheriff, according to the Constitution of 1799. The record says, "Whereupon a County Court was begun and held for Lewis County." It is styled in the record book "The April Court of 1807." This record book is in good state of preservation in the county clerk's office in Lewis County. The corners of its cover are protected by "buckskin," and it is well bound, but has no lines ruled in the paper. It shows the evidences of the "goosequill pen" of that day. It has a home-made index, which is well executed. The first order appoints Walker Reid as clerk. He produced his certificate from the Court of Appeals, which the Constitution required, before his appointment. He gave bond in the sum of one thousand dollars for the discharge of his duties. His bond was attested by George Fearis, presiding justice— there was no county judge under that Constitution—the magistrate oldest in commission, present, presided at any court. The second order was "That Samuel Cox and Jonathan Kenyon be recommended to the governor for surveyor of the county."

The following constables were appointed: Geo. N. Davis, Murdock Cooper, James McClain, Elijah T. Davis, and Baldwin Bane.

COURT-HOUSE AND SOLDIERS' MONUMENT.

John G. Heath was appointed commonwealth attorney.

The following road reviewers were appointed and all reported at the next term of court: William George Wilson, Thomas McIlvain, Robt. Robb, and Wm. Kennard for the road from Lewis to Mason County.

Elijah T. Davis, James Martin, William Sutherlain, and Robt. Voiers, from Sutherlain's, on Quick's Run, to the Ohio River, passing by Catt's and Cumming's mills.

Robert Taylor, William Watkins, Daniel Hendrickson, and Daniel Swearingin from Swearingin's mill, on Cabin Creek, to Salt Lick Road where it crosses to Williamsburg (now Orangeburg).

Hugh Hannah, Thomas Collins, Henry Smith, and Joseph Donovan for the road from Salt Lick to Oharrow's mill.

William Harper, James Wilson, Landen Calvert, and John McDaniel for the road from Gunpowder Gap to intersect Salt Lick Road below McDaniel's.

Samuel Cox produced his commission from the governor as coroner for Lewis County.

Aaron Stratton and George Fearis were authorized by the governor to "celebrate" the rights of matrimony.

John McDowell was licensed to ferry from

Vanceburg to the Ohio shore, etc., "according to law." John Stevenson also established a ferry from the mouth of Sycamore (Concord) to the Ohio shore.

Oke Hendrickson, of Poplar Flat, where the court was held, was granted tavern license.

The May term was held at the same place, and gives the following restrictions to tavern keepers as to charges:

"RATES"

"For Warm breakfast........................25 cents
　" 　Cold　　"　 ....17　 "
　" 　Warm dinner............................25　 "
　" 　Cold　　 "　 ....17　 "
　" 　Warm supper...........................25　 "
　" 　Cold　　"　 ....17　 "
　" 　Oats or corn by the gallon............. 8　 "
　" 　Hay, blades, and stableage for 24 hours...25　 "
　" 　Pasturage for 24 hours................. 8　 "
　" 　Lodging in clean sheets................. 8　 "
　" 　French brandy per half pint............37½ "
　" 　Madeira wine　 "　　"　　"　 ....50　 "
　" 　Any other kind of wine per half pint.....37½ "
　" 　Peach brandy　　　　 "　 "　 "　 ....12½ "
　" 　Whisky　　　　　 "　 "　 "　 ....12½ "
　" 　Cider, Royal, per quart................17　 "
　" 　Cider　　　　 "　 "　 ....12½ "
　" 　For Holland gin per half pint...........25　 "

The last will and testament of James Savage was admitted to probate, May term, 1807. At the same term William Cordingly was "natural-ized" as a citizen of the United States and of Kentucky. His grandsons, John and Frank Cordingly, still live on "Kinny."

The report of David Ballenger, Cornelius Hall, and William Fleming, commissioners appointed by the act forming Lewis County, gives the following place and boundaries for a seat of justice for Lewis County: "Beginning at a beech tree marked W. F. D. B. C. H., standing on the bank of the Ohio River, north 65 west 38 poles from the mouth of Quick's Run; north 65 west to a dogwood, marked as before; thence south 25 west 20 poles to a beech tree, also marked as before; thence south 65 east 12 poles to a beech sapling, marked with the same letters; and from thence to the beginning, containing the quantity of one acre and eighty poles." There is a plat of this survey and rates explaining it in the order book.

The court then appoints some road overseers and allots hands, each of whom is named on the order, except in one instance, where there seems to be a numerous family of the same name, and then the order says "all the Looneys."

The minutes are signed by George Fearis as presiding justice, with a skill in penmanship hard to equal in these later days of educational advancement—this signing was done by the

7

clerk. The June term appoints the officers of the next general election, as follows:

John Dyal and Aaron Stratton, judges in Salt Lick precinct, and Jonathan Kenyon, clerk; Ohio precinct, George Fearis and George Brown, judges, and Walker Reid, clerk. There seems to have been only these two precincts, but the elections were held for three days, so that everybody might have a chance to vote. The only persons voted for at that time were representatives, senators, and governor and lieutenant governor. Magistrates, coroners, sheriffs, and other county officers were appointed by the governor on the recommendation of the magistrates.

In order to weave into our history the names of those people living in the county, and to show their locality therein, we give the record of the court in regard to road overseers and allotment of hands, who are usually named. On the East Fork and main Cabin Creek Road the names of James Barkley, overseer, and Samuel Cox, David Peters, Humphrey Bell John Archard, Robt. Robb, William Robb, John Brownfield, Thos. McIlvain, William Murphy, John Murphy, Robert and Jack Roberts, Neal and John Wallingford as hands appear. As this road extended from East Fork to main Cabin Creek, we know that these people lived in that section of the county.

WHARF SCENE AT VANCEBURG.

On the road from Wilson's Ferry—that is, Wilson's Bottom—to East Fork of Cabin Creek we have John Boyd, overseer, "all the Hilter-brands," the Pitts's, the Looneys, James Vandegraft, Widow Wilson's hands, Samuel Wilson, William George Wilson as hands enumerated by the court.

On Cabin Creek, below Swearingin's mill, were William Graham, David Fenwick, George Brown, Edward Chaney "and his own and John Swearingin's hands." On the road above the forks of Quick's Run at Widow Davis', Richard Elson is overseer, "and all the hands above the forks." On the road from Sycamore to Salt Lick—up the river—the following landholders are mentioned by the viewers of the road: John Stephenson, Samuel Cummins, Rebecca Cummins, William Aills, Rebecca Aills, John Aills, Graham Bedinger, and Alexander K. Marshall, the last at mouth of Salt Lick, and the others in order of their lands from Concord up to Vanceburg.

In order to show what the Lewis County people were doing in those days before the War of 1812, and to find the succession in office, we follow the County and Circuit Courts still further by their record. In the June term of the County Court, held at Oke Hendrickson's home on Poplar Flat, Samuel Cox presented his commission as surveyor, and took the oath, gave bond, etc., and became the surveyor of Lewis County.

In October the county levy was laid at $1.75 on 506 tithes (polls), and amounts to $775.50. The whole county expenses, including the surveying of the county line, the election, and the commissioners to fix a place for a county seat, amounted to only $175.70, leaving a balance in the hands of the sheriff of $709.80.

At the December term it developed that James McPike had objected to a road through his land, and a jury had fixed his damage at $13. The court decided that to be "enormous," and finally, to get the road, the following gentlemen decided to pay it themselves:

G. N. Davis	$1.50
Landen Calvert	4.50
William Harper	2.50
John McDaniel	1.50
Plummer Thomas	1.50
Walker Reid	.50
Total	$13.00

William Roper appears as an attorney in the Lewis Circuit Court, and is allowed $66.66 for prosecuting the pleas of the Commonwealth in the Lewis Circuit Court. His order was made on the sheriff of Lewis County.

William P. Fleming's claim against the

METHODIST EPISCOPAL CHURCH, VANCEBURG.

county as attorney, since its organization till January, 1808, was only $28.12½.

Court of January, 1808.—Anna McKenzie was appointed guardian of Thomas, Anna, Sally, Alexander S., and Hannah H. McKenzie, her children, and orphans of Alexander McKenzie, deceased.

"Ordered that John Dyal be appointed commissioner assessor of the revenue tax for the year 1808." Bond of two thousand dollars was given, with John Stephenson as security.

Elizabeth Harrison was released from tax for the future on her negro man named "Peter."

David Gooding was appointed constable.

It appears to have been the duty of the sheriff to collect taxes, as we find a record of Plummer Thomas coming into this court and "taking upon himself" the collecting of the revenue and county levy, and of his then and there giving a bond of ten thousand dollars for the revenue and fourteen hundred dollars for the levy.

We find the Stricklett family mentioned in this court—one, Peter Stricklett, being old and infirm, was released of county levy.

In the militia of the State, Lewis County was represented by the 69th Regiment, and Thos. Parker was commissioned by the governor as paymaster of that regiment.

The death of John Thompson is noted in this court.

James Rowland was appointed road overseer some place in the Tolleboro neighborhood, with Joseph and James Fitch, John Salisberry, Peter Giddyns, and Lewis Giddyns as hands allotted; and Wm. Carr connected with him as overseer from North Fork of Licking on the Fleming Road.

When a case was appealed from a magistrate's court to the County Court, the appellant became subject for costs, and had to pay up if it was continued. We note that in one case it was ordered that Jonathan Ruggles pay Mathew Burris "two shillings and one penny" for one day's attendance as witness. In fact, that was the price fixed when no mileage was counted.

In a case of perjury of which Ally Alexander was charged on account of her having sworn that she saw somebody carrying one of her father's hogs on a "dutch mare," the evidence was about such as is rendered in a present day court, and Miss Ally was discharged. This case is found in the March term, 1808, and came from Quick's Run.

The Legislature passed another law on the subject of Lewis County's seat of justice, and appointed the magistrates to fix a place. They fixed upon a plat of land given by Oke Hendrickson at Poplar Flat, and ordered a jail built there. Then Mr. Hendrickson deeded fifty acres of land, in trust to trustees, on which to build a town to be called "Mt. Vernon." The jail contract was given to Henry Miers and Adam Tegar at $650. They finally finished the jail, and sued the sheriff for the money; but he beat them, and they were given another order on a new sheriff by the court, and got their money. James Herbert was appointed jailer, and everything would have been all right this time, and Poplar Flat would have been the metropolis, had not John McBride thought there was some other place that suited better, and he brought a suit by his attorney, Marshall Key, and stopped the proceedings in "Mt. Vernon's" history.

In the meantime George Fearis, the presiding magistrate, had been made sheriff and John McDaniel, because of the death of Landen Calvert, had been commissioned justice of the peace, as also had Archibald Boyd, on account of the promotion of George Fearis, the election had passed and the county levy for the second year of Lewis County's existence had been laid at $1.25 and amounted to $727.50. Taxes to the amount of $17.44 had been collected by the clerk, making a total credit to the county of $744.94, from which the expenses, $206.15½, is deducted, leaving $538.78½ still to the credit side of the ledger. But this brings us up to the time when the next move was made at fixing the seat of justice.

It will be observed that the mouth of Quick's Run had been selected and abandoned for Poplar Flat, and now that "Mt. Vernon" had failed, the Legislature, by act of January 28, 1809, appointed Thomas Sloan, John Harrison, Jesse Hard, of Mason; Robt. Morrison, Jas. Reed, of Fleming; Thomas Warring and Charles Lewis, of Greenup County, commissioners to attend to the matter. They selected Clarksburg as the county seat, where it remained till January, 1864. (See Act, Chap. 3.) But the people of the county did not quit living now the court ceased to meet because the seat of justice had left Poplar Flat.

In October, 1808, commissioners had laid off two acres of land at Concord for the purpose of building a warehouse to inspect "hemp, tobacco, and flour," and thus, it seems, Mr. Stephenson, who owned the land and warehouse, started Concord on the road toward becoming a town.

In a settlement made with the sheriff, it was found that he still owed the county $408.02 for the year 1808.

PRESBYTERIAN CHURCH, VANCEBURG.

The record of the court shows cases of felony, larceny, bastardy, murder, etc., but none of the accused are convicted of being guilty, except one case of a Miss Catt, charged with murdering an infant; she was bound for her appearance at the Circuit Court.

Court of 1809.—Rowland T. Parker built the new jail at Clarksburg, and also gave land for the county seat and the town of Clarksburg. He kept a hotel, and gave one room for a clerk's office, "free of charge."

In the May term—May 22, 1809—Mr. Parker was granted tavern license, and at the June term Aaron Stratton, J. G. McDaniel, and Winslow Parker, as commissioners, fixed upon a place for the jail and also plans for building a court house, which was to be of "hewn logs, two good stories high," and 24 x 30 feet—which was done.

We have traced the history of the county up to the removal of the county seat to Clarksburg. Giving the succession of offices and officers; how they obtained them, and also how justice was meted out to the citizens of the county by concrete examples. We have the court, at Clarksburg, in the June term of 1809, commissioning Aaron Stratton, J. G. McDaniel, and Winslow Parker to fix upon a place for the jail and to lay plans for a two-story log court-house, to be 14 x 30 feet in size. This was done.

We now refer you to Chapter 4 for the succession in office of those hardy pioneers who have run so ably and well thus far, and who give to their successors examples of sobriety, veracity, and loyalty to their county that will call forth their best efforts to emulate.

We pass over a few years, as Chapter Four is helping us out, and dwell only on incidents of rivalry between the two thriving towns—Clarksburg and Vanceburg—until we see the times nearly approaching when Clarksburg will lose in the struggle and Vanceburg will win.

I have no doubt in my mind but that the experiences incident to the times intervening between the settlement of the county seat, at Clarksburg, and its change to Vanceburg at a later date (1864), was fraught with large interest to many men. There is always more or less of interest, financially and otherwise, in a small town just coming into prominence; but when that town is favored so generously as to become the county seat it becomes a rival to others and possibly more pleasantly and conveniently located towns. So it was with Vanceburg. She had the advantage of location, and naturally began a campaign for herself.

There was much in favor of Vanceburg, and

each point was given due prominence, I have no doubt. So the rivalry went on until the chances for a change, in the county seat, in favor of Vanceburg, became more of a certainty. Then property began to advance in price; buildings began to improve, and merchants to advertise more extensively until that all-successful December in 1863, when the decision for a change became a fact. Then there was, indeed, rejoicing, not over the loss Clarksburg sustained, but the gain Vanceburg had made. One good thing, in the change of place, was that all having interest in Clarksburg were not so far away but that they could transfer their business with but little cost, comparatively speaking. Fortunate, indeed, were those who had teams of their own. They soon were able to make the transfer and also to help their less fortunate neighbor. Some did not desire to move, and as a result are, or their descendants, living on the old town and court-house site, dwelling in peace and plenty.

REMOVAL TO VANCEBURG. — In December, 1863, the Legislature passed an act for the removal to Vanceburg, and appointed John Thomas Parker, F. M. Carr, and W. R. Stricklett as commissioners to attend to the matter. In January, 1864, the removal of the offices actually took place, and the archives of the

8

county were placed in the Old City Hall, on Main Street.

Then came the rush of attorneys, court attaches, fortune hunters, and adventurers, and Vanceburg rapidly rose from an old meadow, surrounded by a swamp, to an incoporrate city, with streets, alleys, hotels, bar-rooms, business houses, all accompanied with the vim, vigor, and enterprise of that war period, and always the accompaniment of an inflation of currency. Besides, at this time the Legislature was chartering oil companies by the hundred, and this vicinity was not without its part in that great excitement and money-spreading carnival.

The removal to new quarters was a source of trouble and worry to the officers and attorneys, as the records had to find new places of deposit and the change was uncustomary and unhandy, besides the amount of labor it required to handle, sort, and arrange the various books and papers connected with the county and circuit clerk's offices. The want of suitable places for the deposit of all this accumulation of years was keenly felt, and could only be remedied by the building of a new court-house with proper apartments for the various court records and for the accommodation of the officers. But this was to be speedily done, for another act was passed by the Legislature—Jan-

CHRISTIAN CHURCH, VANCEBURG.

uary 30, 1864—empowering the county to issue bonds and levy taxes for the purpose of building the new court-house. F. M. Carr, John Thomas Parker, and John C. Ingrim were appointed by the act as commissioners to let out the contract to build the house. They were also given power to sell the material in the old public buildings at Clarksburg, or to convey suitable parts of it for use in the construction of the new building.

The contract was given to a Mr. Flora, of Bracken County, and the buildings were finished in 1865 at a cost of $25,000. It can be said to the credit of the commissioners, the contractors, and the county that they anticipated the future growing needs of the county, and built a court-house adequate in dimensions for the increasing business of the years to come. They also gave a structure which for solidity and quality of material is not surpassed by any mountain county in Kentucky. For architectural design and adaptability to the purpose for which it is used it is not surpassed by many of the wealthy counties of the State.

It seems that there was one undesirable institution belonging to the county which had never been removed from Poplar Flat—that was the county infirmary. It remained there until about 1879, and also remained a source of distribution of revenue far beyond any good derived from it. In 1880 it was removed to the farm of Colonel G. W. Bruce, on "Kinny," which the County Court had purchased of him, and also made him keeper of the inmates. The inaccessibility of the situation, and other causes, made a reversal of contract necessary, and another appropriation of the people's money became necessary to the proper maintenance of the "unfortunates." As applications for admission to the "poorhouse" had to be passed upon by the county judge, it was thought best to plant the institution near the county seat. Therefore, a deal was made with David Seaman for his farm on Salt Lick, lying within a short distance of Vanceburg. The county retained control of the farm, furnished its teams, seed, implements, and provisions, and appointed commissioners from the magistrates to see to its management. They also appointed a "keeper" and paid him a monthly salary to superintend and work such of the inmates as were able to labor.

Under this system, it has been found, from report of R. H. Fisher, commissioner, that the products of the farm almost support the inmates, and gives them a better living than many of the poor people of the county make for themselves on the outside.

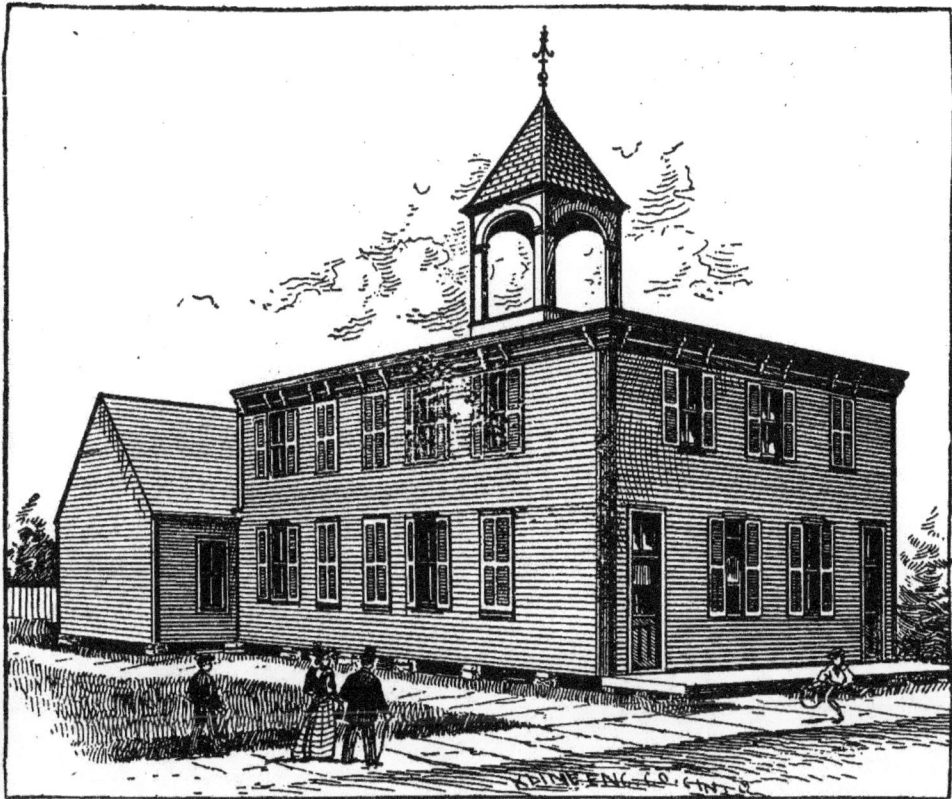

RIVERSIDE SEMINARY.

There was only one part of the old regime that still stuck to the management of the poor which was still detrimental to the interests of the taxpayer, and that was the habit of the magistrates in granting aid to poor people outside of the infirmary; but, happily, that has come to an end. We append the order of Judge Hillis in regard to this matter, of date February 17, 1896.

"MEDICAL AID TO PAUPERS

"Section 3,931 provides that the county judge shall have the power to order a poor person (or persons) to be taken to the poor house, and to cause medical aid to be employed at the public expense for such poor of the county, when admitted, as he may deem proper. The practice of the judge, ordering the doctors to wait on persons outside the infirmary has, like the allowances made heretofore, increased to such an extent as to amount to hundreds of dollars, and Judge Hillis is sustained by not only the county attorney, but all lawyers, in his position that these allowances are wholly unwarranted by law, and that any taxpayer could appeal them and permanently enjoin the payment. Our officials are certainly correct and right in discontinuing these practices, as they are amounting to thousands of dollars and fast absorbing the county's fund. The change may make a hardship for a while as to some extreme cases, but when the doctors fully understand the situation they will no doubt cheerfully aid our taxpayers in bearing the light burden of aiding and assisting the worthy poor of our county. No more orders will be made, except after admittance to the infirmary, on and after the first day of December, 1895. Now let the doctors and people take due notice and govern themselves accordingly."

In order that it may be known to what extent this practice had grown before the above order was promulgated, we append the published allowances made by the Lewis County Court, principally for aid outside, made at the session of April, 1894:

Medical Aid	$453.75
Merchandise	1,007.37
Coffins	46.00
Transportation and care	52.72
Total	$1,559.84

It is probable that of the merchandise item $600 worth was furnished to the infirmary proper, and $172.75 were fees of the physicians at the infirmary; but this still leaves $787.09 expended on the outside, that Judge Hillis has thought it his duty to have a decision of the courts against this leak in the county treasury.

GROWTH OF VANCEBURG.—With the completion of the new public buildings in January, 1861, the city of Vanceburg began to grow with amazing rapidity. Men of wealth saw an opportunity for speculation in town lots, and, in fact, there seemed to be a sort of general exodus

METHODIST EPISCOPAL CHURCH, SOUTH, VANCEBURG.

from the surrounding country to the city; and as money was plenty and the oil excitement raging, quite a number of citizens concluded that raising corn and hogs was a process too slow in getting rich. None of them made a million, and many of them, launching into some business they did not understand, and meeting a counteracting current after the war, closed, went down in the general wreck that follows most town booms.

A few men with means to "stay on," and a knowledge of the meaning of the phrase "terra firma," put their money into town lots, and then aided enterprises, such as turnpikes, that help build up a town, and have been rewarded by the accumulation of wealth by others as well as by themselves. Among those who have built houses and aided in upbuilding the city, may be mentioned Joshua B. Fitch, Judge G. M. Thomas, L. B. Ruggles, Socrates Ruggles, Henry C. Bruce. W. C. Halbert, Wm. and Mart Plummer, Wm. and Thos. Stricklett, G. W. Stamper, John Cox, Thomas H. Carter, and Clark & Hammond. Many others have built splendid residences such as that of Senator S. J. Pugh's built by J. R. Pugh, and the home of Chas. Hammond, H. K. Cole, G. W. Stamper, G. T. Halbert, and W. B. Fisher, besides a lot of cottages built by Miss Mary Halbert; and, in fact, single residences too numerous to mention which now adorn the city and show the taste of their owners and the architectural skill of the mechanic who put them together. Besides the private residences and business houses, lately there has been a church-building mania "on" in Vanceburg. The Methodist Episcopal Church was destroyed by fire several years ago, and that congregation turned itself loose and put up an edifice superior to any that then existed in the city. The contagion spread, and the Presbyterian congregation wanted a church, and they got up a model, though less in dimensions than that of their Methodist brethren, yet surpassing it in unique designs and finishing touches. Then the Christian Church, being a large congregation, began to plan for a new building. They soon found out the railroad trains made too much noise, and that their church was too close to the depot, so they proceeded to build a house that would not only be a fine structure, but with several departments to accommodate any phase of the Church work they might undertake. Thomas Carter, dead lately, built a three-story hotel of brick, with finishing touches in Italian marble, and the Church members argued that if business can have such a house as that in Vanceburg, religion should have a place of worship equal to if not more beautiful than any. But space does not permit an enumeration of the various and single efforts at building which now make up this compact little city. But we must not fail to note the splendid school building, erected by Professor L. Rolf, as Riverside Seminary, in the east end of the city. This is a model school building, and evinces the acumen of its projector in the needs of a school.

Vanceburg to-day has a railroad, the C. &. O., running the whole length of Third Street, and crossing over to Second, passes between it and Front through the remainder of the city. In the last few years the streets have all been graded and macadamized with limestone. The sewers and gutters have been completed, and solid stone and concrete pavements are laid on almost all the streets, beside a board and stone walk to South Vanceburg, almost a mile in length, has been in use several years.

There are five church buildings, viz.: the Methodist Episcopal Church, the Methodist Episcopal Church, South, the Presbyterian, the Christian, and the Heinsch Chapel Colored Methodist Church.

The public school building and the buildings of the Riverside Seminary are edifices that denote the intellectual vigor of the citizens, and, together with their effects, these buildings

are a monument to education of which all
Vanceburg citizens are proud. Beside these
there is now open each year a county high school,
under the efficient management of Professor
C. S. Dale and two assistants. Also each year
there is conducted a normal for the benefit
of young men and women wishing to prepare
for examinations.

In the mercantile pursuits there are three
drygoods stores—G. W. Stamper, S. J. Pugh
& Co., and J. T. Ort; M. Marcus, gent's clothing;
three drygoods and grocery stores—E. G. Clark,
and Hike, of South Vanceburg, and E. Heinisch;
and six grocery stores—G. W. Stamper & Co.,
J. M. Donehoo & Co., J. L. Chadwick, John
Cox, Bagby & Co., and D. Boyd, of South
Vanceburg; and two hardware stores—N. G.
Fisher & Son, and Ingram and Foster; one
planing mill—John Cox & Son; one button
factory—The Vanceburg Button Factory Co.;
one canning factory—Vanceburg Canning Factory; one tannery—A. J. Stein & Co.; one
tobacco hogshead stave factory—W. W. Dugan
& Co.; one ice and electric light plant combine
—Vanceburg Electric Light and Ice Co.; two
livery, feed, and sale stables—Sam'l Pollitt &
Son, and Benjamin Stricklett; three blacksmith
shops—William Grote, Huber & Co., ————;
three feed stores—Henderson and Stricklett,

9   HIGH SCHOOL BUILDING, VANCEBURG.

Staggs Bros., and Captain Webb & Co.; three hotels—Carter House, St. Nicholas, and St. Charles; three millinery establishments—G. W. Stamper, Mrs. Powers, and M. Marcus; two furniture stores—John Cox & Son and G. W. Stamper; one printing office—The Vanceburg *Sun*; one poultry commission house—H. A. Staly & Son; one telephone exchange—The Vanceburg Telephone Co.; three barber shops—Hawthorne, Ham and Barnes; two drug stores—The Gem Pharmacy and Opera House Drug Store; one undertaker's establishment—Plummer Bros; one monumental works—The Vanceburg Monumental Works Co. As these pages go to press there is being completed plans for a Loose Leaf Tobacco Warehouse, to be erected inside the city limits.

Professional.—Four physicians and dentists and three lawyers. One magistrate and county attorney and circuit judge and the county judge; the sheriff and circuit clerk; coroner and county surveyor. There are four resident ministers—two Methodist, one Presbyterian, and one Disciples minister; eight teachers in the city schools, and the county superintendent of schools has his home and office here.

The city has seemed to be able to pass through all the close, panicky times without serious damage.

Compared with other cities of like dimensions (Vanceburg is a city of the fifth class) and wealth, Vanceburg seems to be in better condition than many others. (For taxes, debts, officers, etc., see table at end of this chapter.)

This city has hitherto drawn its support from the timber resources of the adjacent country, but that supply is nearly exhausted, and other means must be found to continue the growth and prosperity of the city. One important industry started in the country near is fruit growing. The canning establishment now being operated in the city, which will be an impetus to that industry, already of no mean proportions, and will give spirit and enterprise to all kinds of business from the money it will disseminate.

The County Fairground is located one mile south of Vanceburg—a cut of which is shown on page 135.

Some Incidents of Note.—The land for the county buildings was donated by W. C. Halbert, Sr. Probably the first bonds issued by Lewis County were those issued by County Clerk Thos. W. Mitchell for the purpose of building the court-house, in 1864. There were no stubs left of these bonds, and it is not certain just how many were issued, but it is known that the buildings cost $25,000. Bonds were a new sort of investment in Lewis County, and capital seemed a little chary of them; but Judge Thomas came forward and subscribed for $1,500 worth of them, and then afterward they went lively, for then, as now, people put confidence in the judgment of the judge in all financial transactions.

Joshua B. Fitch was the sheriff to whom was intrusted the collection of the additional levy to pay off this bonded debt. Socrates Holbrook, whose picture hangs in the court-house as a souvenir of kindly remembrance by Lewis County people, was county judge at this eventful period in our county's history.

W. C. Halbert, Sr., who donated the land for the buildings, was county attorney, and to him the people are indebted for the decent public buildings they now possess, and it may be said for the very existence of Vanceburg as anything more than a one-store town, with a hitching rack and two good-sized mudholes; for it was to his indefatigable effort in securing a petition with the names of all the voters in the county and presenting the same to the Legislature that the act was passed to remove the county seat from Clarksburg to Vanceburg. Just think of Clarksburg as a county seat after a railroad was built along the river, and see how Lewis County was helped to the front by the removal in 1864. In fact, the act of Judge Thomas in subscribing for bonds, the push and vim of Mr. Halbert, and the industry, energy, and honesty with which the county officials, as a body, did their whole duty, brought Lewis County to the front, and made the county town equal to those more wealthy districts of the State.

SCENE ON THE VANCEBURG FAIRGROUNDS.

CHAPTER III

LEGISLATIVE ACTS IN FAVOR OF THE COUNTY.

ACTS OF 1808: An Act establishing academies in the Counties of Lewis and Clay.

First.—Be it enacted by the General Assembly that Winslow Parker, Robert Robb, Aaron Stratton, William Walker, John Radford, James Barclay, and Rowland Thomas, gentlemen shall be, and are hereby constituted a body politic and corporate, to be known by the name of the trustees of the Lewis Academy, and by that name shall have perpetual succession and a common seal, with power to change or alter the same at their pleasure; and as a body corporate, shall be authorized to exercise all the powers and privileges that are now enjoyed by the trustees of any academy or seminary of learning within this State; and, on the death, resignation, or other disqualification of any of the trustees aforesaid, or their successors, a majority of the remaining trustees shall fill such vacancy, and the person so appointed shall be vested with the same power and authority as if specially named by this act; and the by name and style of the trustees of the Lewis Academy may sue and implead, or be sued and impleaded in any court in law or equity, or before any tribunal having cognizance of the same.

Second.—The said trustees and their successors shall have power in their corporate capacity to purchase, or receive by donation, any lands, tenements, inheritance, moneys, rents, goods, and chattels, and to hold same by the name aforesaid to them and their successors forever for the use of said Academy, and to sell, alien, or transfer any such lands, goods, and chattels and apply the proceeds thereof to the use and benefit thereof.

Third.—The said trustees are entitled to locate, survey, and patent the quantity of six thousand acres of vacant land, on the terms and conditions prescribed in an act entitled, "An Act to establish and endow certain academies," and the several acts amendatory thereto; and for that purpose, any contract with any person or persons, to locate and have the same surveyed, for which services they are authorized to give and convey to such person or persons a part of said lands, not exceeding two thousand acres, and may also dispose of one thousand acres for the purpose of erecting the necessary buildings and providing books and other apparatus for the use of the said academy.

Fourth.—The person first named herein, or,

in his absence or refusal to act, the next, shall notify the time and place for the first meeting of the trustees, and on an attendance of a majority thereof they shall appoint a chairman and clerk, who shall severally take on oath "well and truly to execute the duties of their office," and thereafter the board may be called by the chairman or any two of the trustees. The said trustees shall have power to adjourn from day to day, to make and ordain such laws, rules, and ordinances as they may deem proper, not inconsistent with the laws of this Commonwealth; and moreover, to fix on a proper place for erecting the buildings for the said academy. Provided, that a majority of all the trustees shall be necessary to attend on the making of any contract, by-laws, or fixing the permanent seat for the same.

Fifth.—A majority of the said trustees shall have power to engage and employ a competent number of masters and professors to said academy, to fix their salaries and the salary of their clerk, as also the terms of tuition; and, on the misconduct of any master, professor, or student, may dismiss or expel such master, professor, or student from the said academy.

ACTS OF 1809: An Act allowing additional justices of the peace in certain counties.

First.—The County of Lewis shall have one

in addition to the number already allowed by law.

An Act for fixing the permanent seat of justice of Lewis County.

Whereas, it is represented to the present General Assembly that the seat of justice for Lewis County is improperly fixed; for remedy whereof,

First.—Be it enacted by the General Assembly that Thomas Sloo, John Howison, and Jesse Hard, of Mason County; Robert Morrison, James Reed, of Fleming; Thomas Warring, Sr., and Charles Lewis, of Greenup, be and they are hereby appointed commissioners, or a majority of them, to fix upon and establish a place for the permanent seat of justice in said County of Lewis.

Second.—Be it further enacted, that the said commissioners or majority of them, after having severally taken an oath before some justice of the peace for said county, that they will well and truly execute the trust confided by this act, without favor, affection, or partiality shall meet at the present place of holding court in said county, on the third Monday in March next, or any such day thereafter as may best suit, and having so assembled, shall proceed to view so much of the said county as in their opinion will be necessary to form a correct knowledge of the probable population thereof, and such review being made, shall proceed to fix upon a place for a permanent seat of justice in said County of Lewis.

Third.—And be it further enacted, that the said commissioners or majority of them, having so fixed upon a spot for such permnaent seat of justice, shall make out their report in writing, signed and sealed; therein laying off, by proper miles and bounds, one acre of land, designated for the establishment of public buildings; which report shall be returned to the next County Court of said county, to be entered on the record therein.

Fourth.—And be it further enacted, that the County Court of said county shall immediately thereafter proceed to contract by purchase, or otherwise, for said acre of land; as soon as may be, have the necessary public buildings erected thereon for the use of the county, which shall thereafter be the permanent seat of justice for said County of Lewis.

Fifth.—And be it further enacted, that each of the commissioners attending under this act shall be entitled to two dollars per day for each day they may be employed in the execution thereof, to be levied and paid out of the next county levy of said county.

ACTS OF 1809: An Act to alter the time of holding certain Circuit Courts.

SECTION 6.—The Circuit Court of Lewis County shall commence and be held on the third Monday in March, in every year, instead of the fourth, and may, at such time, continue six judicial days, if the business thereof require it.

ACTS OF 1810: An Act to alter the holding of the Lewis County Circuit Court.

First.—Be it enacted by the General Assembly of the Commonwealth of Kentucky, Section 3, that the Circuit Court for the County of Lewis shall be held on the third Mondays in June and September instead of the fourth Mondays in July and October. And the County Courts for said county shall, after the first day of March next, be held on the same Mondays in every month, in which Circuit Courts are respectively directed to be held, except the months in which the Circuit Courts are holden.

There seems to be no acts in favor of Lewis County in the years of 1811-12. In 1813 we find an Act, approved January 8, 1814, authorizing one additional justice of the peace in Lewis County; also an Act approved January 30, 1812, changing the Circuit Courts to the fourth Mondays of April, July, and October in each year, and the County Courts to the same days, except the months in which the Circuit Courts are held. (See Act of 1812, p. 55.)

ACTS OF 1814: There is an Act on page 292 of the Acts of 1814 establishing an election precinct in Lewis County.

ACTS OF 1815: There were no Acts in favor of Lewis passed at this session, so far as can be determined from the record.

ACTS OF 1816: We find an Act, approved February 4, 1817, changing the time of holding the Lewis Circuit Courts to the third Mondays in April, July, and October. (Acts of 1816, p. 240.)

ACTS OF 1817: An Act to authorize the County Court of Lewis County to lay an additional levy.

WHEREAS, it has been represented to the General Assembly of Kentucky that the jail in the County of Lewis was consumed by fire since the sitting of the last levy court in said county, and in consequence thereof the citizens of said county are subject to considerable inconvenience: For remedy thereof, Be it enacted, etc., that the County Court of Lewis County be, and is hereby authorized, at their next February court, to lay an additional levy and make an appropriation for the erection and building of a jail in said county, a majority of all the justices in commission for the county being present at said court.

ACTS OF 1818: An Act to establish election

precincts, Section 3. Be it further enacted, that the place of holding the election in the first precinct in Lewis County be changed, and that hereafter the election in said precinct shall be held at the house of John D. Everitt.

There seem to be no Acts in 1819-20-21-22.

ACTS OF 1823: An Act to declare "Kinniconnick," in part, a navigable stream.

WHEREAS, it is represented to the present General Assembly that it would be of great advantage to a portion of the citizens of Lewis County to declare Kinniconnick a navigable stream, so far up from its mouth as Jeremiah Moore's mill.

Therefore, Be it enacted, etc., that from and after the passage of this Act the said stream, known by the name aforesaid, in the said County of Lewis, shall be, and the same is hereby declared, a navigable stream from its junction with the Ohio River so far up as the mill of said Jeremiah Moore, and any person or persons who may be convicted of felling timber into said stream, or otherwise obstructing or in any way injuring the navigation thereof, from its said junction with the Ohio River to the aforesaid mill, shall be subject to all the pains and penalties now imposed by law for a like offense, in relation to any other navigable waters within the Commonwealth; Provided, however, that rights of any person or persons now owning or possessing any mill, or other machinery, upon said stream shall not hereby be impaired or lessened.

ACTS OF 1823: An Act to allow additional justices of the peace.

SECTION 12.—That there be allowed to the County of Lewis one justice of the peace, in addition to the number now allowed by law, to reside on the waters of Kinniconnick Creek, in the neighborhood of Solomon Thomas.

ACTS OF 1825: An Act to authorize the trustees of Lewis Academy to sell the lands belonging to that institution.

The trustees are authorized to sell and convey the lands of the institution, and to take bond from any agents they may appoint to sell the land. (See Acts of 1825, p. 26.)

ACTS OF 1826: Chapter 70 is an Act for the benefit of Margaret Alice Tracy, nee Norman, relieving her of marriage vows with Isaac Tracy, who was spending her fortune in Indiana. She had left him and started back to Lewis County, Ky., but he overtook her at Cincinnati and had her remaining property, by an order of court, vested in a trustee in said city; and she was unable to get it while she was legally his wife. For this reason she was granted divorce.

ACTS OF 1827: CHAPTER 101.—"That town

10

of Vanceburg in Lewis County shall be, and hereby is established, a town, by the name aforesaid; and that it shall be the duty of the County Court to appoint five trustees for said town as soon as practicable: the said trustees to meet at the house of R. T. Parker, in said town, and take the oath of office of trustee aforesaid, form a board, appoint a clerk, and cause a survey to be made in conformity ' to the original plan of said town," etc. This is the first legislative charter for Vanceburg, and was approved January 24, 1827.

ACTS OF 1828: An Act to establish election precincts, etc.

SECTION 4.—Be it further enacted, that all that part of the County of Lewis included and lying on the waters of Kinniconnick Creek, and between said creek and the Greenup County line, and including what is called Upper Kinniconnick, shall be an election precinct in said County of Lewis, and that the elections be held at the house now owned and occupied by William McEldowney, Esquire.

ACTS OF 1829: An Act to change the time of holding Circuit Courts in certain counties.

SECTION 3.—Be it further enacted, that the Circuit Court for the County of Lewis shall commence on the third Mondays in March, June, and September in each year, and sit, at each term, six judicial days, if the business thereof shall require it; and all writs, subpœnas, recognizances, attachments, or other process, which has been or may be made returnable to the next term of the Lewis Circuit Court, shall be returnable to the same at the time herein provided for its sitting.

ACTS OF 1830: An Act to change time of holding Circuit Court, etc.

SECTION 4.—Be it further enacted, that the Circuit Court for the County of Lewis shall hereafter sit on the fourth Mondays in the months of March, June, and September, and may sit six judicial days if the business requires it.

Act Act for the benefit of Archibald Frizzell, coroner of Lewis County.

Be it enacted, etc., that Archibald Frizzell, coroner of the County of Lewis, be, and he is hereby, allowed until the first day of April next to renew his official bond, which may be given at any time before said time; and any forfeiture, which may have taken place on account of failing to renew his bond aforesaid, is hereby released.

ACTS OF 1831: An Act to change voting precinct, etc.

SECTION 2.—Be it further enacted, that the place of voting in the election precinct in Lewis

County, "Kinniconnick" precinct be, and the same is hereby changed to the house of John Thompson; and it shall be the duty of the County Court of Lewis County to appoint judges and a clerk of the election, who shall meet at the house of the said John Thompson and conduct the elections according to the laws of this Commonwealth regulating elections.

An Act to change the time of holding Circuit Court in Lewis County.

Be it enacted, etc., that hereafter the Circuit Court for the Lewis Circuit shall commence on Wednesdays succeeding the fourth Mondays in March, June, and September; and that all process and bonds, or recognizances returnable to the March term of said court, and heretofore held, shall be taken and considered returnable to the time fixed by the Act for holding the said March term.

ACTS OF 1832: An Act to change the time of holding Circuit Courts, etc.

Be it enacted, etc., that the Lewis Circuit Court shall hereafter commence on the second Monday in April, the second Monday in June, and the second Monday in October, and continue six judicial days, if the business thereof require it.

An Act to change places of voting, etc.

SECTION 1.—Be it enacted, etc., that the

place of voting in the election precinct called
Everett's, in Lewis County, be changed from
the house of John D. Everett to the town of
Concord, and the same rules and regulations
shall be observed in voting and comparing polls
as now directed by law.

SEC. 2.—Be it further enacted, that the
place of voting in Forman's Bottom precinct,
in Lewis County, be changed from the house
formerly occupied by Green Smith to the house
now occupied by William Marshall, and the
same rules and regulations shall be observed in
voting and comparing polls as now directed by
law governing election in this Commonwealth.
(The session of 1832 passed an act authorizing
the Legislature to meet on the last day of December in each year.)

ACTS OF 1833: There is a long Act passed
by this Assembly relating to land warrants to
be issued and laid on vacant land in the county
for the purpose of improving the State Road
from the North Fork of Licking, via Clarksburg and Vanceburg, to the Greenup County
line. For this purpose James Hannah, John
McDaniel, and Pleasant M. Savage were appointed commissioners. Also for the improvement of the road to Concord from Barton Lee's
to the town of Concord. Joseph Cox and
Samuel Stevenson were appointed commis-

sioners for this work. One hundred and fifty dollars worth of land warrants to be issued for the Concord road and three hundred and fifty for the first-named road. The commissioners were prohibited from selling the warrants for less than "Five dollars for one hundred acres."

ACTS OF 1834: An Act allowing additional justice.

SECTION 1.—Be it enacted, etc., that there shall be allowed an additional justice of the peace to the County of Lewis.

NOTE.—Justices were appointed by the governor until 1850, the Legislature authorizing a certain member to be appointed in each county, according to populations, etc.

ACTS OF 1835: An Act to change the holding of the Greenup and Lewis Circuit Courts.

SECTION 2.—Be it further enacted, that the Lewis Circuit Court shall hereafter commence on the first Mondays in April, July, and October, and shall continue five judicial days if the business of the court require it.

ACTS OF 1836: It was enacted by the Legislature of 1836 that Lewis Circuit Court be changed to last Mondays in March, June, and September.

An Act to establish an election precinct, etc.

SECTION 1.—Be it enacted, etc., that all that part of Lewis County, including the voters 'living on the waters of Laurel and Grassy Creek, shall be an. election precinct, at which the elections shall be held at the house of ——— Staggs, Sr., under the same rules and regulations that elections are held in other precincts of said county.

SEC. 2—That hereafter the place of holding the elections in the Kinniconnick precinct shall be at the house of William Heath, in said precinct.

ACTS OF 1837: There were four Acts passed at this session relating to Lewis County—one to appoint commissioners to make the line between Lewis and· Greenup Counties, two Acts for the benefit of the sheriff, giving him more time to collect his fees; and one for the benefit of the jailer.

ACTS OF 1838: One additional justice of the peace was allowed Lewis County, and an Act for the benefit of Thompson N. Stratton, late sheriff, was passed at this session.

ACTS OF 1839: In this session Mower's precinct was established, and the place of voting fixed at the house of Jacob Mowery. An Act was passed for the benefit of W. B. Parker, late sheriff, allowing him to list his claims with the present sheriff for collection, as he had moved into Mason County. An Act for the benefit of Charles Cain, sheriff, was also passed, and one for the benefit of William Watkins, surveyor.

ACTS OF 1840: The session of 1840-41 passed Acts for an additional constable in Lewis County, for the benefit of Thomas Mitchell, jailer, allowing him to live in another house than the county jailer's house, and to collect fees during the time he had no bond in force. Also two Acts for the benefit of Sheriff Chas. Caines, and W. B. Parker.

ACTS OF 1841: More Acts for the benefit of the sheriffs of Lewis County, one allowing Thos. Parker more time to settle with the auditors, and also requiring the auditor to settle with Chas. Caines, late sheriff of Lewis County for the year 1840.

ACTS OF 1842: The voting place in Forman's Bottoms was changed by an Act from the house of William Marshall to that of Nathaniel Garland, February 28, 1842; also the voting place in Laurel precinct was changed from the house of Joseph Staggs to that of Josiah W. Staggs.

ACTS OF 1843: There appears to be no Act concerning Lewis County in this year. Our representative, Socrates Holbrook, probably thought we had enough Acts for the benefit of the sheriff and changing the time of holding Circuit Court.

ACTS OF 1844: An Act to allow one additional justice of the peace to reside on Lurel or Grassy Fork of Kinny was passed on February 16, 1844.

ACTS OF 1845: Chapter 295 reviews the Act of January 25, 1833, in relation to the town of Concord, and Section 2 appoints Arthur Stephenson, Thos. A. Duke, John Lovel, B. D. Taylor, and Henry Grimes as trustees to continue in office until May, 1846.

One Act for the benefit of Thomas Parker, Alexander Bruce, John Johnson, and Charles Caines, allowing further time to collect fees as sheriff and late sheriffs of Lewis County, is all we find in 1844-45.

ACTS OF 1846: An Act for the benefit of Daniel O'Neil and Sarah Graham, allowing Lewis County Court to appropriate money for their support.

ACTS OF 1847: Four Acts were passed in the session of 1846-47. One adding a justice of the peace to reside in the town of Clarksburg, an Act to prevent persons not residents from seining on Kinniconnick.

A special term of the Circuit Court of Lewis County was authorized to be held beginning on the second Monday in June, 1847, for the trial of chancery and criminal cases. Also an Act changing the time of holding the county court, April and October terms, to the first Mondays in said months.

ACTS OF 1848: An Act legalizing the acts of John P. Pell, surveyor, and giving more time to execute bond, etc. Also an additional justice at Esculapia Springs.

CHAPTER 116 in the Acts of 1848-49 incorporates M. T. C. Gould, William C. Halbert, Mark Wallingford, and their successors as the Esculapia Mineral Spring Company, with an authorized capital of fifty thousand dollars. The Act was approved January 26, 1849.

The State Road, between Anderson M. Garland's and Robert Meredith's, was authorized to be changed by this Legislature.

ACTS OF 1849: Section 3, Chapter 455, Acts of 1848-49, appoints Thomas Marhsall, Mark Wallingford, M. T. C. Gould, James McCormick, John McDowell, and S. Holbrook as commissioners to build a turnpike road through Lewis County, to be known as the Maysville and Lewis County Turnpike, and to extend from Maysville by way of Esculapia to Vanceburg. This is another of the bubbles which bursted coincident with Gould's Mineral Spring scheme.

The Legislatures of former years were rich in "vacant lands," and many were the acts trying to get rid of it; for instance:

"Be it enacted, etc., that the Lewis County Court shall apply the proceeds of the vacant lands of said county to the removal of obstructions in Kinniconnick River and to the improvement of the navigation of said stream."

ACTS OF 1850: There are only two Acts concerning Lewis County passed at this session. Both relate to roads; one changes the charter of the Maysville and Lewis County Turnpike Company so as to allow the company to use plank instead of gravel on said road, and the other authorized the Lewis County Court, on petition of Henry Adair, to change the State Road through his lands.

ACTS OF 1850: An Act appointing Isaac Middleton, J. R. Duke, U. R. McKellup, George M. Thomas, Joseph Sparks, Judge Baldwin, and N. R. Garland to divide Lewis County into eight magisterial districts was passed and approved December 12, 1850.

ACTS OF 1851: An Act placing Lewis County in the tenth judicial district, together with Bath, Fleming, Greenup, Carter, Lawrence, Montgomery, and Morgan.

An Act appointing Hesekiah Jenkins, Thomas Glascock, Thomas Marshall, and Mark Wallingford commissioners to remark and survey the time between Mason and Lewis Counties.

CHAPTER 528 changes the places of voting

in district number five from the house of Stephen Nowland to Josiah Staggs, and lays off the boundary of district number six, and leaves the voters to decide whether the polling place shall be at John B. Fenley's house or at the town of Tollesburg.

An Act to organize County Courts fixes the time for the court of Lewis County on the second Monday in March, June, September and December.

NOTE.—Under the Constitution of 1850 the Legislature met biennially.

There were no Acts for 1852.

ACTS OF 1853: An Act giving Wm. S. Parker, sheriff of Lewis County, further time of two years to collect taxes, fee bills, and muster fines.

ACTS OF 1854: An Act for the benefit of J. M. Todd, sheriff of Lewis County, releasing him from all damages upon a judgment standing against him for failing to pay over the revenue of 1852, he having already paid the full amount of revenue, interests, and costs.

An Act to prescribe the time of holding the Greenup and Lewis Circuit Courts.

SECTION 2.—That hereafter the Lewis Circuit Court shall commence on the Mondays succeeding the termination of the May and November terms of the Greenup Circuit Court in each year, and continue twelve judicial days, if the business thereof require it.

An Act placing Lewis County in the Ninth Congressional District passed February 24, 1854, over the veto of the governor.

Chapter 665 reads as follows: "Be it enacted by the General Assembly of the Commonwealth of Kentucky, that after the passage of this Act the April and October terms of the Lewis County Court shall be held on the third Monday of each month, instead of the first Monday.

There were no Acts for 1855.

ACTS OF 1856: In February, 1856, the Legislature passed an Act authorizing the building of the "Mud Turnpike" from Vanceburg to Mt. Carmel.

ACTS OF 1857: An Act in relation to a road in Lewis and Carter Counties allows further time for collecting tax to build same.

There is also a similar Act on account of a road in Fleming and Lewis Counties—the "Mud Turnpike."

There was also a long Act passed appointing commissioners, laying off road districts, and stating who are exempt from work; also reducing all road laws in Lewis and Greenup Counties. Also an Act to increase the county levy to two dollars for the purpose of building a jail in Lewis County.

There were no Acts for 1858-59-60.

ACTS OF 1861: At a called session held in May, 1861, an Act was passed changing the voting place in Henderson precinct to the school house at Poplar Flat.

An Act incorporating the town of Quincy, in Lewis County, making the boundary as follows: Beginning at a large elm tree at the lower landing on the land of Geo. Fruit, deceased, on the bank of the Ohio River; thence a straight line to the house of Samuel McKee, including the same; thence a straight line to the house of Abram Thomas, including the same; thence running so as to include the saw mill and house of S. Smith to the county road at the mouth of the lane running to the New Hampshire landing; thence with said lane toward the river to the lower line of Labun Woodworth; thence up the river with his line to the upper lane to the upper Woodworth tract, and with the line of the said Woodworth tract down said lane toward the river until it strikes the river; thence down the river to the beginning.

Nelson G. Morse, Wm. S. McKinny, and Henry McKee were appointed judges of an election for town officers, to be held the first Saturday in May, 1861.

An Act amending an Act passed January 30, 1851, granting Lewis County power and right to sell seminary land; the amendment gives Lewis County the right to sue and be sued.

CHAPTER 428: Be it enacted, etc., that Salt Lick Creek in Lewis County, Ky., from its main forks near Adam Bertram's to the mouth of said creek be, and the same hereby is, declared a navigable stream.

This Act shall take effect from and after its passage.

An Act paying Geo. T. Halbert twenty-five dollars as State Agent in collecting taxes on the lands of Moylan's heirs, in Lewis and Carter Counties.

ACTS OF 1862: This session was prolific in Acts for Lewis County. In the first place we have an Act for the benefit of J. R. Garland and his sureties as sheriff. Next, an Act granting the trustees of the Tollesboro school district time until the first day of February, 1862, to teach and report the free school.

ACTS OF 1863: An Act amending the charter of Concord. Wharfboats and other boats shall not occupy the public grade without license from the town trustees. Trustees may charge not exceeding thirty dollars for use of said grade, per annum. A fine of five dollars for disregarding Act to be collected before any justice or police judge.

An Act changing the voting place in Kinni-

connick district to the Jefferson schoolhouse;
also another Act incorporating the Kinniconnick Bridge Company, authorizing Geo. W.
Bruce, Jubes Fruit, and other persons to build
a bridge or finish approaches to the railroad
bridge, and charge toll upon the same until
they had received the money expended and
ten per centum thereon, when the County Courts
shall declare the bridge free to public travel.

An Act to incorporate the Salt Lick Bridge
Company makes Wm. H. Taylor, James Hiner,
James C. Cole, Jackson Norris, Robert Bedford,
W. C. Halbert, N. B. Webster, J. C. Ingrim,
Thos. H. Thomas, John McCall, and Thos. D.
Parker corporators and authorizes a capital
stock of $3,000, in shares of $10 each, to open
subscription book, and when $1,000 is sub-
scribed, to call meeting and hold an election
for officers. The stockholders were then to
pay for the stock and to begin work on the
bridge. When the bridge was completed they
had power to collect tolls and pay dividends,
etc.

An Act allowing the sureties of James M.
Todd to replevy the judgment held against them
by the Commonwealth.

An Act for the benefit of the Vanceburg
school district, allowing till June 1, 1862, to
the public school.

CHAPTER 778 incorporates the Vanceburg Male and Female School, with W. C. Halbert, Thos. D. Parker, Geo. M. Thomas, Thos. H. Thomas, and H. Ingrim as corporators. This is the beginning of the public school building now in use in this city. (Page 446.)

CHAPTER 1049 legalizes the election of trustees in the town of Vanceburg, on account of some irregularity in holding the election.

ACTS OF 1864: An Act for the removal of the seat of justice for Lewis County.

Be it enacted by the General Assembly of the Commonwealth of Kentucky:

First.—That the seat of justice for Lewis County be, and the same is hereby, removed from the town of Clarksburg and established in the town of Vanceburg.

Second.—That John Thomas Parker, F. M. Carr, and W. R. Stricklett be, and they are hereby, appointed commissioners to select, in the town of Vanceburg, a suitable site and grounds for the erection of a court-house, jail, and other necessary public buildings, not to be less than one acre. Said commissioners shall have power to contract for the land for said public buildings, upon such terms and at such prices as they may agree upon, or to accept a donation of same. The land selected by the commissioners, and purchased or donated, shall

11

be conveyed by the grantor or donor by deed to
the Lewis County Court, and their successors
in office. The sum agreed to be paid for the
land shall be allowed by the next succeeding
Court of Claims for said county, and payment
thereof provided by the county levy. The said
commissioners shall also procure suitable rooms
in the town of Vanceburg for holding courts
and clerk's offices, to be used for such purpose
until suitable buildings are erected; so soon
as such buildings are procured, and a deed of
conveyance made for the land selected for
public buildings, the commissioners shall make
a report to the Lewis County Court, together
with a deed, which shall be recorded. When
the commissioner's report shall be filed as aforesaid, it shall be the duty of the clerk of the
Circuit and County Court, and the judge of the
Quarterly Court, within twenty days thereafter,
to remove all books, records, and papers belonging and appertaining to the respective officers aforesaid to the rooms provided therefor
in Vanceburg; and the Circuit, County, and
Quarterly Courts for said county shall thereafter be held in Vanceburg, at the time prescribed by law: Provided, that until the removal of the records, etc., as above provided,
the courts for said county shall be held at
Clarksburg.

Third.—It shall be the duty of the judge of the County Court, at the first term of said court held in the town of Vanceburg, by order, to cause the justices of the peace for said county to be summoned to attend at the next term thereafter of said court, at which time, if a majority of the justices in said county be not present, the court shall adjourn from day to day, until a majority of said justices are present, and may issue attachments to compel attendance; and when a majority of said justices are present, they shall take the necessary steps and make all necessary provisions for the erection of public buildings for said county.

Fourth.—That the County Court of Lewis County, a majority of the justices being present in court, shall have full power and authority to make sale, to the highest bidder, at public auction, on such credit as the court may determine, of the public ground, and buildings thereon, in the town of Clarksburg in said county; and they shall take bond from the purchaser for the price, with good personal security, payable to the said County Court, and their successors in office, which bond shall have the force of a replevin bond. They may appoint a commissioner to make the sale and prescribe the terms, but such sale, if made by a commissioner, shall be subject to the approval and confirmation of the County Court. The justices of the peace for said county, a majority being present in court, and concurring, shall have the power and authority to remove the public buildings, or any part thereof, that they may wish to use in the erection of new buildings at Vanceburg, and to sell what may remain, as above provided. The County Court shall appropriate the proceeds of the sale to the erection of public buildings in Vanceburg.

Fifth.—That, upon payment of the purchase money for the public grounds, and such of the public buildings as may be sold, the county judge shall execute to the purchaser or purchasers as deed of conveyance therefor, vesting in the purchaser or purchasers such title as the County Court may hold to said property.

Sixth.—That any two of the commissioners named in the second section of the Act, concurring, shall have full power to perform the duties required of the three. And in case said commissioners should fail or refuse to act, or die, it shall be the duty of the County Court of Lewis County to appoint others—such appointments to be made not later than the February term, 1864, of said court; and the commissioners, so appointed by said court, shall have all the powers of those named in the second section of this Act.

Seventh.—This Act shall take effect from its passage.

An Act providing for the erection of public buildings in Lewis County.

Be it enacted, etc.:

First.—That an ad valorem tax of ten cents is hereby levied upon each one hundred dollar's worth of taxable property subject to taxation for State revenue, in Lewis County, for the purpose of building a court-house, clerk's office, jail, and jailer's house in the town of Vanceburg, Lewis County, which tax shall be levied for and during five years in succession, commencing with the year 1864, which shall be the first year.

Second.—The sheriff of Lewis County shall collect the tax authorized by the Act, and pay the same over as ordered and directed by the County Court of Lewis County. The sheriff shall execute bond, in the Lewis County Court, with good security to be approved by said court, conditioned to faithfully collect and pay over said tax as the said court may direct; and he and his securities shall be liable on said bond for all money collected or which he could have collected under this Act, which he shall fail to pay over when due, and ordered to do so, by the County Court of Lewis County; and suit may be brought on said bond, in the name of

Lewis County Court, in the Lewis Circuit Court for any failure of his duty under this Act. The said tax shall be due from the sheriff, at the same time that the State revenue is due. He shall receive and retain in his hands the same compensation for collecting said tax as is allowed by law for collecting the State revenue.

Third.—It shall be lawful for the clerk of Lewis County Court to issue the bonds of the County of Lewis in one, two, three, four, and five years, bearing interest at six per centum per annum, and payable annually, for the purpose of building said court-house, clerk's office, jail, and jailer's house. The bonds aforesaid may be sold by said County Court clerk on such terms as to him may seem right and proper; and the tax authorized to be collected by Act is hereby pledged to the payment of said bonds and the interest thereon. The said clerk may issue said bonds and hand them over to the contractor upon the order of the commissioners authorized to let out the contracts for the public buildings, which bonds shall be in such amounts as said commissioners may direct; and the money arising from the sale of said bonds shall be paid over to the contractors, upon the order of said commissioners. Before said County Court clerk shall receive the money on said bonds, he shall execute a covenant with good security, to be approved by the County Court, to the County Court of Lewis County, for faithful performance of his duty under this Act, which bond shall be executed before and attested by the county judge, and filed in the Lewis County Court clerk's office; and suit may be brought on said bond by said County Court for any failure of duty by said County Court clerk.

Fourth.—That F. M. Carr, John Thomas Parker, and John C. Ingram, or any two of them, shall have full power and authority to let out the contract for the erection and completing the public buildings authorized by this Act; and shall have power and authority to enter into such covenants from contractors as shall be necessary; and shall see that the covenants of the contractors are complied with before any money shall be paid. Said commissioners shall have full power and authority to remove to the town of Vanceburg for the purpose of using same in building public buildings, all or any portion of the material in the old court-house, clerk's office, jail, and jailer's house, in Clarksburg. If the commissioners, or any of them, should die or refuse to act, the County Court of Lewis County shall, at its next term after such death or refusal, appoint suitable persons to fill such vacancy and shall, from time to time, fill such vacancies, and make such orders as become necessary to carry out this Act. Said commissioners shall receive and appropriate to the erection of said buildings all donations and subscriptions made for that purpose.

Fifth.—That the County Court of Lewis County, a majority of all the justices of the peace in and for said county being present in court, and a majority of those present concurring, shall have power to increase the county levy to any sum, not exceeding two dollars on each tithe, and may do so for five years.

Sixth.—This Act shall take effect from its passage.

An Act to amend an Act passed March 30, 1861, to incorporate the town of Quincy, in Lewis County.

Be it enacted, etc.:

First.—That an Act incorporating the town of Quincy, Lewis County, Ky., approved March 30, 1861, is hereby amended, that the boundary of the said town of Quincy shall be as follows: Beginning at the upper line of a tract of land owned by Eifort, Dodge & Co., at the low water mark of the Ohio River, and running back with said line so as to exclude the tracts of lands of Samuel McKee, James Lewis, Abraham Thomas, John J. Hackworth; thence with said line of

Hackworth, George Aumiller, and Woodworth's; thence with said Aumiller and Hackworth's line to the Ohio River; thence with the meanderings of the river, at low water mark, to the beginning, containing an area of about three hundred acres.

Second.—Thus W. S. McKinney, William Hackworth, and Wm. B. Thompson shall be the trustees of said town of Quincy till the regular election takes place, on the first Saturday in May, 1864.

Third.—That said trustees, or their successors, shall have power to lay a tax on so much of the real estate within said boundary, so incorporated, to open streets and grade a wharf, as they may see proper; and in all other respects the laws of the State concerning laws regulating and governing towns shall apply to and govern the town of Quincy, and be a part of its charter.

Fourth.—This Act shall take effect from and after its passage.

An Act establishing a new precinct on Kinny.

Be it enacted, etc.:

First.—That the Lewis County Court shall have power, and are authorized, to make a new election district on Kinny Creek, out of parts of Laurel Fork precinct and the precinct known as the "Crossing of Kinny" precinct, and to locate and fix the place of voting in said precinct; and, when said court shall affix the boundaries of said district and appoint the place of voting in it, and enter the same on the records of said court, the said district is declared established.

Second.—That at the next regular election after the making of said district, two justices of the peace and a constable for said district shall be elected, as prescribed by the Constitution and Laws of the State, who shall hold their offices until the next regular election of said officers in said district.

Third.—This Act shall be in force from its passage.

An Act to change voting place from Clarksburg to Vanceburg.

Be it enacted, etc.:

First.—That hereafter the place of voting in election district number three, in Lewis County, be and is hereby changed from Clarksburg to Vanceburg, in said county.

Second.—This Act to take effect from its passage.

ACTS OF 1865: The first page of the Acts of 1865 reveals the Kinniconnick oil excitement, as there we read of James D. Smith, William Overend, Samuel Bate, and Henry J. Smith made corporators of the "Kinniconnick Central

Oil and Mining Co." Mr. Samuel Bate, now of this city, will take pride in telling you of the wells they bored, and he can actually show you some oil in that locality yet.

The "Kinniconnick and Salt Lick Petroleum Co." came into existence with George M. Thomas, Wm. C. Halbert, John P. Willim, Thos. W. Mitchell, and Thos. D. Parker as incorporators. They had a capital stock of $500,000, divided into shares of from $5 to $50. They had power granted open books, and when $20,000 was subscribed the company might proceed to business.

Judge Thomas did not make his money out of oil, this Act to the contrary notwithstanding.

CHAPTER 1304 gives Seth Parker, late sheriff, more time of two years to collect his fee bills, etc.

ADJOURNED SESSION OF 1865: CHAPTER 849 corporates Wm. S. Rand, Seneca W. Ely, William Halbert, Jacob W. Rand, George Halbert, Thos. J. Davis, and their successors, as the Vanceburg and Kinniconnick Railway Company, with a capital stock of one million dollars.

CHAPTER 1018 incorporates the Lewis County Petroleum Co., with John R. Morton, John McLean, Jas. R. Hawley, John G. Wells, Robt.

E. J. Miles, L. Barney, and E. L. VanWinkle as corporators.

NOTE.—This company was probably intended to furnish freight for Colonel Rand's railway, as above noted.

An Act to change the voting place in Laurel Precinct from Brightma's to William Stafford's, and to make two places in the crossing of Kinny precinct, one at Briery schoolhouse and one at McKinney schoolhouse, was approved January 27, 1865.

An Act for the benefit of J. R. Garland, giving him two more years to collect his fee bills, etc., or place them in the hands of proper collecting officers, was passed February 3, 1865.

ACTS OF 1866: CHAPTER 41.—Be it enacted, that the voting place in Mower district in Lewis County be, and the same is hereby, changed from Temperance Hall to the house of Jacob Mower.

CHAPTER 414 establishes an additional voting place at the house of William White, in Esculapia district.

CHAPTER 421 establishes an additional voting place at Kinny Mills and tanyard, in the Elk Fork district, and changes the boundary of said district so as to extend down Kinny to Straight Fork, including the house of John Peckelsimer, persons living on Straight Fork to be in the Laurel precinct.

CHAPTER 426 compels Vanceburg to levy a tax in aid of the construction of the bridge over Salt Lick Creek.

CHAPTER 505, p. 426, Acts of 1865-66, makes Vanceburg a city, and gives the following boundary: "Beginning at the mouth of Salt Lick Creek; thence up Salt Lick Creek to the mouth of Dry Run; thence up Dry Run to the mouth of the branch running into Dry Run between Kaleher's land and N. B. Webster's land; thence up said branch to the head; thence a straight line from the head of said branch to the head of the Southeast Fork of Slate Branch; thence down Slate Branch to the Ohio River; thence down the Ohio River, with its meanders, to the mouth of Salt Lick Creek, the place of beginning."

The new Constitution has rendered void most of the remainder of this Chapter, and therefore we do not copy it further.

CHAPTER 410 places the farm of James H. Darragh in Vanceburg voting district, and those of Anthony Evans and Thos. Nolan in the Crossing of Kinny district.

CHAPTER 277 gives the first charter for a "Deposit Bank" in Vanceburg. The incorporators were Jas. C. Cole, James Hiner, Joshua B. Fitch, George T. Halbert, William R. Stricklett, John P. Willim, Thos. W. Mitchell, Thos. D. Parker, and Thos. B. Harrison, or rather they were appointed commissioners to raise a capital stock of $100,000 by subscription at $100 per share. Evidently that was too much money for Vanceburg, and the whole scheme collapsed. The Deposit Bank of Vanceburg is not that bank.

CHAPTER 500 incorporates the Vanceburg Flouring Mill Co., with John P. McAndrew and William C. Halbert as the incorporators, allows them a capital of not over $100,000, the use of a common seal, and the right to build a grade and wharf the entire length of their land on the Ohio River.

This is one of the corporations that actually did something, as the mill and grade testifies by yet remaining as a monument of their work.

CHAPTER 501 produces another corporation in the persons of Wm. R. Stricklett, James R. Garland, and Warner Clary, known as the Vanceburg Hotel Co. The capital of this company was to be $50,000, divided into shares of $25 each.

The probable outgrowth of this charter is the "St. Charles Hotel," on Second Street, in Vanceburg.

CHAPTER 287 is an Act allowing any school district to vote a tax in aid of the common school. Section 5 relates to Vanceburg as follows: "That the election in the Vanceburg district shall be held at the schoolhouse of the Vanceburg Male and Female School; and the free school for said district shall be taught at said house, and the trustees of said high school shall be deemed the trustees of said common school district; and three of said trustees may sign the notices with the common school commissioner and do all other acts required of trustees of common schools under this Act and all the laws in regard to common schools of this State."

CHAPTER 285 is an Act amending an Act providing for the public buildings in Lewis County. It authorizes the county judge to call the County Court into session and have it levy an increase of the ad valorem tax to 30 cents on the $100 worth of property, and gives power to increase the poll tax to $3 on each tithe, and the same was to remain in force until the debts due on the public buildings were all paid.

CHAPTER 425.—An Act authorizing Lewis County Court to levy a tax to create a bridge fund for Lewis County.

Be it enacted, etc., SECTION 1, That the County Court of Lewis County (a majority of the justices of the peace for said county in commission being present in court, and a majority of those present concurring) shall have power and are hereby required, to assess and collect a tax annually, of not more than ten nor less than five cents on each one hundred dollars worth of property assessed for State purposes, for the creation of a fund for building and repairing bridges in said county; this tax shall be perpetual, and be dedicated to the purpose of building and repairing bridges, and not diverted to any other purpose."

This is the law yet in force in the county. It requires the sheriff to collect the tax, and requires the county judge to appoint commissioners, and first build or repair the bridge most in need of it.

ACTS OF 1867: An Act allowing J. R. Garland two years to collect his fee bills as sheriff of Lewis County.

Seth Parker, late sheriff, was also given two years to collect fee bills.

Thos. W. Mitchell, clerk of the Lewis County and Circuit Courts, was allowed to list his fee bills with any officer and given time of two years to collect same.

An Act giving Seth Parker two years, as administrator of John T. Parker, late clerk of Lewis County and Circuit Courts, to collect fees, etc.

An Act for the benefit of Seth Parker and his sureties, releasing them from damages included in a judgment against them, and also released of $687.76 military tax for the year 1862.

Alfred Harrison was allowed two years to collect fee bills as surveyor of Lewis County. Chapter 237.

CHAPTER 157 continues the ad valorem tax of thirty cents on the one hundred dollars, to aid in furnishing public buildings to the county, and applies it to building turnpikes: Provided, that the Act was ratified by the people at an election.

An Act to amend an Act to levy a tax to aid in building turnpike roads in Lewis County.

Be it enacted, etc., that an Act entitled an Act to levy a tax to aid in building turnpike roads in Lewis County, approved March 5, 1867, be so amended that the tax directed to be levied and collected by said Act, and by an amended Act passed at the present session, shall be collected and paid upon each one hundred dollars worth of real estate within the distance prescribed in said Act and amendment; that said tax shall be collected on all real estate within two miles of the commencement of said road at or in the city of Vanceburg, including the real estate in said city.

This was the turnpike road year for Lewis county. The following roads were chartered:

"Mt. Carmel, Esculapia, and Kinniconnick," with G. A. Henderson, Charles Nute, Alex Foxworthy, N. A. Glascock, John Bateman, and W. C. Power, incorporators; "Concord and Tollesboro," with R. D. Taylor, R. B. Lovel, John Lovel, John M. Myers, and Jesse Markland, incorporators; "Lewis and Mason," with a company to be organized after stock was subscribed; "Vanceburg, Quick's Run, and Concord," with T. B. Harrison, Wm. R. Stricklett, J. C. Cole, Thos. J. Bruce, Robert Bedford, Thos. H. Mitchell, and Thos. D. Parker as corporators; "Vanceburg, Salt Lick, Tollesboro, and Maysville." As the last named was the first chartered road, and as the charters of the others were modeled by it, we will give that Act entire as a sample of Turnpike Legislation for Lewis County:

CHAPTER 1347.—An Act to incorporate the Vanceburg, Salt Lick, Tollesboro, and Maysville Turnpike Road Co., in Lewis County, and to establish a Sinking Fund Board for said County.

Be it enacted by the General Assembly of the Commonwealth of Kentucky.

SECTION 1.—That a Company is hereby formed and created a body politic and corporate, by the name and style of the Vanceburg, Salt Lick, Tollesboro, and Maysville

Turnpike Road Company, to consist of a president and five directors, with other stockholders, for the purpose of making a turnpike road from Vanceburg, in Lewis County, up Salt Lick Creek to Mason County line; and from thence to intersect some turnpike road leading to Maysville, the place at which the road shall reach the line between Lewis and Mason Counties to be selected by the board of commissioners hereafter named in this Act. Said road shall be built upon the macadam plan. Said company, by said name, shall have perpetual existence and succession, and all the rights and privileges and franchises incident to such a corporation; and shall be capable of taking and holding their capital stock, and the increase and profits thereof; and of purchasing, taking, and holding, to them and their successors and assigns, and of selling, transferring, and conveying, in fee simple, all such lands, tenements, and hereditaments and estate, real and personal, as shall be necessary to them in the prosecution of their work; and to sue and be sued, plead and be impleaded, answer and be answered, defend and be defended in all courts of record, or any other places whatever; to contract for, buy, and own the right of way for said road; to have a common seal, and to do all and every other act and thing whatever within the object and scope of their incorporation, which body politic or corporate may lawfully do.

SECTION 2.—That the capital stock of said company shall be one hundred thousand dollars, and may be increased to any sum necessary to build the roads and branch roads authorized by this Act, to be divided into shares of twenty-five dollars each. Books for the subscription of stock shall be opened on the third Monday in March, 1867, or as soon thereafter as commissioners may direct, at the clerk's office of the Lewis Circuit Court, in Vanceburg, and continue open until the stock shall be subscribed, or until the board of directors may see proper to close them. The books shall be opened under the direction of Thos. W. Mitchell, J. B. Fitch, Geo. M. Thomas, Geo. T. Halbert, J. R. Garland, and Thomas D. Parker, any two of whom may open the books at said place, and are hereby empowered to act and are appointed commissioners for that purpose; said commissioners shall procure books, and the subscribers shall enter into the following obligation: "We, whose names are hereunto subscribed, do respectively promise to pay to the president and directors of the Vanceburg, Salt Lick, Tollesboro, and Maysville Turnpike Road Company the sum of twenty-five dollars for each share of

stock set opposite to our names, in such proportions and at such times as the said president
and directors may require."

SEC. 3.—So soon as ten thousand dollars are
subscribed to the capital stock of said Company
(or sooner, if the commissioners judge best), it
shall be the duty of said commissioners to give
notice, in writing, to the stockholders for a
meeting of said stockholders, at such time and
place as they may designate, for the purpose
of electing a president and three or more directors, not to exceed five; the said officers shall
be elected from among the stockholders, and
one vote shall be allowed for each share of stock,
and the said officers shall continue in office
one year, and until their successors are in like
manner duly elected. A majority of the directors shall be competent to transact business.

SEC. 4.—So soon as said company is organized by the election of officers, the president
and directors shall possess all the powers, rights,
and privileges, and shall and may do all acts
and things necessary for laying out and causing
a survey of the most practicable route for said
road, and for carrying on and completing said
road; and may have and enjoy all the rights
and privileges and be subject to all the duties,
qualifications, and restrictions hereinafter provided for.

SEC. 5.—Said president and directors shall fix and regulate the elevation and grade of said road, width or part thereof to be covered with stone, and the width or part thereof to be elevated and graded, and left uncovered with stone; they shall designate the place for the erection of gates, not exceeding one for every five miles of said road; and they may charge and receive the same tolls which are allowed by law to the Maysville, Washington, Paris, and Lexington Turnpike Road Company, as amended by Act of the Legislature, approved January 29, 1829: Provided, the width of said road shall not exceed sixty feet, and the part covered with stone shall not be less than twelve feet.

SEC. 6.—The president and directors may call on the subscribers of stock for any portion of their stock subscribed, not exceeding one-fourth of the total amount at a time, nor on shorter periods than three months after the first call; the first call of one-fourth may be called for and payment enforced at any time after said board is organized, until all the stock subscribed shall be paid in by the subscribers of stock.

SEC. 7.—The president and directors shall deliver a certificate, signed by the president, and countersigned by the treasurer, to each stockholder for the shares by him held, which certificate shall be transferable on the books of said board, according to the order, in person or by attorney in fact of such stockholder; but no share shall be transferred until all calls or arrearages thereon are paid. On the transfer of any share, the original or existing certificate shall be surrendered and a new one issued in the name of the purchaser thereof, who shall thereupon become one of the corporators, and be entitled to all the rights, privileges, and benefits of the corporation generally.

SEC. 8.—That the president of the board may call meetings of the board at such times and places as he may think proper, and a majority of the directors shall be necessary for the transaction of business; said board shall keep a record of its proceedings, to be entered in a book to be provided for that purpose; and each day's proceedings shall be signed by the president or presiding officer; and they may adjourn from time to time, as it may be necessary in the judgment of the board.

SEC. 9.—That the board of directors shall have power and authority to agree and contract with, and appoint all such surveyors, engineers, superintendents, artists, and officers as it shall judge necessary to act within the authority of the board, and fix and pay, all salaries thereof; to prescribe the time, manner, and proportions in which the stockholders shall make payment on their respective shares, subject to the conditions hereinafter prescribed; to draw orders on their treasurer for all moneys necessary to pay the salaries or wages of persons employed, and for materials and labor furnished; and to do all other matters and things as by this charter, or by the by-laws under it, said board is authorized to do; and the president shall give twenty days notice of the amount of the call on each share of stock, and of the time of payment. And if any stockholder shall refuse or neglect to pay his proportion of said stock for the space of twenty days after the time appointed for the payment thereof, every such stockholder shall be subject to suit by warrant before a justice of the peace, or in the quarterly or Circuit Court for the amount or amounts so called, and shall pay interest upon it from the time it should have been paid, at six per cent per annum, until paid. And in the event of said corporation failing to make any portion of any share of stock, the whole amount which shall have been paid thereon shall be forfeited to the company, and passed to the general items of profits.

SEC. 10.—That the said road shall be located by the president and directors, commencing at

Vanceburg, and from there up Salt Lick Creek to the headwaters thereof, and thence the most practical route to the line between Lewis and Mason Counties; said board may give preference to that route upon which the citizens and property holders give the most liberally and subscribe the most stock. Said road shall be laid out and graded as president and directors may order; and they, their surveyors, engineers, and other agents, are hereby authorized to occupy, use, and own any public road, or any part thereof, between the termini of the road to be built for all purposes necessary to the construction and use of said turnpike road on the macadamized plan, making reasonable provision for travel on said public roads while said turnpike is being constructed. Said company may also go upon any lands or inclosures contiguous thereto, to examine any lands, quarries of stone, or other material necessary for the construction or use of said road, and the board of directors and the owners of said land, quarry, stone, or material can not agree upon the price which shall be made by the company for the same, application shall be made on behalf of the company to the County Court of Lewis County for a jury to assess the value of the same; and, after return and confirmation by said County Court of the inquest made by said jury, said company shall make payment of or tender the value of any land, quarry, stone, or other material, and shall thereupon proceed to occupy, appropriate, and use the same in the construction of and for the use of the said road; and all persons employed in the construction of said road with wagons, carts, and all other necessary implements shall have free ingress and egress to and from said lands, quarries, stone, and other materials for the purpose aforesaid; and the directors shall have power to agree with the owner or owners of any lands, quarry stone, and material for the same or the use thereof.

SEC. 11.—That when said road, or any continuous section of two and one-half miles of said road, shall have been completed, the board of directors shall have power to erect a gate and collect half toll—that is, one-half the amount for five miles, according to this Act.

SEC. 12.—The tollgate keepers shall be appointed by the president and board of directors; said board shall also appoint a clerk and treasurer, the latter of whom may be required to enter into a bond, with good security; said bond shall be made payable to said company. The clerk shall keep in a well-bound book a record of the proceedings of said board, which shall at all times be open to the inspection of any stockholder. The bond of the treasurer shall be conditioned that he will faithfully discharge his duties as treasurer, and that he, at all times, will pay over any money in his hands to the order of the president and directors of said board; suit may be brought on said bond in the name and president and directors of said company for any default of said treasurer in any court having jurisdiction of the amount claimed to be due from said treasurer.

Sec. 13.—The president and directors may let out any portion of said road as soon as four thousand dollars are subscribed, and the balance of said road, or an additional part thereof, at the discretion of the board, as soon as the capital stock is subscribed to an amount sufficient to build the road to Cabin Creek, or a less distance. Said board may let out the building of any portion of said road from one to fifteen miles as fast as the money is subscribed to build the same. As soon as said road is finished to Salt Lick Creek, and a suitable bridge erected across said stream, they may erect a tollgate and collect toll for that portion of said road. The charge for toll shall be in conformity with the general law of the State regulating tolls on turnpike roads; they shall only be authorized to charge toll for so much of said road as shall be completed and in good repair for traveling.

SEC. 14.—If any person shall go around or turn off said road with the intent to avoid the payment of tolls, as fixed by the president and directors, he, she, or they shall, on conviction thereof before any justice of the peace or other magistrate, be fined five dollars, to be collected, and other sums, under the jurisdiction of said officers.

SEC. 15.—The president and directors shall have power to construct branch roads from the principal road, and for constructing said branch roads, on any one of them, the president, directors, and company shall have the same powers and privileges that are given to them in this charter to construct the main road.

SEC. 16.—That all suits, pleadings, and process, there shall be no change in the name or style of the president, directors, and company of the Vanceburg, Salt Lick, Tollesboro, and Maysville Turnpike Road Company; and in the management, construction, and government of said main and branch roads, the powers of the company shall be the same in all respects, and all gifts or grants to one may inure to both by consent of the president and directors and stockholders of such branch road.

SEC. 17.—Said company shall have power

to acquire, hold, or sell real and personal estate, so far as deemed by said corporation necessary in the construction, use, and repair of said road or branch roads, to build bridges, erect gates, houses, and do all other acts and things necessary in the exercise of the powers herein expressly conferred.

SEC. 18.—The president and directors of said company are authorized to sell stock in said company to any amount they may judge proper, to any person or persons, and take their obligations, payable in labor on said road, or part in labor and part in money, at such prices as may be agreed on between the parties.

SEC. 19.—The power of holding and conducting the election of the officers of said company shall be vested in any one of the commissioners named in this Act. The first election shall be held at the clerk's office of the Lewis Circuit Court, in Vanceburg; after the first election, the board of directors shall fix the time and place of all future elections, and who shall hold and conduct the same. The president, directors, and other officers of said company, from time to time elected, shall, before entering upon the duties of their office, take an oath, before some officer authorized to administer oaths by the laws of this State, well and truly to discharge the duties of their respective offices.

SEC. 20.—That the president and directors
shall have power to adopt and enforce such
by-laws, rules, and regulations as they may
deem necessary and proper for enabling them
to construct, control, and manage the road, and
all branch roads and property belonging to the
same, contemplated to be constructed by this
Act, it being the intention to confer power on
said company to build said main road, as many
branch roads as said president and directors
may choose and can raise the money to build.

SEC. 21.—It shall be the privilege of each
individual through whose land the main road
or any branch road may pass, who may subscribe stock, to work out the value of his stock
through his land, and adjoining thereto, at the
estimated price for labor done, or he shall have
the preference at the lowest bid; all subscribers
of stock shall have the privilege of working out
their stock subscribed under the direction of
the president and directors of said company, or
their agent.

SEC. 22.—In order to encourage the building
of macadamized roads in Lewis County, it is
hereby made the duty of the County Court of
said county, whenever one-half of the stock of
said company shall be subscribed by responsible
individual shareholders, to build said turnpike
road ten miles of its distance and length, and

proof of such subscription shall be made to said County Court, to subscribe to said Turnpike Road Company one thousand dollars per mile for and in the name of Lewis County; and said county shall, upon such subscription by the county judge of said county, become a stockholder in said company to said amount. The stock of said county shall be represented and voted at any election of officers of said company by the presiding judge of the County Court and the clerk of said court, each voting one-half of the stock of said county at all elections held by said company; and when said county judge is satisfied of sufficient stock having been subscribed by responsible individual stockholders in said company, to build one-half of an additional number of miles of said road, or any branch thereof, not less than three miles in length, at a time; said presiding judge of the Lewis County Court shall again sign for and in behalf of said County of Lewis one thousand dollars per mile to the stock of said road or branch road, as the case may be.

SEC. 23.—That the Lewis County Court is hereby authorized and directed to issue the bonds of said county, payable at not a longer date than twenty years, to bear interest not exceeding six per cent per annum, which bonds may be in such amounts, and principal and in-

terest payable at such place or places, as the
said County Court may direct—the interest to
be paid annually. Said bonds may be sold by
order of said County Court, and the money
paid to the president and directors of said turnpike road company, or said court may order
said bonds to be issued and delivered to said
president and directors; and if so delivered, said
County of Lewis shall thereupon become a
stockholder to the amount of money called for
in the bonds issued and delivered to the president and directors of said company.

Said County Court is also authorized to
issue the bonds of the county, and loan them
to said turnpike road company, in amount sufficient to enable said company to build fifteen
miles of the main road the first year after the
same is commenced; said bonds to draw six
per cent per annum, the interest to be paid
annually; said bonds may be issued to fall due
not more than fifteen years hence. For the
bonds loaned to said company the county shall
have a lien upon said road, and its toll and
revenues, until the county is reimbursed.

Sec. 24.—To meet the annual interest on
said bonds, to pay all expense incident to the
issual thereof, and the payment of principal
and interest, and all expenses incident to the
conducting a sinking fund, and to provide a

sinking fund fully sufficient to pay and liquidate
the principal when due, it shall be the duty of
the County Court of Lewis annually to levy
an ad valorem tax on the property subject to
pay State revenue assessed for taxes in Lewis
County, which, when added to the poll tax,
shall be sufficient to defray the necessary county
expenses, and the expenses before named, and
put with the principal of the sinking fund a
sum annually, sufficiently large, so that it will
be ample to redeem and pay off all the bonds
issued by said County Court for turnpike road
purposes, and bridges, when said bonds shall
become due. Said County Court shall appoint
three discreet persons sinking fund commissioners, and they and their successors are constituted a body, politic and corporate, by the
name of the Lewis County Sinking Fund Commissioners; and as such and by that name may
contract and be contracted with, sue and be
sued; but before the funds of the county raised
for the sinking fund purposes shall be put into
their hands, they shall execute bond to the
Commonwealth of Kentucky, with good surety,
to be approved by said County Court, in double
the amount of funds which may go into their
hands, or be under their control for the ensuing
year; and it shall be the duty of said court to
renew said bond annually; said County Court

13

may issue said bonds, payable not beyond the time named in this Act, but conditioned that said bonds may be redeemed and paid off sooner if said County Court so elects.

SEC. 25.—Said county bonds shall be ordered to be issued by said County Court at a regular term, and shall be signed by the presiding judge of the County Court, and attested by the County Court clerk; and if semi-annual coupons be desired by said court for interest, they shall be signed by the County Court clerk.

SEC. 26.—The president and directors of said company shall have power, and are hereby authorized, to open books for the subscription of stock at any place they may judge best for the interest of said company; and should commissioners all refuse to act, or die, or remove, the County Court of Lewis County is hereby authorized and required to appoint other commissioners to open books for the subscription of stock in said company; and commissioners thus appointed shall possess all the powers of those named in this Act.

SEC. 27.—This Act shall take effect from and after its passage.

Amended March 9, 1867, as follows:

First.—Authorizes the clerk to issue the bonds on demand of the road company.

Second.—To take effect when ratified by vote of the people.

The second section of this amendment was repealed by a later Act.

CHAPTER 1879.—An Act for the benefit of A. E. Cole, late teacher in district No. 11. He made a mistake in his report in regard to the number of his district, and therefore could not draw his salary. The Act authorizes that payment be made to him out of the surplus fund due Lewis County.

CHAPTER 1590.—Changes the voting place in Elk Fork precinct from McEldowney's schoolhouse to Hamrick's mill.

CHAPTER 1676.—Changes the line between Tollesboro and Esculapia precincts to the State Road.

CHAPTER 1708.—Is the Act authorizing a tax of fifty cents to the one hundred dollars worth of land on each side of the turnpike roads in Lewis County.

CHAPTER 1746 changes the time of holding the Court of Claims from the third Monday in October to the third Monday in April.

CHAPTER 1903 authorizes the trustees of the Union Meeting House, on Cabin Creek, in Lewis County, to sell said land and appurtenances and distribute the proceeds among the Christian Church, the Baptist Church, and the New School Presbyterian Church.

CHAPTER 2035 incorporates the Salt Lick,

Esculapia, and Mt. Carmel Turnpike Road Company. Samuel B. Pugh, Wm. F. Jones, David Arthurs, Jr., Howard Shepard, W. F. Redden, John P. McAndrew, and Thomas D. Parker were the incorporators.

CHAPTER 2028 is an Act for the benefit of J. B. Fitch, late sheriff, giving him two years time to collect his fee bills.

CHAPTER 1751 is an Act for the benefit of the city council of Vanceburg, validating a contract made by them with the Grade Company, of Vanceburg, and also providing for the election of a mayor for said city.

ACTS OF 1868: CHAPTER 774 changes the Tollesboro and Esculapia precinct line so as to include John M. Spence, Jr., in the Tollesboro precinct.

CHAPTER 1195 changes the line between Carter and Lewis Counties so as to include the residences of William Kinder, Marion Mc-Clung, Alexander Pendland, Wm. Rayborn, Henry Rayborn, George Pendland, Wm. H. Logan, Tobias Logan, O. H. Holland, and James A. Patrick in the County of Lewis.

CHAPTER 1178 enables the qualified voters in Vanceburg Common School District to elect trustees.

CHAPTER 929 is an Act in favor of Samuel Ellis, late sheriff of Lewis County, giving him till the first day of June, 1868, to finish paying the revenue due from him to the State.

CHAPTER 1855 is an amendment to two Acts in regard to Vanceburg. It changes the time of holding elections to the first Saturday in January in each year, and requires all incumbent officers to hold over till January, 1870. It also gives the city council authority to fill vacancies by appointment.

ACTS OF 1869: CHAPTER 1884 incorporates the Cabin Creek, Springdale, and Maysville Turnpike Road Company.

This charter allowed the company to build a road from Bull Creek up the Ohio to Cabin Creek, up Cabin Creek to the forks; thence up the South Fork to Indian Run, in Lewis County, so as to intersect the Concord and Tollesboro Road, with the right and privilege to construct and keep up a branch from the forks of Cabin Creek by the most practical route to the Ohio River, opposite Manchester, and from thence up the Ohio River to Concord.

The capital stock was to be $75,000, and the incorporators were W. J. Tully, Jackson Sweet, Thos. M. Fry. Headly Harrison, Samuel West, J. D. Tully, Jno. McNutt, P. B. Vauden, Robt. A. Cochran, Henry C. Barkley, Robt. Means, Robt. Lovel, David W. Fearis, Thomas Wilson, Pres. Moore, and John Purcell.

Every road named in this charter has been built except the one to Concord, and it is now building. The company has also extended its charter and roads with a branch from East Fork to Main Cabin Creek, and from D. W. Fearis' house, on East Fork, to the head of said creek and to intersect the C. & T. Road, near Salem Church. There is also an extension up Indian Run to the V. S. L. T. & M., at the head of Salt Lick, near Herrin's blacksmith shop.

CHAPTER 2067.—Be it enacted that Samuel Ellis, sheriff of Lewis County, shall have until the April County Court, in 1869, to make out and return his delinquent list.

CHAPTER 1254 defines the limit in which taxes shall be collected for the benefit of the Vanceburg, Salt Lick, Tollesboro, and Maysville Turnpike Road. As the taxes on the road have ceased, we deem it useless to copy the long Act.

CHAPTER 1394 is an Act in favor of J. B. Fitch, giving more time to collect his fee bills, etc., and allowing him to list with other officers.

CHAPTER 1482 is an Act to reduce into one all Acts in regard to the town of Concord. The boundary is to remain the same as in the original town plat. All the concerns of the town are vested in five trustees, who are to be elected annually by the voters who have paid their taxes. A police judge and marshal is also to be elected and hold office one year. The returns of said election are sent to the County Court, which shall certify the same to the governor, who is to issue commission to the police judge. The said judge must take oath of office, and has the same jurisdiction as a justice of the peace, but only in the limits of the town. He has the power of commitment to the county jail. He shall hold his court on the first Saturday of every month, and continue till the causes are all disposed of. The right of appeal from his court is granted to all parties in the same manner as from the justice's courts. The chairman of the board of trustees is to preside when the police judge is absent, for any reason, from his court. If a vacancy occurs in his office, the trustees are to recommend some suitable person to the governor for his commission for the unexpired term. The police judge must execute bond, with security, to the town trustees for the payment of all money coming to his hands and belonging to the town. The marshal must serve all processes, warrants, etc., collect fines and taxes, and has the general powers of a constable. He is also inspector of streets and alleys, but the trustees may appoint a commissioner instead of him.

All taxes were made due from the marshal on the first of August, and he is to make settlement with the trustees at the regular meeting in that month.

The trustees have a right to appoint a clerk, who shall keep a record of the meeting and all ordinances passed by the board. They are also required to appoint an assessor, with duties usual thereto.

The trustees have the power to levy a poll and ad valorem tax, to tax shows, charge wharfage, license hacks, etc. They shall have a lien on property for taxes, and the marshal shall advertise and sell the same.

The trustees have power to charge venders of spirits fifty dollars as a license fee, and the County Court is prohibited from granting license to sell liquors in said town without the consent of the board of trustees. The trustees may do all other things in the town of Concord that any well-regulated town is authorized and required to do, but which are too numerous to be here repeated.

CHAPTER 1500 incorporates the Vanceburg, Dry Run, and Kinniconnick Turnpike Road Company, with the following persons as commissioners to open books for subscription of stock: Thos. W. Mitchell, Thos. B. Harrison, F. H. Rice, and Wm. Pell, at Vanceburg; and Jacob W. Rand, Samuel Bate, and Thos. Bate at the house of J. W. Rand.

The general provisions of other turnpike legislation was made applicable to this road, and it is another of the finished roads in the county, and extends, under this Act, from Vanceburg to Thos. B. Harrison's place on Kinny.

CHAPTER 1503 incorporates the Vanceburg, Quincy, and Springville Turnpike Road Company. The commissioners appointed were Thos. W. Mitchell, James McDermott, J. R. Garland, of Vanceburg; Samuel Kibby, B. F. Branham, N. G. Morse, of Quincy; and Samuel Yeager, Champ. Osborn, and Dr. Fulton, at Springville.

This road was built about three miles from Vanceburg, and then failed.

CHAPTER 1502 is an amendment to the charter of the Concord and Tollesboro Road, but as that road has been taxed to death, it is useless to go into details in regard to this Act. Said road is now a "free county road."

CHAPTER 1657 diverts the taxes raised under an Act to finish public buildings to aid for building turnpikes in Lewis County. It also authorizes a poll tax of three dollars on all citizens over twenty-one years of age, which, after paying ordinary county expenses, is to be in aid of the roads. And in order to avoid a separate Act for each road, it was enacted herein that each mile of turnpike road building in Lewis County shall have one thousand dollars in bonds of the county in aid of its construction.

CHAPTER 1662 is an Act to protect birds and game in Lewis County. It is unlawful under this Act to pursue, kill, or hunt, or in any manner injure any birds commonly known as the bluebird, swallow, martin, robin, wren, or any other bird whatsoever, at any season of the year, or at any time, or under any circumstances, without the consent of the owner of the lands. The Act also makes it unlawful to hunt for other game mentioned on the premises of another without his consent, and makes it a fineable offense to offer such game, so taken from the premises of another.

CHAPTER 1725 incorporates the Cabin Creek Road Company, which was to build a road from the C. & T. Road, down Cabin Creek to the Mason County line. Under this charter the road was built. The commissioners were Asa McNeil, D. M. Dunbar, Thomas Henderson, Geo. W. Rowland, John H. Reganstine, Alex. McKensie, A. J. Hendrickson, John D. Tully, and Wm. Fenwick.

CHAPTER 1726 is an Act to amend the charter of the Mason and Lewis Turnpike Road Company. It authorizes the company to extend their road from Burtonville to Kinniconnick Creek, in Lewis County, and to connect with roads in Fleming County, if expedient. It authorizes more taxes, but the road has never reached Kinny yet. (A. D. 1896.)

ACTS OF 1870: CHAPTER 882 amends the law in regard to stockholders paying taxes of the V. S. L. T. & M. Road. It requires stockholders of said road living between Cabin Creek and the Mason County line to pay taxes just the same as non-shareholders.

CHAPTER 986 repeals an Act allowing voters of school district No. 46 to vote on a proposition to levy a tax.

CHAPTER 755 authorizes the Vanceburg, Salt Lick, Tollesboro, and Maysville Turnpike Road Company to borrow money, issue bonds, etc., in order to complete the road to the Mason County line. The act also requires the county judge to issue a bond of one thousand dollars as fast as each mile was completed. It also authorized the company to establish a tollgate within one mile of the court-house in Vanceburg.

CHAPTER 759 incorporates the Fleming and Lewis County Turnpike Road Company.

Said turnpike road has not been built.

Cabin Creek, Sand Hill, and Manchester Road. John Sullivan, Robert Hoop, Geo. W. List, James Nash, David Craig, Andrew Wilson, Geo. M. Tolle, Thos. Biggar, Ellis Tucker,

John T. Hendrickson, and David W. Fearis, incorporators.

This road has been built, and several branches, as stated in another place in this volume.

CHAPTER 723 incorporates the Vanceburg Male and Female Academy. The trustees appointed by the act are G. M. Thomas, W. C. Halbert, Thos. D. Parker, Thos. W. Mitchell, Geo. Little, Henry C. Bruce, James R. Garland, Andrew Smalley, Thos. B. Harrison, John Armstrong, and John C. Ingrim. They were authorized to levy a tax. The trustees had the right to appoint a faculty and were to keep a number of professors in the several chairs.

This was the beginning of the public school building which now is the sole property of the Vanceburg Common School District. There are other Acts, hereinafter produced, which brought about the effect.

CHAPTER 749 amends the charter of the Cabin Creek Road Company, and allows them to levy a tax of fifty cents on each one hundred dollars worth of property within one-half mile on each side of said road. Provided, the taxpayers should assent.

CHAPTER 350 authorizes the Lewis and Mason Road Company to charge the same tolls as charged by the Maysville, Orangeburg, and Mt. Carmel Turnpike Road Company.

CHAPTER 580 extends the Concord and Tollesboro Road to Mt. Carmel, and changes the title accordingly.

CHAPTER 685 charters the Cabin Creek, Sand Hill, and Manchester Turnpike Road Company, with a capital stock of $30,000. The following commissioners were appointed to open books: Headly Harrison, D. M. Dunbar, Thos. M. Fry, Pascal Vawter, T. H. West, Thos. J. Himes, Jacob P. Mower.

ACTS OF 1871: CHAPTER 1302 is an Act authorizing William L. Fitch to be granted license to practice law before he had attained to the legal age.

CHAPTER 1303 is an Act authorizing a tax for a bridge fund in Lewis County, not more than ten nor less than five cents to be laid on the one hundred dollars.

CHAPTER 1294 is an amendment to the Concord and Tollesboro Road. Authorizes the county judge, under certain conditions, to issue bond, to each mile, of one thousand dollars.

CHAPTER 1403 is an amendment to the Act incorporating the Vanceburg Male and Female Academy. It releases personal property from taxation, and changes the schoolhouse to a house for the common school of the district.

The house must not cost over four thousand dollars. The tax on real estate and the poll tax was extended to the whole school district outside of the city as well as in it.

CHAPTER 1519 requires all the turnpike road companies to make settlement with the County Court, showing an itemized account of all receipts and expenditures, annually. The first settlement must show all receipts and expenditures from the commencement of their work on the road. The county clerk is required to keep a record of the same. This act was approved March 13, 1871.

CHAPTER 1571 amends the Concord and Tollesboro Road charter by allowing the company to issue bonds of the road and sell the same at par, to aid in the construction of the road. The taxes and tolls, after paying for repairs, were to be applied in payment of said bonds. This Act also requires the company to settle with the County Court. These bonds were issued, and finally got the people and the purchasers into trobule.

CHAPTER 1596 amends the charter of the Cabin Creek, Sand Hill, & Manchester Road Company. Allows them to issue bonds, borrow money to the extent of six thousand dollars, and pledge the bonds in payment with ten per cent interest attached in coupons, secured by mortgage on the road, its taxes, and tolls till the same is paid.

CHAPTER 1636 incorporates the Quick's Run and Sout's Landing Turnpike Road Company, and appoints F. M. Carr and James Stout as commissioners to receive subscriptions to the stock, the capital being authorized at $50,000.

CHAPTER 1638 incorporates the town of Tollesboro in the following language: "That the town of Tollesboro, of Lewis County, be, and the same is hereby, established and incorporated under the name of the "Town of Tollesboro," with the following boundaries, to wit: The eastern boundary to run with the farthest limits of T. J. Barkley's farm; the western boundary with the farthest limits of Lewis Middleton's farm; and the northern and southern boundaries running parallel with the Vanceburg and Tollesboro Turnpike, extending one quarter of a mile on each side of the pike."

SEC. 2.—That W. N. Wallingford, Geo. W. Jordon, and W. B. Perkins are hereby appointed trustees of said town, to hold their offices until trustees are elected or appointed and qualified as their successors, under the general law regulating towns established by County Courts.

SEC. 3.—That all power conferred by law on trustees of towns established as aforesaid are hereby conferred on the said trustees and their successors; and, in addition thereto, they shall have exclusive, and full, and complete power to regulate or prohibit the sale of spirituous, vinous, or malt liquors by tavern keepers, coffee house keepers, merchants, or others, within said town.

SEC. 4.—This Act shall not relieve the Vanceburg and Tollesboro Turnpike Road Company from the duty of keeping up their road through said town, nor prevent the said company from charging toll as heretofore.

SEC. 5.—This Act shall take effect from its passage.

ACTS OF 1872: CHAPTER 46 is an act appropriating part of the public school money of district No. 8, in Vanceburg, to a school taught under the patronage of W. C. Halbert, and the rest to a school taught in the Methodist Church, under the direction of the trustees of said district.

This Act was repealed by the same session in Chapter 489. As Mr. Halbert had received part of said money before the Act was repealed, suit was brought by Jos. A. Sparks, commissioner of common schools, for the recovery of said money. The suit was decided in favor of the commissioner.

CHAPTER 208 is an amendment to the charter of V. S. L. T. & M. Road, and limits the land subject to taxation from Bertram's farm, on Salt Lick, to Esculapia.

CHAPTER 293 incorporates the Cabin Creek Turnpike Road Company, and appoints J. E. Hall, Geo. W. Rowland, John D. Tully, and Robert Gillespie as commissioners to open books and receive subscriptions.

This is the charter under which the road was built.

CHAPTER 772 appropriates $140.25 to the keeping of two lunatics in the Lewis County jail, and authorizes the payment of the same to Lewis Plummer, jailer of Lewis County.

CHAPTER 825 amends the charter of Cabin Creek, Sand Hill, and Manchester Road. It allows the company to issue bonds and borrow money in the sum of $12,000.

CHAPTER 968 amends the charter of the town of Quincy. This Act extends the limits of the town to Kinny Creek, and prohibits the sale of liquor in said town.

CHAPTER 969 regulates the payment of turnpike taxes so as to be paid to the treasurers of said roads in Lewis County, and if not paid before November must be listed with the sheriff of the county.

CHAPTER 981 directs the auditor to draw his warrant on the treasurer for the sum of fifty dollars, in favor of John P. McAndrews,

14

for conveying Lewis Kirk, a lunatic, to the asylum, at Lexington, Ky.

ACTS OF 1873: CHAPTER 150 releases the sheriff of Lewis County from collecting taxes for the Lewis and Mason Turnpike Road Company, and authorizes the company to appoint a collector.

CHAPTER 169 authorizes the Vanceburg Male and Female Academy to sell part or all of the land purchased by them, and to buy five acres more land, if all is sold, and to use the proceeds in the erection of building; and also to use $634.95 of money proceeds of former seminary land belonging to Lewis County, which was in the hands of W. C. Halbert. The land and building not to cost more than $10,000.

CHAPTER 198 reduces the county levy from three dollars to two dollars per tithe, and requires the sheriff to return his delinquent list of 1871 and 1872 to the county clerk, who shall record the same and list them with officers for collection.

CHAPTER 199 authorizes the Lewis County Court of Claims to levy an ad valorem tax of ten cents on the one hundred dollars worth of property for the purpose of repairing or building a new jail, and purchasing a lot for the site thereof. The court was also directed to use the money due the county from Samuel Ellis, late sheriff, in furtherance of this object. The act allows bonds to be issued and the tax thus anticipated, but pledges it in payment of the bonds if so issued.

CHAPTER 215 issues the bonds of Lewis County for one thousand dollars to build a bridge across Salt Lick Creek, at Bertram's farm, on the Salt Lick, Esculapia, and Mt. Carmel Road.

CHAPTER 289 legalizes the Acts of a special term of the Lewis County Court, held June 28, 1872.

CHAPTER 291 legalizes an order made by W. S. Parker, acting as special judge of Lewis County, in favor of J. R. Garland, and authorizes the sheriff, who has paid said order, to be allowed the same in his settlement.

CHAPTER 313 authorizes the County Court to make an allowance to the Circuit Court clerk for cross indexing the suits in the Circuit Court. The Act states that hereafter the claim shall be allowed annually.

CHAPTER 451 authorizes R. B. Lovel, late sheriff, to list his fee bill and tax receipts with the constables for collection, gives the constables same power in collecting as held by the sheriff, and makes them liable on their bond for such collections as shall be made.

1873—VOL. 2: CHAPTER 531.—All taxpayers

on any turnpike road may pay their taxes to
the collectors of said road on or before the first
day of November in each year; but if not so
paid they shall be listed with the sheriff, and
ten per cent added.

CHAPTER 532 compelled the tavern keepers
to pay a license of from fifty to one hundred
dollars to the trustees of the Vanceburg Male
and Female Academy for the privilege of selling
ardent spirits to people outside of the city
limits. Said money was to be used in building
the schoolhouse.

CHAPTER 555 defines the limits of the fifth
ward in the city of Vanceburg.

CHAPTER 563 authorizes the court to increase
the ad valorem taxes fifty cents on one hundred
dollars, and appropriates the same to the payment of the county debts. It also requires the
county clerk to procure a book and make an
entry of all the bonds issued by the county,
the date and amount thereof, and the road issued
to, and when due; the clerk shall furnish the
sheriff, each year, the bonds due in that year,
and the sheriff shall pay the bonds in the order
they fall due. The additional taxation authorized by this Act shall first be used in paying
bonds hereafter issued, and the taxes so collected
shall be pledged to redeem the bonds hereafter
issued, and the bonds shall draw ten per cent

interest, payable annually. The bonds hereafter issued shall be used in aid of turnpike
roads and bridges, and are to be paid in the
order in which they fall due.

CHAPTER 589 authorizes the Cabin Creek
Turnpike Company to cross Cabin Creek at
Wm. Henderson's, and requires the county to
subscribe one thousand dollars to aid in building the bridge.

CHAPTER 603 authorizes Lewis County to
subscribe fifteen hundred dollars to the stock of
the Cabin Creek, Sand Hill, and Manchester
Road for the purpose of building bridges across
Cabin Creek and Crooked Creek in the line of
said road.

CHAPTER 619 authorizes the Lewis County
Court to subscribe two thousand dollars to build
bridges on the line of the Vanceburg, Salt Lick,
Tollesboro, and Maysville Turnpike Road. The
company was given the right to appoint an
assessor, who must return his book to the
County Court for revision, etc.

All laws exempting stockholders from paying
taxes were repealed by this Act, and after the
road should be completed the president is to
be allowed fifty dollars per year as salary.
The directors have their toll free during their
continuance in office.

CHAPTER 673 gives the Concord Road their

bridge grub of one thousand dollars from the county, and authorizes the company to issue bonds of said road to two thousand dollars per mile, and pledges the taxes to be collected for payment. This Act also allows the company to charge persons hauling logs with double team a double toll.

CHAPTER 866.—An Act for the benefit of Lewis Plummer, jailer of Lewis County, pays him seventy-nine dollars out of the treasury of the State.

CHAPTER 1019 gives the Kinny Bridge on the V. Q. & Springville Pike the usual one thousand dollars from the county, but authorizes the court to appoint commissioners to put the money in the bridge.

CHAPTER 1021 is an amendment to the Vanceburg and Quick's Run Road charter, but the main point is to get three thousand dollars from the county to build a bridge across Salt Lick Creek. Said bridge is built.

CHAPTER 1056 releases R. B. Lovel from a five per cent assessment of $156.65 against him by the auditor, he having paid into the treasury the full amount of the revenue due the State from him for the year 1871.

ACTS OF 1874: CHAPTER 28 prohibits the Cabin Creek Turnpike Company from collecting taxes off people who have been assessed by the Concord Road Company.

CHAPTER 119 is an Act to regulate the sale of liquor in Lewis County. It requires that no less quantity than two gallons shall be sold. It was voted on and approved by the people November, 1874.

This stopped the open sale of liquor in Vanceburg, until 1876, when a new city charter was granted admitting the sale and placing the money to the credit of the city schools. Judge Hargis, of the Criminal Court, decided that the granting of license against the expressed voice of the people at the polls was illegal and void. And this closed the bar-rooms again until an Act was passed allowing the citizens of Vanceburg to vote on the proposition of license, March 1, 1880. "For license" won by a majority of 29, and since that time the "dispensaries" have been open.

CHAPTER 143 amends the Vanceburg, Dry Run, and Kinniconnick Turnpike Road Company. Changes the tax to be levied to five cents per acre on lands lying along the road, etc. (Page 178, Acts of 1873-74.)

CHAPTER 173 gives Seth Parker, Samuel Ellis, and R. B. Lovel, late sheriffs of Lewis County, two years more time to collect fee bills, etc.

CHAPTER 213 amends an Act in regard to the county levy in aid of turnpikes, makes the taxes collected under this levy subject to the payment of the county indebtedness already incurred, and prohibits its use otherwise. The county judge is to appoint a turnpike commission under this Act, who is to inspect all roads that are reported built, or parts thereof.

CHAPTER 243 advertises sales of real estate or personal property by the sheriff, under execution from the court, all notices of the sittings of Master Commissioner for settlement of the estate of deceased persons in the Vanceburg *Kentuckian.*

CHAPTER 282 exempts "Riverside Academy" in Vanceburg, from all city, county, and local taxes for the year 1874.

CHAPTER 380 appropriates the money for tavern license—fifty dollars—for the use of the common school in the town of Concord.

CHAPTER 25 amends the charter of the Concord and Tollesboro Turnpike Road. It prohibits teamsters from "rough locking" their wagons, and requires them to use a "rub lock."

This Act also authorizes the County Court, if petitioned by the taxpayers, to levy fifty cents additional on the one hundred dollars to pay off the bonds at sixty cents on the dollar. The taxpayers probably did not petition, as the bonds were the cause of several suits, and finally the road reverted to the county for the stock it held in it.

CHAPTER 30 makes the special taxes listed with the sheriff in favor of the Cabin Creek Turnpike Road, due and payable on the first day of February following the time of listing.

ACTS OF 1875-76: CHAPTER 45 amends an amendment to the Concord Road, makes all fines collect payable to the treasurer of the road.

CHAPTER 145.—An Act for the benefit of Madison Thomas, appropriating three hundred dollars for the support of a lunatic.

CHAPTER 272 prohibits a greater interest than six per cent on any future bonds of the county, appropriates the taxes of thirty cents on one hundred dollars exclusively to the payment of the turnpike bonds and interest; prohibits a greater levy than five cents on the one hundred dollars for bridges, except by the unanimous consent of the magistrates, but in no case to exceed ten cents. All claims are to be paid out of the county levy, unless otherwise specially provided for, the county levy to be due on the 31st day of December, of each year. Other taxes due, one-half on December 31st and one-half on April 1st. Statement of all moneys collected the previous year to be made by the county judge on June 1st and published in the county paper.

CHAPTER 692 reduces into one all the Acts

in regard to the city of Vanceburg. This chapter leaves the boundary the same as heretofore, lays the city off into five wards, makes the officers consist of a mayor, nine councilmen, marshal, city attorney, assessor, collector, and treasurer, city clerk, street commissioner, gauger and weigher, coal and wood inspector. The mayor and council are to be elected by the people, for one year, and the others appointed by the council.

This is the famous charter which contained the license clause—Section 22—and which was decided illegal by Judge Hargis.

It is also the charter under which the city was governed until 1891. Having been superceded, it is too long to copy for its worth to this volume. It can be found on page 433, Acts of 1876, Vol. 2.

CHAPTER 776 incorporates the Tollesboro Cemetery Company. The incorporators are Dr. Nesbitt Taylor, W. N. Wallingford, Isaiah Grigsby, James Barkley, Alex. M. Rummins, and Maudly Trussell.

ACTS OF 1878: CHAPTER 87 authorizes the trustees in school district No. 26 to report a four month school instead of five, and to receive the money for same.

CHAPTER 435 amends the charter of Vanceburg by making the city attorney, marshal, street commissioner, and assessor elective offices by the qualified voters.

CHAPTER ·501 authorizes the Lewis County Court to sell the "poorhouse farm," and to buy other property. This Act was approved March 16, 1878, and under it the poorhouse was· removed to Kinniconnick.

CHAPTER 558.—An Act to incorporate "The Woodland Cemetery Association," of Vanceburg, in Lewis County.

The incorporators are H. C. Bruce, S. Ruggles, L. B. Baird, T. B. Harrison, T. B. Stricklett, J. W. Darrow, James R. Pugh, John C. Ingrim, T. W. Mitchell, and W. C. Halbert, Jr.

The beautiful cemetery on the hill above Vanceburg is the result of this Act.

CHAPTER 760.—Be it enacted, that the turnpike laws of Lewis County be so amended as to require all persons holding evidences of indebtedness against the Cabin Creek, Sand Hill, and Manchester Turnpike Road Company be required to produce such evidences of indebtedness to the County Court of Lewis County, on three months' notice, to be given by the county judge of said county, by posting a written notice on the front door of the court-house of Lewis County, and by publishing said notice in the Vanceburg *Courier* and Maysville *Bulletin* for at least three months.

Said evidences of indebtedness, when produced, shall be registered upon the record book of said court, and any person failing to produce any evidences of indebtedness as above, shall forfeit their right to any interest they now be entitled to receive on said evidences of indebtedness.

SEC. 2.—This Act to take effect and be in force from and after its passage.

This Act was never advertised, as it requires. Perhaps it was un-Constitutional in that it aimed to vitiate a contract.

CHAPTER 763 is an Act to amend the charter of the Cabin Creek, Sand Hill, and Manchester Road. It reduces the officers from five to two.

CHAPTER 929.—An Act appropriating five hundred dollars to W. T. Warder, sheriff, and to the family of John Ruggles for the capture of Jesse Underwood. We give a full account of this in another chapter.

CHAPTER 962 authorizes the State treasurer to pay H. T. Warder, sheriff of Lewis County, $37.50 on account of payment made by him to Edward Stone, committee of Laural Stone, a pauper idiot.

CHAPTER 1031 changes the time of holding the Criminal Court. In Lewis County it is to be the fourth Monday in June and third Monday in November in each year.

ACTS OF 1879: Makes W. R. Hull, John McCormick, James Thomas, Isaiah Grigsby, J. Win Parker, S. G. Hillis, Geo. W. Davis, S. D. Gardner, M. W. Wallingford, and all other persons who may hereafter hold policies in this corporation, in the manner herein prescribed, be, and are hereby incorporated, etc.

This was a mutual, pro rata assessment company, and, of course, went to the wall after a few barns were burned and assessments made.

CHAPTER 150 gives the County Court power to grant tavern license to sell ardent spirits in the city of Vanceburg.

CHAPTER 202 gives the taxpayers on the C. & T. Turnpike Road until the first of December to pay their tax.

CHAPTER 422 authorizes the Court of Claims in Lewis County to levy an ad valorem tax of ten cents on one hundred dollars worth of property for county purposes, and to raise the levy of poll tax to two dollars.

CHAPTER 605 permits persons whose lands have been sold for taxes due the Vanceburg, Dry Run, and Kinniconnick Turnpike Road to redeem same within twelve months from date of sale, by the party paying to the purchaser the amount of purchase money and ten per cent interest on the same.

CHAPTER 711 appropriates thirty-four dollars

to T. B. Bullock, late deputy sheriff of Lewis County. The Act does not say what the appropriation was for.

CHAPTER 775 repeals part of an Act in regard to selling liquors in Lewis County—insofar as it refers to the town of Concord. The Act requires the trustees to take a vote as to whether the citizens want liquor sold; and, if they do, then the vendor is to pay fifty dollars license-fee to go into the school fund.

CHAPTER 781.—Amendment to the city charter of Vanceburg. Allows the officer to take out his fees from any fine paid first, and the remainder to be credited to the fine imposed.

CHAPTER 792 authorizes the trustees of the Vanceburg Common School District to issue bonds to finish the schoolhouse begun by the Vanceburg Male and Female Academy. Also a tax of fifty cents on the one hundred dollars worth of realty, beginning with the year 1880, and to continue till the house is paid for. The bonds were to be signed by the county clerk, and taxes to be paid out by him—some more lame legislation.

CHAPTER 930.—An Act for the benefit of J. W. Parker, or rather of school district No. 30, whose trustees had failed to list forty-two pupils. The Act directs the auditor to pay said Parker, as teacher, $81.06.

CHAPTER 1168 amends Sec. 22 of the Vanceburg City Charter, by substituting "Common School Commissioner" for "Treasurer." This is in regard to tavern license fees to sell whisky in Vanceburg.

CHAPTER 1174.—An Act for the benefit of H. T. Warder, sheriff, allowing him to list his fee bills with the officers.

CHAPTER 1188 gives justices of the peace jurisdiction in all cases where the matter in controversy, exclusive of interests and costs, does not exceed one hundred dollars.

CHAPTER 1292 relates to advertising by master commissioners and sheriffs, and fixes the times and rates therefor.

CHAPTER 1294 fixes a fine for "dead locking" and injuring the Vanceburg, Dry Run, and Kinny Turnpike.

CHAPTER 1304 authorizes Lewis County to construct a bridge across Salt Lick Creek on the line of the Vanceburg, Salt Lick, and Tollesboro Turnpike Road, at the Caine's farm; issue bonds, more taxes, ten cents on the one hundred dollars, and the county to have stock to the amount invested in the bridge.

ACTS OF 1881: CHAPTER 123 makes the Laurel Fork of Kinny a "navigable stream" below the mouth of Grassy.

CHAPTER 781 incorporates the "Kinniconnick Creek Turnpike Road Company," with L. A. Muleer, Wm. Hardy, Jonathan Easham, Samuel McEldowney, Joseph D. Rredden as the incorporators. This Act repeals that part of the Vanceburg, Dry Run, and Kinny Road as should cover the same ground as this charter.

CHAPTER 791.—This is the Act which finally transferred the Male and Female Academy to the trustees of the common school, in Vanceburg. The "whereas" shows that, beside paying for the lot, the building cost about seven thousand dollars. Being still in debt, at the passage of the Act, in the sum of six thousand dollars, the trustees were authorized to levy a tax of one dollar on each one hundred dollars worth of property subject to taxation for State revenue, lying in the district, and to continue said tax till the debt was paid. The school is to be free to all children at least five months each year, and is to receive the public school money, together with fines and liquor license fees, etc.

The trustees have power to have a higher grade school taught after the five months' free school, and to regulate the attendance, tuition, and course of study therein. The name and title of the school is the "Vanceburg Public School and Seminary." They also have the right to select teachers, same as the common school trustees of other districts.

CHAPTER 874 is the charter of the Vanceburg and Concord Turnpike Road Company. The incorporators are L. B. Baird, John Moore, John Monteith, Thos. J. Bruce, F. M. Carr, Lewis B. Ruggles, and L. A. Grimes. This road is to run from Vanceburg, down the Ohio River, to Concord. Two and one-half miles of it have recently been built, from Vanceburg to Quick's Run Creek.

CHAPTER 900 is the incorporation of "Riverside Male and Female Seminary," at Vanceburg, Ky. The principal, H. K. Taylor, and trustees, Samuel J. Pugh, A. H. Parker, H. C. Bruce, L. B. Piersal, T. B. Harrison, Dr. J. M. Wells, A. L. McKay, and F. M. Taylor, are mentioned in the Act. The institution has the right to confer degrees of "Maid of Science," "Bachelor of Science," "Maid of Arts," "Bachelor of Arts," and further honorary degree for a three years' course in literature.

CHAPTER 1217 incorporates the Vanceburg, Quincy, and Springville Turnpike Company. Geo. T. Halbert, Isaac Voiers, A. P. Frizzell, Leonidas Darragh, A. I. Yancy, A. F. Moore, W. W. Agnew, and B. F. Branham were mentioned as incorporators.

CHAPTER 1332 amends the Vanceburg city charter. Gives the treasurer only three months

15

after his successor is qualified to make complete settlement with the city.

CHAPTER 863 is the charter of the Tolesboro and Mt. Carmel Turnpike Road Company. A. D. Pollitt, Isaiah Grigsby, J. Win Parker, A. H. Pollitt, James Thomas, G. W. Reader are appointed commissioners to open books, etc.

CHAPTER 1149.—J. Win Parker, R. W. Pollitt, and G. P. Bane, and their successors be, and are hereby incorporated, under the name and style of Robert M. Owens Lodge, No. 588, of Free and Accepted Masons. This lodge has built a neat house at Tollesboro.

CHAPTER 1271 incorporates the Tollesboro and Esculapia Road. James Toncray, Jackson Teager, Thos. Ruggles, Hiram Warder, James Hull, and William Jones are the incorporated board of directors.

CHAPTER 836 is an act to establish a road law in Lewis County, but we think it has been superseded by another General Statute law, and is, therefore, unimportant.

CHAPTER 840 is the incorporation and charter of Poplar Flat and Indian Run Turnpike Road Company. Thompson Henderson, Horace Applegate, George Herron, Moses Ruggles, Aaron Hamlin were constituted a board to act until the first election.

This road has been built.

CHAPTER 1197 amends the Act authorizing the sale of the poorhouse farm. This Act requires the court to levy and collect taxes authorized in the former Act, before the farm is bought, so as to have the money ready.

CHAPTER 1165.—An Act for the benefit of John F. Pollitt. It authorizes the payment of $28.95 out of the school fund belonging to Lewis County.

CHAPTER 992.—Because S. H. Parker, assessor of Lewis County, had his book and blotter destroyed by fire on the 7th day of February, 1882, and thereby lost over five hundred lists, he is allowed thirty days additional time to make up his book to be returned to the auditor, and is allowed fifty dollars additional pay for the extra service in remaking the book.

CHAPTER 1320.—The Court of Claims of Lewis County is by this Act authorized to levy ten cents tax on the one hundred dollars to build a bridge across Kinny, at the upper Blankenship Ford. The bridge is built.

ACTS OF 1883-84: CHAPTER 6.—An Act in relation to a bridge over Salt Lick Creek at Vanceburg. Authorizes a tax and bonds for the purpose.

CHAPTER 56 incorporates St. Mary's Lodge of Free and Accepted Masons, at Concord. R. M. Owens, S. G. Hillis, L. A. Grimes,

B. T. Wells, and John Freeman are the incorporators.

CHAPTER 56 enacts that John D. Tully, Amos Means, Mandley Trussell, and J. W. Tully be created a body politic and corporate, by the name of "The Ebenezer Cemetery Association, of Lewis County."

CHAPTER 60 enacts that John M. Myers, Benjamin Biven, S. G. Hillis, James H. Barkley, and the present trustees of East Fork Christian Church be, and are, created a body politic and corporate under the name of "The East Fork Cemetery Association."

CHAPTER 59 enacts that B. T. Wells, S. G. Hillis, L. A. Grimes, W. Traber, Jas. H. Garrett, William Sparks, and J. T. Hines be, and are, created a body politic and corporate by the name of "The Concord Lodge, No. 260, I. O. O. F.

CHAPTER 156.—An Act for the benefit of J. Win Parker. Gives him $81.06 as teacher, and repeals a former Act for the same purpose.

CHAPTER 248 establishes the Vanceburg Deposit Bank, and appoints Geo. M. Thomas, Socrates Ruggles, Wm. M. Bireley, A. H. Parker, and W. C. Halbert commissioners to open books and receive subscriptions to the capital stock of said bank, which is $25,000. The stock was subscribed, and the bank established, and is in good condition and all O. K.

CHAPTER 448, for the benefit of Mrs. J. K. Carr, appropriates $35.75 to finish paying her as teacher, in district No. 14, because the trustees failed to properly take the census.

CHAPTER 541 amends the Act incorporating the Tollesboro and Mt. Carmel Turnpike by extending the time to take subscriptions to July, 1884.

CHAPTER 584 amends the Vanceburg and Quincy Turnpike by making said road begin in the center of the bridge in Slate Creek. And, it seems, it also ends there.

CHAPTER 558 amends the Mason and Lewis Turnpike Company by allowing a branch road to be built from Beech Lick, via Mrs. R. H. Lee's, Mrs. Man Davis', and to Farrow's mills. Lewis County to take one thousand dollars per mile stock.

CHAPTER 477 amends the Cabin Creek, Sand Hill, and Manchester Road; allows a branch road up East Fork to the C. & T. Road, near Salem Church. The road has been built.

CHAPTER 624.—Another "oversight" in the trustees in district No. 2 causes this Act to be passed by the Legislature in order to secure $44.33 to the district.

CHAPTER 709 amends the charter to the city

of Vanceburg; first, by making the marshal perform the duty of street commissioner, and secondly, making a "qualified voter" in said city only those who had paid the poll tax.

CHAPTER 750 incorporates the Poplar Flat, Indian Run, and Salt Lick Turnpike Road Company. Geo. W. Hevin, Alex. Harrison, Horace Applegate, W. K. Hampton, Thompson Henderson, and A. J. Hendrickson are the incorporators. The road is built.

CHAPTER 858 releases J. W. McNeal from State and county taxes on account of his being a paralytic.

CHAPTER 1052 gives the Vanceburg public school trustees to issue more bonds and levy taxes to protect the school property on the river front.

CHAPTER 1421 amends the Tollesboro and Esculapia Road charter by authorizing a county subscription of one thousand dollars to the mile when the road is let to contractors and one mile is made. Books were to be opened prior to September 1, 1884. Said road has never been let.

CHAPTER 1577 levies a tax of twenty-five cents on the one hundred dollars worth of all taxable property in V. S. L. T. & M. Road district, for the purpose of building approaches to the bridge at Caine's farm, on Salt Lick Creek.

ACTS OF 1885-86: CHAPTER 28 repeals an Act of May, 1884, in regard to levying a tax on the people along the line of the V. S. L. T. & M. Road, to build approaches to a bridge.

CHAPTER 149 authorizes the County Court to build a bridge across Kinny, near the mouth of Trace, and to issue bonds and levy a tax to pay the same.

CHAPTER 282 authorizes the Lewis County Court to appropriate out of the bridge fund, and pay to the officers of Cabin Creek, Sand Hill, and Manchester Road Company, the sum of one thousand dollars for the purpose of erecting two bridges on said road.

CHAPTER 291 authorizes the Poplar Flat, Indian Run, and Salt Lick Road Company to elect officers as soon as two hundred dollars is subscribed.

CHAPTER 433 incorporates the Esculapia Springs Company. W. F. Jones, W. W. Bean, A. R. Mullins, J. W. Baldridge, John Gates, B. A. Wallingford, Geo. T. Hunter, Joseph Power, Harvey Parker are the incorporators. Busted!

CHAPTER 438 directs the judge of Lewis County Court to issue bonds of the county in the sum of six thousand dollars, and subscribe same to the stock of the Maysville and Big Sandy Railroad Company, said bond to be issued in paying for the right of way in Lewis or other counties. The bond shall draw interest at six per cent, and a tax of five cents on each one hundred dollars' worth of property is levied to pay them. CHAPTER 969 of the same session amends this Act by increasing the bonds to $10,000.

CHAPTER 550 enacts that the trustees of the Methodist Episcopal Church, in Vanceburg, may convey lot No. 48 to T. M. Games, S. Ruggles, B. W. Parker, Alfred Harrison, and L. B. Piersal, and their successors, in trust for the benefit of said Church.

CHAPTER 686 provides that a fee of ten cents for each suit entered on the general and cross index to suits in the Lewis Quarterly Court. This claim is to be allowed the county clerk each year.

CHAPTER 807 incorporates the Sand Hill and Concord Turnpike Road Company. The incorporators are Jackson Norris, B. T. Wells, John M. Freeman, G. S. Doyle, and W. S. Jeffers.

CHAPTER 880 incorporates the Manchester, Crooked Creek, and Covedale Turnpike Road Company. The incorporators are A. M. Lang, John M. Myers, Amos Means, G. S. Doyles, J. H. Garrett, and Jas. G. Wilson.

CHAPTER 899 amends the Cabin Creek, Sand

Hill, and Manchester Road charter. Permits them to build a branch from Thos. M. Rea's, via Bink Gilbert's and Mrs. L. Crawford's, to John McCarahan's house, on Main Cabin Creek. Said road is allowed one thousand dollars per mile county subscriptions, and was built for that amount.

ACTS OF 1887-88: CHAPTER 14 empowers the County Court of Claims to levy twenty-five cents instead of ten cents as per Act March 10, 1880.

CHAPTER 15 authorizes the County Court to issue bonds and levy twenty cents on the one hundred dollars to build a bridge at the mouth of Montgomery and over the stream of Kinniconnick.

CHAPTER 278 authorizes and charters the Cabin Creek, East Fork, and Concord Turnpike Road Company. This road was to run from Thos. M. Rea's, on East Fork, via East Fork Cemetery to the C. & T. Road, near the lands of Jeremiah Wellman.

Cornelius Hughes, Jonathan Truesdell, Saml. Fry, T. M. Rea, D. H. Boyd, and F. M. Truesdell were appointed commissioners, etc. This road was not built.

CHAPTER 439 authorizes the Cabin Creek Road Company to build a branch road up Clear Creek to Tollesboro. They did not do it.

CHAPTER 866 amends the charter of Vanceburg so that the assessor shall begin his duties
on the 10th day of September, each year. He
shall report his completed work in November
to the council, which shall appoint three super-
visors. They are to report in December. The
city clerk shall list the taxes with the collector
by the 15th day of January. After the first
day of May the collectors shall advertise and
sell property for taxes, and may be redeemed
at any time within two years by cost and thirty
per cent interest.

CHAPTER 1185 authorizes the circuit clerk
to make a general, direct, and revised index to
suits off the docket.

CHAPTER 1462 divides the V. S. L. T. & M.
Turnpike Road into two sections, and allows the
election of officers on each section. Section
No. 1 extends from Vanceburg to the Cabin
Creek bridge, including the bridges; and No. 2
from said to the western terminus. It also
authorizes the building of a branch road from
Tollesboro one mile toward Richland.

ACTS OF 1889-90: CHAPTER 143 amends the
charter of the Quick's Run and Ohio River
Road so that the road may run to Vanceburg,
or to Carr's Landing, on the Ohio.

CHAPTER 218, for the benefit of J. C. Willim, sheriff, allowing him further time to make

official bond, said right having been forfeited by an oversight in neglecting .to obtain his quietus.

CHAPTER 325 amends the title to the Cabin Creek, East Fork, and Concord Road, making said road begin at the residence of Jacob Mower and run along Chalk Ridge to E. F. Courtney's, and thence to the C. & T. Road, at the residence of Cooper Means.

The usual ration of county bonds is prescribed.

CHAPTER 373 incorporates the Kinniconnick and Freestone R. R. Company. The road is to run from the Ohio River, up Kinny and through Carter or Rowan Counties, to intersect the Lexington and Big Sandy R. R.

The incorporators are all persons who become stockholders, and the commissioners to open books are A. H. Parker, J. W. Sweet, C. B. Houghton, and George W. Bruce, Jr., of Lewis County.

CHAPTER 450 changes the boundary line of Lewis County as follows: "Beginning at a point where the line now crosses the Orangebury and Tollesboro Turnpike Road; thence with said road east 36 rods and 10 poles to a corner of the lands of Samuel Hull and S. D. Gardener; thence with their line north 196 rods to a corner in the lands of Humphrey Marshall

and S. D. Gardener; thence west with said
Gardener's line 12¾ rods to its intersection with
the present line between the two Counties of
Mason and Lewis; all lands lying to the west
of above named line shall hereafter be in Mason
County.

CHAPTER 463 permits the Cabin Creek Road
Company to build a branch from Cottageville,
in Lewis County, to Rectorville, in Mason
County, and prescribes the usual one thousand
dollar county bonds for both counties.

CHAPTER 499 amends an Amendment to
the V. S. L. T. & M. Road, properly naming
the boundary of the two divisions of said road.

CHAPTER 504 makes it a misdeamor finable
in the sum of twenty-five dollars or imprison-
ment not less than fifteen days for any person
to take intoxicating liquor to a church or
school. This Act applies to Lewis County and
a few others.

CHAPTER 685 amends the charter of the city
of Vanceburg so as to allow the city to dispose
of lands that she may own.

CHAPTER 912 authorizes Lewis County to
levy a tax of ten cents on the one hundred
dollars for the purpose of building a bridge
over Kinny Creek, at the mouth of McDowell.

This Act has never been carried into effect.

CHAPTER 1034 incorporates the Vanceburg

and Stout's Lane Turnpike Road Company. The incorporators are W. J. Willim, B. F. Bradford, T. J. Bruce, John Hammond, G. K. Cole, J. C. Cole, E. Falls, A. H. Parker, and W. C. Halbert.

CHAPTER 1014 makes it unlawful to vend, sell, loan, or give away any kind of intoxicating liquors within two miles of Oak Ridge Baptist Church, in Lewis County, or to engage in dancing within the same distance. The Act makes the offense a misdeamor finable from ten to fifty dollars.

CHAPTER 1158 amends an Act for the benefit of county clerks, in so far as Lewis County is concerned. It changes fees from fifty to twenty-five dollars.

CHAPTER 1244, for the benefit of school district No. 75, authorizes the trustees to levy a tax to build a schoolhouse.

CHAPTER 1459.—Covedale and Ohio River Turnpike Road Company is hereby incorporated, with Dyas Pence, Amos Means, Isaac T. Hines, Henry C. Myers, and B. F. Wells as the incorporators. The road is to run from Covedale to the Pence schoolhouse, on the Ohio River.

CHAPTER 1590 authorizes Lewis County to levy a tax to build a bridge over Scaffold Lick, in Quincy Precinct. The tax authorized is twenty cents on the one hundred dollars' worth of property in the county.

This bridge has been built, and is an excellent one.

CHAPTER 1663 incorporates the "Petersville and North Fork Bridge" Turnpike Road Company. Dyal D. Lykins, Peter D. Lykins, John F. Lang, Dyal Gullett, Landen C. Brown, Edward Becket, and Jesse Miner are the incorporators. The road has been built; it was finished in 1895.

CHAPTER 1761 amends the charter of the town of Quincy. Makes the election for trustees, police judge, and marshal to be held on the first Saturday in April of each year. It prohibits the sale of intoxicating liquors under any license except druggists', and that must be on prescription signed by regular practicing physician, stating the reason therefor. From sixty to one hundred dollars was the fine fixed.

ACTS OF 1891-92-93: This is the long session immediately after the adoption of the new "Constitution of 1890." It did not deal in any special legislation, except to repeal several local Acts.

The new Constitution prohibits the Legislature from passing any special legislation, and, therefore, our chapter on "Acts" necessarily ends here. But before closing this chapter, we

must say that local legislation has been the
bane—the curse—to the State of Kentucky.
During its existence it was impossible to tell
whether the law in one county was the law in
another, or whether the General Statute was not
modified by certain legislation from being effective in some localities; but a worse effect of
it was that a few people in a certain locality
wanting a turnpike road, for instance, would
get a charter and subject the people of the whole
county, who had no interest in their scheme, to
pay a tax on county bonds for the benefit of
that locality. It made the county pay taxes to
raise capital for a corporation to do business
on, and then give it the power to continue the
tax by charging the public for services rendered
from institutions produced mainly by their own
capital. If "turnpiking" is a business done
for profit, the profit ought to accrue to those
who furnish the capital, but some of the roads
have been built on the county bond alone, and
the people who paid the taxes have also paid the
toll, and have never received a cent in return;
in fact, there is only one road in the county
that ever paid a dividend, and that is the Lewis
and Mason Road, from Burtonville to Maysville.
We firmly believe that these roads ought to be
turned over to the county, it being the largest
stockholder, and made free to the use of all
citizens of the county.

CHAPTER IV

SUCCESSION OF OFFICERS—LIST OF REPRESENTATIVES—
POLITICS—ISSUES IN THE VARIOUS CAMPAIGNS—
DELEGATES TO THE CONSTITUTIONAL CONVENTIONS.

THE CONSTITUTION OF 1799, under which Lewis
County was organized, did not name a county
judge, but the oldest magistrate presided at
the County Courts, which were held once a
month. George Fearis seems to have been
that magistrate from two reasons—he signed
the court records as presiding justice, and he
was first appointed sheriff in the county, custom
requiring the magistrate oldest in commission
to be appointed. Some seem, however, to think
Landen Calvert was first; but the evidence
above refutes that idea.

Landen Calvert, however, was the first
grown person to die on Salt Lick; the date is
not given, but I find that he was last in court
of June 27, 1808, and his successor was appointed in January, 1809, so that he must have
died between those dates. The old graveyard
where he is buried has been turned into a
pasture, to the shame of Lewis County, be it
said, in thus neglecting to commemorate her
pioneers by even a decent graveyard.

SUCCESSION OF OFFICERS: At first there

were only two election precincts—Salt Lick and Ohio precincts—but the election lasted for three days, if any one of the candidates desired it. There was an election every year for the purpose of electing one representative in the Legislature and one senator. The senators, after the first election under the Constitution of 1799, were to serve four years. The first senators elected were divided into four classes by lot, one class going out each year, and a new member taking his place.

There was no election of the judiciary or minor offices of the county. The magistrates composing the County Court were appointed by the governor, with a "during good behavior" tenure of office. There was only three ways to get them out—bad conduct, death, or promotion to sheriff. The two oldest magistrates were always recommended to the governor by the court for sheriff, who, it seems, from the various appointments, held office for two years. There is nothing in the Constitution of that day in regard to his term of office, and we judge from the appointments made that the term was two years. The coroner, jailer, and surveyor stayed in during good behavior, unless they resigned, which several of our county's first officials in these offices did.

The court appointed the clerk, constables,

16

jailer, and county attorney, and the governor
appointed the justices, sheriff, coroner, and
surveyor. Generally one person held both of
the last named offices, though not always.
When we come to consider the expanse of territory covered by Lewis County, and think that
it was most a wilderness untouched by the ax
in the period of which we write (1807 to 1810),
and that neighbors might be only ten miles
apart, we cease to wonder that the court would
lay off a road from Salt Lick to Washington
(Mason County) with the same self-satisfied
information as a Vanceburg citizen would speak
of an alley between Second and Third Streets.
The sparseness of population can be judged
somewhat by the number of polls listed for
taxation each year, from 1807 to 1820:

1807....	Tithes in Lewis County				506
1808....	"	"	"	"	581
1809....	"	"	"	"	489
1810....	"	"	"	"	535
1811....	"	"	"	"	545
1812....	"	"	"	"	569
1813....	"	"	"	"	572
1814....	"	"	"	"	593
1815....	"	"	"	"	640
1816....	"	"	"	"	655
1817....	"	"	"	"	671
1818....	"	"	"	"	702
1819....	"	"	"	"	789
1820....	"	"	"	"	831

This included not only the white males over twenty-one, but also the colored people, over sixteen, on whom their owners had to pay taxes.

In resuming the narrative of succession in office, that chapter two carried up to the June Court of 1809, we will begin in November, at the taking of the third county levy, as there was no change of officers or other important events in the interim that calls our attention.

November Term of Court of 1809.—The third county levy, as shown on the record of the County Court, is as follows:

```
382 white tithes, per $1.25............$573.00
102 black    "     "     "   ............ 153.00
Taxes, etc.......................... 39.42½
                                      _____
    Total.........................$765.42½
    Claims allowed.................$214.58½
                                      _____
       Balance...................$550.84
```

April Term of Court of 1810.—Joseph Robb was made county clerk, Joseph B. Reid having followed the example of his brother, Walker Reid, and resigned. Walker Reid afterward became the noted Judge Reid, of Kentucky.

Mr. Robb served Lewis County as clerk for forty-four years, and this fact is made part of an epitaph on his tombstone in the Clarksburg Cemetery.

The fourth county levy was made in the October Term, 1810:

535 tithes, at $1 . . . . $535.00
Taxes, etc 8.68

Total $543.68
County Claims $287.44

Balance $256.24
The sheriff's salary was $40.00
The county attorney's salary was 34.00
The. Commonwealth attorney's salary
was 100.00

They were given an order on the sheriff to be paid when collected.

The following commissioners of revenue (assessors) were appointed for the coming year, February 11, 1811:

Thos. Mitchell, in the bounds of J. G. McDowell's Company of Militia;

W. B. Parker ("Red Buck"), in Rowland T. Parker's Company.

Garret Smith, in John Radford's Company.

James McClain, in John Cummin's Company.

George Fearis, in Thos. McElvain's Company.

John Donovan, in George Means' Company.

Wm. P. Ball, in John Phillipp's Company.

This shows a peculiarity of the institutions of that day, which may need a little explanation. Every able-bodied man was a militia man, and belonged to some company. Those living nearest together belonged to the same company, and the bounds of that company were limited like a voting precinct is now. The captain had the name of all his men, and the assessor could get to them easily, being himself a member of the same company which he assessed. Each man had to give in his property to the commissioner or be called into court for contempt. Every able-bodied man had to pay a tithe muster, be fined, or furnish a substitute. The fines collected and reported in county settlements were mostly from this source.

There seems to have been seven companies in Lewis County in February, 1811, and the regiment was known as the 69th Kentucky Militia.

February Term of Court of 1811.—The County Court ordered a "Stray Pen" built at Clarksburg, and appointed, first, Garland S. Parker, and afterward James Winter, keeper. It was for the purpose of impounding strayed stock so that their owners might recover them.

August Term of Court of 1812.—John R. Chitwood was made county attorney, and Joseph Robb was clerk of both County and Circuit Courts.

October Term.—Mr. Robb presents this account of taxes to the County Court:

Taxes on 5 County Seals, per 50 cents . $2.50
Taxes on 38 Deeds, per 50 cents........ 19.00

Total............................$21.50
Commission, 5 per cent........... 1.07½

Due County................$20.42½

CIRCUIT COURT:
Taxes on 33 writs, per 50 cents.......$16.50
Taxes on 4 Chancery supb., per 50 cents. 2.00

Total..........................$18.50
Commission..................... .92½

Due Commonwealth.........$17.57½

The name of David Johnson, in a probate to his last will and testament, appears in the October court. Whether he is progenitor of the large family of that name is for them to determine.

Lewis County had not yet got started on her career of debts and bonds, for we notice the Fiscal Court, in October, 1812, only allowed claims to the amount of $395.67½, and levied $426.75 with which to pay all expenses.

William Cottingham's name figures in this court. He objected to a road being established

through his land, and a jury awarded him
21½ cents, which was immediately paid in
open court by Arch. Frizzell, and the road to
Catt's mill, on Quick's Run, was ordered to
be opened.

November Term.—David Brown, as attorney,
represented the Commonwealth against Esquire
James McClain, in the November Court, 1812.
It seems, from the record, that some new law
in regard to magistrates returning fines in their
hands was not understood by them, and the
county attorney brought suit to teach them
their duty in a way they were not likely to
forget.

January Term of Court of 1813.—Aaron
Owens got his commission as sheriff, and Fred
R. Singleton was appointed his deputy.

The Commonwealth attorney was ordered
to bring suit against Benjamin Aills, contractor
to build a court-house, but the commissioners
came to his rescue and changed the contract
somewhat, and accepted his work with a proviso
that a stove be furnished instead of stone
chimney. In a short time afterward, the stove
failing to appear, the court ordered the chimney
built, and the next session was held in the
new house.

February Term.—Some more new names
appear in the February session of the court, *viz.*

Christiana Lantz, George and Ferdinand Fry, John Hymes. They are mentioned as being on the road from Wilson's Bottom to "Big East Fork" of Cabin Creek. The descendants of these still hold the fort in that neighborhood.

March Term.—Jonathan Kenyon had a ferry privilege on the Ohio side, at Vanceburg, in 1812, and in March, 1813, John McDowell got the same privilege from the County Court in Lewis.

April Term.—Henry C. Bruce was commissioned April 8, 1813, as justice of the peace, and Richard S. Wheatly was appointed county attorney.

June Term.—On June 28 Israel Thomas was appointed administrator of the estate of George Halbert, deceased, and John Radford was commissioned surveyor and coroner of Lewis County, June 3d.

August Term.—August 23d John Hamlin and James Swearingin had a suit in court, and Mr. Hamlin let his temper get away with his judgment, and used profane language in court, and was therefore fined one dollar, which he paid.

September Term.—Harry Parker emancipated William Moore, a slave, and had the paper recorded in the court.

November Term.—In November of this year the name of Jesse Hamrick appears as a citizen of Lewis County, he being allowed a claim by the County Court of Claims.

February Term of Court of 1814.—James Winters, a boot and shoe maker, had a boy apprenticed to him. The names of some more of our county citizens appear at this session— James Boyd, in a last will and testament; Robt. Juck, as a constable; Samuel Reiley and Robt. Rayborn, as road overseers; Joseph Lyons and Robert Rea, as hands on a road from Salt Lick to forks of Cabin Creek.

August Term. — A colored man, named "Harry," was tried for felony, he having stolen a gun and powder horn from Jno. W. Leach. At his first call into court his owner, Mary Lewis, of Mason County, did not appear in his defense, and the case was continued to next term, when he was tried before a jury and found guilty, and a verdict that he should have thirty lashes on the bare back was rendered. The court ordered that the sheriff execute the sentence immediately, and remanded the prisoner to jail until the sentence was executed.

September Term.—We find the names of James Dazier and David Vance connected with a road order from Concord up the left fork of Sycamore, and extending from John Stephenson's mill to Joseph Taylor's blacksmith shop.

The county levy in this year was only fifty

cents on each poll, but it was thought sufficed
to build a stone chimney to the log court-house
at Clarksburg.

January Term of Court of 1815.—The court
refused to pay twelve dollars for damages to
land by opening a road.

John Dyal about this time demanded his
seat as justice of the peace, but the court refused.
He took the case to the Circuit Court, and obtained an order that they show said court their
reasons for such action. At the next meeting
of the County Court the justices rendered their
reasons: That the said John Dyal had been a
regularly enlisted soldier in the United States
Army, and that he had gotten a furlough from
his commanding officer; that he had failed to
return when his furlough expired, and had been
in hiding until he had, by promising to pay
certain moneys to the Court of Lewis County,
been discharged from the army; that he had
not paid said money, and therefore they refused to seat him. This statement went before
the Circuit Court, but he obtained a mandamus
against the County Court and was allowed
his seat.

February Term.—February 27th G. N. Davis
presented commission, dated January 27, 1815,
from the governor, making him coroner of Lewis
County, and John G. McDowell presented a

commission as sheriff, and Thomas Mitchel was appointed his deputy.

John G. McDowell owned the land at the whirlpool at Vanceburg, where the mill and the west end of the city now stand, and was endeavoring to establish salt works there. He had commissioners to view a way from C. Greenup's salt wells back of Vanceburg through the lands of Moses Baird and Robt. H. Grayson to the river at the whirlpool, and also a jury to assess damages on a writ of *ad. quad dannum*. He got the way for salt water pipes.

March Term.—Frederick R. Singleton was commissioned as surveyor and Joseph Robb renewed his bond as clerk, a thing which he continued to do for forty years.

May Term. — Aaron Stratton and Thos. Mitchell had built a cabin at the mouth of what was then called Hazel Hollow, and they also got a right of way for salt water from C. Greenup's wells. There is an old salt well on Hazel yet. The property is owned by Mr. Thompson Kenyon.

The names of Baily Bryant, John Spence, and John Purcell appear about this time as citizens of Lewis County.

June Term.—Robt. Bagby and Thos. Shain, justices of the peace, were appointed judges of the election in Kinniconnick precinct; Winslow

Parker and John McDaniel, in Clarksburg; and Hugh Hannah and Arch. Boyd, in Cabin Creek precinct. This shows three election precincts in the county in 1815.

John G. McDowell, it appears, was continued sheriff, with J. W. Leach, deputy.

August Term. — Charles Fetters was appointed overseer on the road from Taylor's horse-mill to the South Fork of Cabin Creek, and William Kelly on the State Road toward Fleming County. Besides these, the following gentlemen were found living in Lewis County, according to the record in August, 1815: On the road up the river above Kinny to Rowland Thomas' farm, James Stephenson, Sr., James Stephenson, Jr., Thos. Mahan, William Burk, the Forman's, Jonas Hare, Josh. Baily, Wm. Bilderback, Wm. Harmon, Robt. Bagby. Jacob Scott, Ed. Scott, Wm. Dorch, David and Wm. Shain, Robt. Shain, J. W. Leach, and Thos. Shain. From Rowland Thomas' up to Greenup County, James Laughlin, James Applegate, Joseph Huston, John Hardy, Anthony Thompson, Thomas Veach, John S. Laird, David Hudson, Wm. Hudson, Levy Connelly, Michael Stockwell, Christian Staily, and Rowland Thomas, Jr., Abraham Dean, Israel Halbert, Jas. Moorehouse, and William Cottingham are neighbors on Salt Lick.

September Term.—At this session of Lewis

County Court, held at Clarksburg, began a trial which resulted in the only case of capital punishment that has been legally performed in Lewis County.

The culprit was a negro slave named George. He was the property of James Hill, of Bath County, and was charged with attempt at rape on the person of Mary Davis, a girl eleven years old, daughter of Walter Davis. The witnesses against him were John Harrison and Thos. Mitchell. A jury consisting of Henry Halbert, Geo. Thomas, Larret G. Smith, Archibald Frizzell, William Cottingham, John Fry, Thomas Gayle, Plummer Thomas, Robert Voiers, Samuel Cummins, Elias Stalcup, and James Martin, were empanneled, and the prisoner was allowed counsel (who failed to appear). The jury found him guilty as charged in the warrant, and then his owner appeared with his attorney and endeavored to get an appeal on account of error in the proceedings; but the court overruled his motion, and, on the 27th day of September, 1815, he was sentenced to be hanged. The negro was valued at five hundred dollars and recommended to the mercy of the governor, but was at the same time sentenced to hang on the 27th day of the following October. The sheriff was immediately ordered to build a gallows for the execution, which was to be between the hours of 10 A. M. and 3 P. M. of the day appointed. John G. McDowell was the sheriff at the time, and the execution took place on the hillside opposite Clarksburg.

About this time Mr. Henry C. Bruce died, as we find on the order book where Polly Bruce relinquished her right to become administratrix, and John Bruce and Joseph Morgan were appointed.

The county claims for 1815 amounted to:

Fines, etc., to	$82.92½
640 tithes, at 50 cents	320.00
Total	$402.92½
Debtor	248.41½
Balance due county	$154.51

December Term.—David Looney made application to the court to build a mill on Crooked Creek, near what was then known as Massie's Fork. We think it was the same mill site which was lately owned by the Ruark family.

January Term of Court of 1816.—William G. Bullock was made deputy surveyor. This is not the W. G. Bullock who was deputy sheriff under Thos. Wilson a few years ago; but it is one of his relations.

February Term. — The family names of Brewer, Osborn, Hillis, and Myers, who still have representatives in the county, are found in the order book of the Lewis County Court, in February, 1816. Edward Brewer made application for permission to build a mill on Cabin Creek, and Samuel Hillis (or Hillhouse) was one of the jury appointed to condemn the land for the site of the mill. Jacob Myers was an overseer of the road from Sycamore to Crooked Creek. John Means had his property improperly listed, and was released thereof, and Richard Conway was an overseer on Cabin Creek Road.

August Term.—Thurston Wollen is made constable, and Arch. Frizzell took the oath as coroner of Lewis County.

William Worthington appears as an attorney in a case between James Winters and G. N. Davis. John Stockholm also had a suit with Reuben Plummer, who, it seems, from an alias warrant, lived in Fleming County. John Halbert was appointed commissioner on a road from Salt Lick to Quick's Run. Thos. Bragg was a witness in a cause between Wm. Watkins and Daniel Swearingin.

September Term.—The last will of Wm. Graham was presented with James and William Barkley as witnesses, and Robt. Robb and Geo. Fearis as executors named. George Maple and James Rowland were appointed appraisers of the property. These parties all lived on Cabin

Creek, and all except Maple have representatives still living in Lewis.

Evan Harry was allowed four dollars for an armchair for the court-house, and Andrew Moore allowed witness fees. The Harry family lived on the mountain, between Mudlick and Burtonville, and the Moores lived on the head waters of Mudlick. The irrepressible J. T. Harry is still a resident of Kinny, and Amos Harry lives near Burtonville. Both these gentlemen are now old men who can look back over sixty years and still not see the ancestor mentioned in this section. The author can remember seeing Uncle Jimmie Moore, an old man on crutches, who used to visit his father in 1853. He was the grandfather of Lewis Moore, now residing near Esculapia, and of Elder E. L. Moore, of Honey Landing.

John Montgomery, on Quick's Run; David Arthurs, on the State Road; John and George Fry, East Fork of Cabin Creek, are all mentioned in the November term of the court. Their children's children are still here.

COUNTY LEVY FOR 1816:

655 polls at 50 cents	$327.50
Fines, taxes, etc	46.34
Total	$373.84
Allowances	208.12½
Balance due county	$165.71½

November Term.—The names of the following citizens are found: G. W. Bruce, Solomon Fuller, Daniel Olds, Martha Zornes, Catharine Olds, Richard Clary, Joseph Clary, the first part of whom lived on Kinny; but the Clarys lived on the road from Cabin Creek to Phillips Creek, and were appointed commissioners to view a roadway there.

January Term of Court of 1817.—This court was held at Benjamin Wood's house, in the town of Clarksburg. There seems to have been something the matter with that "stone chimney" to the court-house, as several times when the time indicates that the weather might have been cold the court was held at other places than the court-house.

Andrew Wilson was made a justice of the peace, and John Stephenson became sheriff at this session. Squire McClain had Elizabeth Brown, a pauper, under his care, and he had ordered fifty pounds of meat and 3 bushels of corn to be given her from some of the citizens for her sustenance. William Hull was allowed one dollar in this court for the corn.

March Term.—Thomas Marshall announced his commission and took the oath as a justice. The Kinny precinct had been formed by Act of the Legislature, and made four voting places in the county.

17

November Term.—This year William Pitts got permission to build a mill on Quick's Run, and Tavenor Moore's stock mark was recorded. John Taylor also died this year.

The court made the following levy:

By 671 polls, at 75 cents............$503.25
By fines, etc.......................... 35.64¾

Total...............................$538.89¾
To claims allowed.............. 292.05

Balance "depositum".......$246.84¾

Jacob Myers was made overseer from Sycamore to David Looney's, on Crooked Creek, and Moses Irvin from James Dixon's, on Sycamore, to the "two-mile tree," near Moses Bevins' farm. The court also contracted to build a clerk's office on the public square.

By reference to the Acts of the Legislature we find that the jail was burned after the county levy had been laid. The Act authorizes the court to lay an additional levy to rebuild the same. There was a peculiar custom of the court in those days which might have had something to do with the burning of the jail. When a man became involved in debt more than he could pay on demand he was placed "in bounds," that is, he might not go outside of a certain boundary till he had paid his debts.

If he did so he was to be jailed. It is probable that the man "in bounds" thought if there is no jail there is no jailing. In February, 1818, Winslow Parker, Aaron Stratton, and Ben. Woods were appointed commissioners to build the jail or to have it done. The jail was to have two apartments, one for debtors and one for criminals, with a hall between them. The part for debtors was built out of hewn logs twelve inches square, and the room for criminals was to have double walls of logs, filled between with stone. The jail was built by Joel Stratton, building contractor, for $730. W. B. Parker was jailer at that time, and had charge of the prisoners if there were any.

About this time the names of Joseph Sparks, Geo. Sparks, Elias Gilbert, and James Nash are shown to be citizens of the county by a road order appointing them to work on a road from the "Sand Fields," near Wilson's Ferry, up Crooked Creek.

The old "cloth mill" seems to be established at or near George Fearis', as he had a boy, David Mackelroy Gosset, bound or apprenticed to him to learn the "trade and mysteries" of fulling and finishing domestic cloth.

The Tolle family are represented in the person of John Tolle, who resided near or on Phillip's Creek.

On the motion of John Thompson, whom, it seems, lived on Kinny, a road was opened from the fork of Kinny to Spurgin's mill, on Salt Lick.

February Term of Court of 1818.—Alexander Bruce was given a certificate of "honesty, probity, and good demeanor" as a lawyer.

March Term.—The court had the road from Wilson's Ferry to Sycamore viewed and laid out. This was the first public highway along the river from Wilson's Bottom to Concord.

The family name of Ruark is first mentioned in the person of Jordon Ruark, who was paid as a witness for Joseph Ward in a case between him and John Brewer.

May Term.—Jacob Colvin, in the records, presents the name of that family in Lewis County, and in August the name of John Tully appears on record.

November Term.—The Court of Claims met and made the following levy:

702 tithes, per 70 cents	$526.50
Fines, licenses, etc.	219.94
Total	$746.44
Claims allowed	230.57½
Balance due county	$515.86½

That stone chimney to the court-house had two fire-places—one downstairs, 4½ feet wide at the back, and one upstairs, "3 feet in the clear." It was built by Henry Halbert at a cost of $129.50.

It appears in evidence that John McDaniel was a hatter, as one, John Clem, was apprenticed to him to learn that trade.

In the same court (November) Charles Queen was made road overseer from Kendrick's, on Salt Lick, to Vanceburg.

December Term.—This session turns to view some of the wealth owned in those days. The assessor had not been able to get the list of John and Horatio Bruce, and they were called into court to give in their list, which shows some wealth for those days. It is as follows:

2 white males, over 21 years; 10 black, over 16, and 2 other blacks, total, 12 blacks; 7 horses, 400 acres of second rate land, valued at $10 per acre; 350 acres of second rate land, valued at $10 per acre; 350 acres of second rate land, valued at $25 per acre; 6,500 acres in Mason County, valued at $7 per acre; 175 acres in Bourbon County, valued at $40 per acre; 100 acres in Garrard County, valued at $20 per acre, with a total valuation of $77,600.

January Term of Court of 1819.—Hugh Hannah produced his commission as "High Sheriff" of Lewis County, and W. J. Simspon was appointed deputy sheriff.

March Term.—This year Aaron Stratton is engaged in the salt business at Vanceburg, and had a way viewed by commissions to convey salt-water from Greenup's wells to a lot in the town.

Samuel Redman was appointed road overseer from Clarksburg to Cottingham's branch. W. B. Parker qualified as assessor under the new Act, and Benjamin Aills was admitted to the bar as an attorney. Rowland T. Parker removed to Vanceburg, and got tavern license there. Thos. Bragg was also allowed tavern license at Vanceburg.

June Term.—W. B. Parker resigned as jailer, and Thos. Mitchell was appointed in his stead.

John and Horatio Bruce, in this month, were also trying to increase that wealth by making salt at Vanceburg.

August Term.—John Stephenson presented to the court his commission as justice, and took his seat. Robt. Meridith's will was probated, with his wife, Rebecca, as administratrix.

"Old Ebenezer" in, August, 1819. The congregation elected George Means, George Maple, Archibald Boyd, Samuel Boyd, and William Robb as trustees and certified them to the court as proper persons to whom deed for the church property might be made, and the court recognized them as such.

Elijah Moore built a mill on the East Fork of North Fork of Licking, adjoining the property of Jonathan Wilson—at least he got permission from the court, in August, 1819, to do so. This mill ought to be found somewhere near Burtonville.

September Term.—Wm. B. Parker returned his lists as assessor, also his account for services rendered. It took him seventy days to take all the lists, at the cost of one dollar per day. He also was allowed ten dollars for making out the list, amounting in all as salary the sum of eighty dollars.

The county was laid off into districts in September, as follows: Beginning at the mouth of Kinny, and including all settlements on it to the mouth of Laurel, thence up Laurel, including all settlements on it; thence a straight course to the Greenup County line, to be one district to be called District No. 1, or Kinny precinct.

No. 2. Beginning at the mouth of Kinny, thence down the Ohio River to the first branch above Samuel Cummins; thence a straight line to the dividing ridge between Sycamore and Quick's Run, and with same ridge, dividing the waters of Salt Lick and Cabin Creek, and the waters of North Fork and Kinny, following the highest points of said ridge to the Greenup

County line; thence with said line to the boundary of District No. 1, and with said boundary to the beginning, to be one district, to be known as District No. 2, or Clarksburg precinct.

No. 3. Beginning at the top of the dividing ridge between Thos. Parker and Joseph Watkins, on the State Road, and with the said road to the forks of the same at the Williamsburg Road, and with the Williamsburg Road to the Mason and Lewis County line, at Dr. Alexander Duke's. Thence with Mason and Lewis County line to the mouth of Crooked Creek, and thence up the Ohio River to the first branch above Samuel Cummins'; thence with line of District No. 2 to the beginning, to be one district, known as District No. 3, or Cabin Creek precinct.

No. 4. Beginning at Dr. Alex. Duke's, thence with the Lewis and Mason County line to North Fork of Licking, at the corner of Mason and Lewis Counties; thence with the North Fork and Fleming and Lewis County line to where the Greenup County line strikes the same; thence with the Greenup and Lewis County line to where it intersects the line of District No. 2, on the ridge, and with said ridge to the beginning of District No. 3, to be one district, known as No. 4, or North Fork precinct.

November Term.—Edward Kelly got permission to build a mill on Little East Fork of Cabin

Creek. Thompson Ward was admitted to the bar as an attorney in Lewis County. / John Thompson was appointed constable in District No. 1, Murdoc Cooper in District No. 2, William Boyd in District No. 3, James W. Singleton in District No. 4.

In November the court made its levy on

789 tithes, per $1	$789.00
Fines, licenses, etc	18.65½
Total	$807.65½
Claims	466.55½
Balance due county	$341.10

December Term. — The Polly family, of Quicks Run, are first mentioned in this session, in the name of David Polly, who is authorized to keep an insane brother at the county's expense.

James McCormick, of McCormick Springs on the head of Salt Lick, is mentioned as a road overseer from John McDaniel's to the top of the mountain above Gunpowder Lick.

January Term of Court of 1820.—The court laid off an additional magisterial district, to be called Sycamore District, and numbered it No. 5. John and Andrew May and Joseph Spence are named as being on the boundary line in said district.

May Term.—Bushrod Fry was appointed constable in the Sycamore precinct, and John M. Logan, at Clarksburg, at the same court above mentioned.

Samuel Criswell, living on Kinny, at the mouth of Grassy Fork, made application for a road over to Clarksburg.

The name of William Chapman appears at this time as a Lewis County citizen.

Joseph Ruark was released as overseer on the Three Island Road. Mr. Waugh and Joseph Lane are mentioned in connection with a road from Boyd's horsemill to Mason County line.

June Term.—The school trustees at Clarksburg were permitted to have a school taught in the court-house.

Fred R. Singleton was commissioned surveyor for the county.

September Term.—The last will of William Cottingham was admitted to probate and his wife, Polly Cottingham, named as executrix, with George Thomas, Stephen Halbert, and John Halbert as securities.

Christopher Fort, as a citizen of Lewis, is mentioned as a juryman to assess damages on a roadway. An old lady, Peggy Fort, lived with Alex. Vance, near Concord, in 1837. She was one hundred and five years old when she died, and had been blind for a number of years.

She was Mr. Vance's mother-in-law and the grandmother of Mr. George Vance.

December Term.—Mr. Robb presents the following bill for blank books:

Mr. Joseph Robb bought of Edward Cox, Maysville, Ky.:

1 Record book, 6 quires	$12.50
1 " " 4 "	7.00
1 Small blank book	2.25
1 " " "	1.00
Total	$22.75

Received payment,
EDWARD COX.

Thomas Marshall's estate was valued in a court assessment at $34,600.

A road was established from the mouth of Holly Fork of Kinny to McDaniel's, on Salt Lick. Solomon Thomas had a cabin at the mouth of Holly, and John Fowler is reported to the court as the owner of the land up Holly, through which the road passed.

January Term of Court of 1821.—John Dyal received his commission as sheriff, dated November 26, 1820, and became sheriff in January, 1821. He had Nathan Halbert appointed deputy.

When a justice died, or was promoted to sheriff, he brought all his books and papers to court and they were turned over by the clerk to the nearest magistrate to the one deposed, and retained by him till a successor was appointed.

February Term.—Daniel Wood, a tanner, had Richard Wilson Lee apprenticed to him to learn the trade.

The March term failed to meet, and, in May, Jesse Truesdale was appointed overseer on road from Boyd's horsemill to Robt. Rea's.

A road from Scott's branch of Laurel to Grassy Fork of Kinny, and thence on a road already established, to Clarksburg, was laid out at this time. Also a road from the Greenup saltwells to the mouth of Trace, on Kinny.

June Term.—Henry Halbert was commissioned as justice of the peace, and John Carter made overseer of road from Quick's Run to Heath's mill, on Salt Lick.

The following citizens appear on the roads designated: On the Quick's Run Road, William McCann, Thomas McKinny, Thos. Oliver, Valentine V. Crawford; on Cabin Creek Road, Jonathan Laish, James West, John West, James Richards, John Riggs, John Brownfield, Peter Hoover, Jas. Graham, Sam'l Lane, Wm. McNutt, John Hoover, John Downey, Richard and William Fry; on Andrew Henderson's road, James Dickson, James Calhoun, Andrew Sherdine, Chas. Wood, Francis Henderson, James Henderson, William Boyd, Simon Kinnard, Ferdinand Fry; on a road from McKenzie's to Concord, or some place in that neighborhood, are John Piper, John McKenzie, John Thompson, Thomas Taylor, John McClain, John Carson, Amos Means, Thomas Yapp, Robt. Means, and King D. McClain.

On a Crooked Creek and Little Fork Road are Jesse Truesdale, John Gilbert, Elias Gilbert, Abraham Bilyen, Joseph Taylor, and Daniel Sexton.

Jacob, Michael, and Chas. Fetters, John, David, and Samuel Riggs, Henry Myers, Peter Looney, and "all the Pittsis'" worked on the road on Crooked Creek.

On the road from Sycamore to Crooked Creek, Jacob Myers, as overseer, had John and William McCandless, John Dyal, Alex. Dyal, Simon Dyal, John Kellum, Stephen Dwiar, Robt. Myers, James Wiley, Thomas Wright, and John Stevenson.

On the road from Concord, John Stephenson, as overseer, had John Bilyen, Thos. Bedford, Ben. Bedford, John Reid, John Trent, James Bivins, Ed. Stevenson, Joseph Means, John and William Reed, Thos. Berryman, Paul Bilyen, Paul Vanhorn, Pres. L. Stevenson, Alex. Davis, and David Dyal.

W. P. Ball had as hands John Feagans, David Gault, Wm. Yancy on some road back of Concord or Poplar Flat.

On the road past Thos. Marshall's are Peter Duzan, Gabriel Peed, Ezra Toncraye, David Toncraye, Wm. Walker. On Cabin Creek and Brown's Run are Alex. Osburn, Thos. Gillespie, David Maple, John and Thomas Hines.

August Term.—It is made a matter of record on the order book that Thos. Marshall had married the widow of John Boyd, and he wanted the administrator of her estate to show cause why he did not settle with the court. At the next session the said administrator settled and paid over nine dollars he had received for rent.

Thompson Ward was appointed county attorney.

November Term.—The court levied 75 cents on 896 polls, and allowed claims amounting to $486.14. The levy amounted to $672.

The August term authorized a road to be viewed from the mouth of Grassy, on Kinny, near Benjamin Cole's farm, and thence up Kinny to the head and over the ridge to Mudlick; thence down same to North Fork.

The commissioners appointed to view that road the following citizens living on the route: Benj. Cole, Samuel Criswell, William Murphy,

Solomon Thomas, Samuel Spurgin, Andrew Means, John Thompson. Well's Camp, Thomas Thompson, Abraham Plummer, James Silvey, John Maddox, on Kinny; and thence the road went up Sugar Camp hollow to the dividing ridge between Kinny and Mudlick, and followed the path to Mudlick, leaving H. C. Martin's house to the right; thence through John Bell's lands to John Green's farm; and thence down Mudlick past Caleb Taylor, John Hammon and Joshua Powers to William Quintance, on the North Fork of Licking. This is perhaps, the first road up Kinny from the J. B. Harrison farm to Petersville, and thence to Mudlick.

December Term.—John Chambers was a witness to the will of Augustine Cowne, and Green H. Smith and Jacob Neal had a lawsuit which resulted in a judgment of fourteen dollars for Neal.

January Term of Court of 1822.—Francis T. Hood was admitted to the Lewis County bar.

James McCallister, Mathew Thompson, W. H. Calvert, David W. Davis, Robb Robb, Sr., John Piper, Jas. Rowland, David Hendrickson, John Owens, and John Bell are said to live near Mudlick, and were appointed commissioners to value property under execution on that stream.

March Term.—The first school districts in Lewis County were laid off according to an Act of the Legislature. The first district began at the mouth of Slate Creek, above Vanceburg, and thence with a path known as Barrett's trace to the Sandy saltworks to a point where said trace crosses the Lewis and Greenup County line; thence with said line to the Ohio River, and with the river to the place of beginning.

The second district began at the mouth of Slate, and thence, with the Slate Road, to the top of the ridge dividing the waters of Salt Lick and Kinny from Cabin Creek and the North Fork of Licking, and with said ridge to the Lewis and Greenup line to Barrett's trace, and with said trace to the beginning.

Number three began at the whirlpool in the Ohio River, at Vanceburg; thence with the State Road to the top of the mountain above Thos. Parker's; thence with the chain of ridges which divide Quicks Run from Cabin Creek and Sycamore to the Ohio River, so as to strike the river between the mouth of Sycamore and Samuel Cummin's mill; thence up the river to the beginning.

Number four began at the mouth of Sycamore; thence down the Ohio River to the mouth of Crooked Creek; thence with the Lewis and Mason line to the Salt Lick Road at

Alexander Duke's; thence with said road to the top of the hill above Thos. Parker's; thence with the chain of ridges dividing the waters of Quicks Run, Cabin Creek, and Sycamore to the Ohio River, between Cumming's mill and the mouth of Sycamore; thence down the river to the beginning.

Number five—and the rest of Lewis County shall be district number five.

William J. Simpson, on account of contemplated removal from the county, was released as commissioner to settle with the sheriff, and resigned his commission as justice of the peace.

On motion of Joseph Staggs and John Knox it was ordered that commissioners be appointed to view a road up Laurel and Grassy to the Greenup County line.

May Term.—Richard Aills released as road overseer from forks of Quick's Run to Ohio River, and Jonathan Ruggles was appointed.

Isaac Pitts was made overseer from widow McKensie's to Sand Hill.

Richard Pell and Thos. Mitchell were granted tavern license in Clarksburg.

On motion of James McCormick commissioners were appointed to change the Gunpowder Lick Road.

James Carr licensed to keep tavern in Vanceburg.

18

Hugh McIlvaine, a tanner, had Stuart Marshal apprenticed to him to learn the trade.

Beverly Stubblefield and William Hannah were allotted to Wm. P. Ball's road.

Thos. Mitchell presents his account as jailer of Lewis County.

June Term.—Fred R. Singleton resigned the office of surveyor of Lewis County.

John G. McDowell lost his ferry license at Vanceburg by order of the court. He seems to have been away and not to have been attending to his ferry.

There was no court held in August.

September Term.—David Garth and Henry Bedinger were appointed overseers on Salt Lick Roads; John Stalcup on the Ohio River Road, from Cumming's to Quicks Run; and John Halbert from Quick's Run to Vanceburg. Samuel Reily, Nelson Plummer, John and Ben Maddux, Anthony Swim, and Charles Vincent were allotted as hands on a Kinny road.

Aaron Stratton was granted a license to ferry at Vanceburg, and Lucy Bragg license to keep a tavern at her house, above Vanceburg.

Francis T. Hord and Benjamin Aills were practicing attorneys in this court.

November Term.—Daniel Halbert was appointed tax commissioner.

Joseph H. Knapp had Ezinah Ames, a poor

boy, bound to him to learn the carpenter's trade, and Spencer Cooper had John Slater bound to learn the trade of stone-cutter.

John O. Powling had a license granted him to keep a tavern at the White Sulphur Springs. This evidently was the beginning at Esculapia, as it will be seen by the letter of Mr. Calvert, in "Early Settlements on Salt Lick," and that Mr. Powling lived in that section and at the farthest settlement up the creek.

William Cofin was granted a license to keep a tavern at Vanceburg.

The claims allowed in this year amounted to $303.32, and the levy, at 62½ cents on 929 polls, to $576.87½.

January Term of Court of 1823.—William Watkins was commissioned surveyor, and John McDaniel sheriff, with commissions dated November 20, 1822.

William Heath was appointed guardian of Jane Heath, daughter of John Heath, deceased.

Ben Givins was appointed overseer on the road from Farrow's mill to the mouth of Little East Fork of Cabin Creek.

Thomas Mitchell was appointed superintendent of the public buildings at Clarksburg.

John Fry renewed his bond as constable in District No. 5.

Ambrose McDaniel appointed commissioner to view a road from Scott's Branch, up Laurel.

Francis T. Hord, county attorney, was authorized to contract for the first County Seal Lewis ever had. He contracted with Pleasant Beard for the engraving and furnishing of said seal for the sum of twenty dollars.

February Term.—Commissioners were appointed to view a road from Gun Powder Gap, on the Left Fork of Salt Lick, to Truitt's mill, on the State Road, near Aquilla Smith's.

April Term.—In this term Jacob Colvin was made overseer from Clarksburg to Quick's Run. James Singleton renews his bond as constable in District No. 4.

The Gun Powder Gap and Aquilla Smith Road passed through lands of George Graham, Henry Powers, John Kendrick, and Abraham Van West.

Winslow Parker sent from Vanceburg his resignation as justice of the peace, which was accepted.

John Thompson was allowed $91.75 for the maintenance of Peter Nogle, a pauper, for the year 1822.

Samuel B. Victor and William Wilson petitioned the court for a road from Victor's house to the State Road.

William Walker was appointed overseer on

road from the well on Little Stone Lick to where the road from Williamsburg (now Orangeburg) intersects the road to Salt Lick.

Peter Duzan, Henson Tolle, and Gabriel Peed were appointed commissioners to view a road from Phillip's Creek to Salt Lick.

Alexander Young established a mill on Cabin Creek.

Charles Cox was granted a license to keep a tavern at the house lately occupied by Rachael Jack. This was probably near the mouth of East Fork of Cabin Creek.

Thomas Parker and Joshua Powers were recommended to Governor Adair as suitable persons for justices of the peace.

Carr, Davis & Co., mercantile firm, had several suits in court, appealed from the decisions of various magistrates. Henry Bedinger and George Graham were also litigants.

James Chaney was overseer on the road from Lewis and Mason line to Farrow's mill.

Jeremiah Moore obtained permission to build a mill on Kinny, below the mouth of Town Branch.

Thos. Marshall, Esq., gave information against John Hern in favor of Milton Hern, a poor orphan, and also against John Luman for the benefit of his children, to show cause why they should not be bound out to some person able to take proper care of them.

William Peters was appointed overseer on "Three Islands" Road, from Wilson's Ferry to East Fork of Cabin Creek, at Taylor's horse-mill.

Edward Brewer was appointed overseer from John Swearingin's mill, on Cabin Creek, to Lewis and Mason line.

It was ordered that a road be made on Kinny from Thomas Shain's, past Moore's and Bruce's mills, to the mouth of said creek.

James McCormick failed to open the Gun Powder Gap Road, and the court removed him and appointed James Adkinson in his stead.

James Boyd was appointed overseer from Wilson's Ferry, down the river to a bear wallow, near James West's.

James Fearis was appointed overseer from Lewis and Mason line, up East Fork to Humphrey Bell's.

The minutes of this court were signed by James McClain.

May Term.—Hannah Johnson, having married William Williamson, was released from being executor of the estate of David Johnson, her former husband.

Samuel Wilson, overseer on Crooked Creek Road, had the following hands allotted to him:

Curtis Lantz, Peter Heloy, Christian Lantz, Leonard Lantz, Joseph Sparks, John G. Wilson, Jos. S. Wilson, James S. Wilson, and John Hayiman.

William Peters, overseer, had the following hands allotted to him: John Wilson, Hugh Wilson, Richard Nash, Edward Boyd, John Peters, Aaron Peters, James Adams, Theophilus Latin, John Huffman, Samuel Cax, William Cox, Andrew Wilson, George Switzelm, David Peters, Jr., James McClain, Richard Huffman, William McNutt, and John McNutt.

James Fearis, overseer on East Fork Cabin Creek, had the following citizens on his road: Thos. Hughes, James Haines, Levi Darnell, Daniel Fetters, James Rea, Thomas Rea, Robert Rea, Towsand Hoggins, Noah Pitts, Thos. Vaughn, Eli Vaughn, John Vaughn, Michael Fetters, Lewis Fearis, Thomas Taylor, Charles Cox, James Band, and Ferdinand Fry.

Rev. Samuel G. Lowery, a minister ordained by the Ebenezer Presbytery, was granted a license to solemnize the rites of matrimony.

James Orcutt, Daniel Priest, Sam'l B. Victor, Marmaduke Swearingin lived on the road above Clarksburg.

Stephen Calvert, John Johnson, Jos. Johnson, John Nash were hands on the State Road, under Stephen Halbert, overseer.

July Term.—The following business was done in the July term of court:

Thomas Parker took his seat as a new justice of the peace.

Jacob Frizzell appointed constable in District No. 2, and John Leitch in District No. 1.

Alsea Victor and Stephen Halbert were appointed administrators of the estate of William B. Victor, deceased.

James Price, Thomas Pool, and Alexander Irwin are mentioned as hands on Quick's Run Road.

Ophelia Hunter was apprenticed to Charles Watkins to learn housewifery.

August Term.—Samuel White was appointed road overseer from Catt's old mill to Upper Pond Run, on the Ohio River.

John Kendrick, overseer from Gun Powder Gap (Esculapia) to the house of Aquilla Smith, on the State Road; the following hands were assigned him: William Hannah, Phillip P. Dornan, Samuel Williams, and Henry Powers.

On motion of Richard Evans, Jeremiah Moore, David Evans, Martin Coker, and Basil Burris were appointed commissioners to view a road on Lower Kinny.

On the river road, above the mouth of Kinny, the names of John Forman and Charles Cooley are mentioned, in addition to those already ed on that road.

There was no court held in September.

October Term.—Nancy Carrington and Daniel J. Carrington were appointed administrators of the estate of William Carrington, Sr., deceased.

Joshua Easham was appointed administrator of the estate of Alex. McDaniel.

William B. McDaniel, son of Alex. McDaniel, was apprenticed to Joshua Owins, a farmer.

Claims against the county amounting to $386.94½ were allowed, and a levy of 62½ cents laid on 894 tithes, amounting to $558.75.

Constables and guards had their claims certified to the auditor of State, and were paid from the State treasury. The circuit clerk made settlement with the County Court, but fees received by him were turned into the State treasury.

January Term of Court of 1824.—On motion of Samuel Cox, Joseph Taylor, James Price, Daniel Sexton, and Moses Ormes, Jr., were appointed commissioners to change road from Moses Ormes, Sr., on Quick's Run, to John D. Everett's, through the lands of Thomas Pool and William McCann.

Nothing of importance occurred during the February court, and there was no court held in March.

April Term.—Harry Parker, being sixteen

years of age, selected as his guardian Mr. Plummer Thomas.

Henry Bedinger released and Samuel Martin appointed as overseer on road from Catt's old mill, near the mouth of Quick's Run, to Heath's mill, on Salt Lick.

Woodruff Roberts was appointed overseer from Cottingham's Branch to Clarksburg.

Jesse Hamrick appointed overseer on the State Road from Daniel Carr's to George Truitt's mill, on North Fork.

David Woodruff was appointed constable, vice John Johnson, in the Clarksburg district.

Robert Grant was appointed commissioner to take the tax assessment in the county.

Robert Bagby resigned as justice of the peace, and Joshua Owens and Jno. W. Leach were recommended to the governor for appointment.

May Term.—George Rea was appointed constable in District No. 3.

John Robb was appointed deputy county clerk.

July Term.—The following judges and clerks for the annual election were appointed:

In FORMAN'S BOTTOM PRECINCT: Henry Halbert, Joshua Owings, judges; John Thompson, clerk.

In CLARKSBURG PRECINCT: Aaron Stratton, Thomas Shain, judges; William S. Parker, clerk.

IN CABIN CREEK PRECINCT: James McClain, John Stephenson, judges; Thomas Parker, clerk.

IN NORTH FORK PRECINCT. Archibald Boyd, Andrew Wilson, judges; Asabel Brewer, clerk.

August Term.—John Maddox was appointed overseer on road from Bear Branch to James Silvey's, on Kinniconnick.

On the road up Holly Fork of Kinny, Solomon Thomas was overseer.

October Term.—The claims amounted to $337.73½; levy on 939 tithes, at 50 cents, $469.50.

Geo. W. Bruce gave in a list of his property, amounting to $4,985, which the commissioner had failed to assess.

The court ordered a whipping-post established in the court-yard, at a cost of six dollars.

Francis T. Hood was discontinued as county attorney.

November Term.—Benjamin Aills was appointed county attorney, with no other reward than the use of two volumes of Little's Digest, which were owned by the county.

January Term of Court of 1825.—Rev. Elias Oliver, a minister of the Methodist Episcopal Church, was licensed to solemnize the rites of matrimony. Mr. Oliver lived up the river, above the mouth of Kinniconnick.

Archibald Boyd was commissioned sheriff

October 30, 1824, and presented his commission to this court, took the oath of office, and gave the several bonds necessary to enter upon the discharge of his duties.

William P. Henderson was appointed deputy sheriff.

Thomas Shain, Esq., signed the minutes of this court.

February Term.—The last will and testament of Moses Irwin was proven by John Boyd and John Irwin, and Betsy Irwin and John Irwin were appointed as executors. They gave bond, with Caleb Richards as security, and had Samuel Hampton, Jacob Myers, John Fry, and Thomas Thompson appointed as appraisers of the property.

April Term.—Aaron Stratton, who owned the land on the lower side of Kinny, where the State Road crossed, and Matthew Thompson, who owned the land above Kinny, applied for a ferry license across said stream, and the same was granted them.

James W. Singleton qualified as constable in District No. 4.

Jas. Cooper granted tavern license at his house in Vanceburg.

James Carter the same at Clarksburg, and Amos Spurgin at White Sulphur Springs.

Green H. Smith qualified as constable in the Kinny precinct, and John Fry in District No. 5.

Lewis County was divided into two districts for the purpose of assessing the taxable property. The dividing line was the State Road, from Vanceburg to the North Fork. The side down the river was called the North District, and that above the road the South District. John Halbert was appointed to assess the South District, and William J. Simpson the North District.

Jacob Frizzell was made constable in District No. 2, and Joseph N. Ralston in the Clarksburg District.

Mathias Tolle was appointed road overseer from Wilson's Ferry, on the Ohio River, at Manchester, to George Fearis' shorsemill, on Cabin Creek.

Abraham Carr, overseer from Jonathan Hayden's to Thomas Parker's.

May Term.—John Harrison was released as road overseer on account of age, and Thomas Ruggles appointed in his stead. This was on the road from crossing of Cabin Creek by the State Road to the house of Thomas Parker, on the hill toward Clarksburg.

Geo. W. Bruce had a road established from the river over the hill and down Spy Run to Kinny, to intersect the Moore's mill road on that stream.

July Term.—James Lane Pitts and Samuel

Campbell Pitts were appointed executors of the will of William Pitts.

Alexander Young was commissioned as justice of the peace.

Clifton A. Ganet was admitted as an attorney at the Lewis County bar.

Charles Woods, overseer from the head of Quick's Run toward Concord.

Stephen Bliss as overseer about Sycamore.

There was no court in August.

October Term.—William J. Simpson, commissioned as justice of the peace, took his seat first at this session.

Elizabeth Maddox and Hesekiah Griffith granted administration of the estate of John Maddox, deceased,. with James Silvey, William Heath, James Hughbank, and Humphrey Beckett as appraisers.

This is the first mention of the Beckett family, many of whom lived on the hills between the head of Kinny and Mudlick, and one, Reason Beckett, lived on Mudlick where the Kinny Road came over the hill to that stream. On the hill we can mention Thomas Beckett, William Beckett, and John Beckett. Humphrey Beckett lived on the ridge between Mudlick and the head of Bucklick and Salt Lick.

John Stephenson resigned his commission as magistrate, and Edward Stephenson and Jas.

Johnson were recommended to Governor Desha for appointment.

Joseph Robb renewed his bond as county clerk, with John Stephenson, Samuel Cox, George Boyd, Fred R. Singleton, Aaron Stratton, George Means, and John Piper securities. It seems that Mr. Robb could have given half the county as security, had it been desired. His annual settlements with the court show him honest to the fraction of a cent, the make-up of his records declare him competent, and his leniency in judgments in his favor against hard-pressed sheriffs prove the goodness of his heart. Jos. Robb's official tenure is part of his epitaph, and well might his friends refer to his official character and integrity as a monument more lasting than the marble slab at his grave.

George Means, overseer on the road from Cabin Creek to Williamsburg (name later changed), was released on account of age, and John Teager appointed.

It took John Halbert twenty-six days and cost twenty-six dollars to assess one-half the county, and William J. Simpson thirty-six days to assess the other half. Each received one dollar per day, so that the entire assessment cost the county only sixty-two dollars.

Doctors Duke and Leonard produced an account for medical aid to Ichabod Wheaden, a pauper, amounting to seventy-two dollars. This is ten dollars more than the whole assessment cost, and shows the doctors of that day were "up to snuff." This aid was authorized by Thomas Marshall, a magistrate, and shows a long line of precedents for the actions of later day magistrates and physicians and a practice which the county got rid of in 1896.

The claims this year were $205. Fines, etc., collected, $31.44½; 1,029 tithes, at 37½ cents, $385.87½.

November Term.—In the settlement with the sheriff, Archibald Boyd, it was found that for 1824 he only owed the county the sum of $8.73.

December Term.—The administration of the estate of William Arnold was granted his widow, Nancy Arnold, and Upton Arnold. They gave bond in the sum of $15,000, with Jno. Arnold and Moses Dimitt securities.

John Wallingford was made overseer on road on Kinny, from Bear Branch to James Silvey's.

The records closing up the year 1825 were signed by Aaron Stratton.

January Term of Court of 1826.—Joshua Owings removed to Bath County, and resigned his commission as justice of the peace.

Edward Stephenson was commissioned as justice instead of John Stephenson, resigned.

February Term.—Zachariah Williams, who was a local preacher in the "New Light" Church, is mentioned in connection with Jesse Hamrich, a Methodist Episcopal minister who obtained much notoriety when the slave question split his Church, on account of his strong anti-slavery sentiments. They were appointed commissioners to view a road from Buck Lick to Truitt's mill, on the North Fork.

On petition of Humphrey Beckett, James Moore, Benjamin Plummer, John Wallingford, and Solomon Plummer were made commissioners to view a change in the road from Mudlick, over the hill to Kinny.

The administration of the estate of John Thompson is granted to his brother-in-law, Francis Henderson.

John W. Mavity, who for some reason appears to be at his brother-in-law's, James McCormick's, home, near the head of Salt Lick, is ordered to help work the Gun Powder Gap Road.

Mr. Robb had Harrison Taylor appointed deputy county clerk.

April Term.—David Maple appointed overseer on the Three Island and Flemingsburg Road, from the South Fork of Cabin Creek to the crossing of the road from Clarksburg to Washington, Mason County.

"Pine Hill," on Lower Kinny, had received

19

its cognomen prior to 1826, as shown by a road order in this session.

Sheriff Arch. Boyd was ordered to pay William Barkley $7.50, Hugh Walker $6.50, and George Maple $2.50 out of the levy for 1825.

William Nicholls was granted the administration of the estate of David Powell, with Geo. Means and Thomas Marshall securities.

On motion of Joseph Robb, William Priest was bound to Joseph Hampton to learn "the art and mystery of the manufacture of leather."

Thomas Grover was appointed road over-seer, in lieu of Richard Taylor, released, on the State Road, from Thos. Parker's to Swearingin's mill, and Richard Taylor, Nesbit Taylor, Thomas Boggs, and Thos. M. Grover allotted as hands.

Charles Cox is granted tavern license at his house in Lewis County, and James Carr the same at Vanceburg.

Israel B. Donaldsons, overseer from Quick's Run to Vanceburg.

Harry William, John Cottingham, and James Cottingham are mentioned as having been appointed to use a hoe on the public road on Salt Lick.

From the following order we can gather the change in plan of assessment, the names of company commanders in the militia, and the various assessors for the year: "Agreeable to a late Act of the Legislature, Nathan Halbert is appointed to take the lists of taxable property in the bounds of Captain J. W. Leache's Company; Daniel Halbert, in Captain Robt. Parker's Company; John Thomas, in Captain William Heath's Company; John Halbert, in Captain Nicholas Elson's Company; Simon Dyal, in Captain Ellis Owens' Company; William Barkley, in Captain W. P. Henderson's Company; Anderson Osburn, in Captain Alex. Osburn's Company; William Walker, in Captain John Hendrick's Company; William P. Ball, in Captain Alfred Owens' Company.

Wm. J. Simpson, Esq., granted license to solemnize the rites of matrimony.

May Term.—Peter January made application for tavern license at Esculapia, then called White Sulphur Springs. On account of a majority of the court not being present, his application was deferred till next court, when it was granted. He probably took the place of Wm. O. Powling, who had previously obtained license at that place, and of whom Mr. Dudley Calvert, in "Early Settlements on Salt Lick," says he sold out and went to Maysville. In all probability Mr. January followed his example.

July Term.—According to an Act passed December 21, 1825, the county clerk furnishes

and records a list of all the public law books
in his possession, both in the county and circuit clerk's offices.

This report shows that he never had any
copy of the Acts of the Legislature farther back
than 1808.

He had a few "Reports" and "Digests," by
Little, Marshall, and Bibb, and some volumes
of United States Laws, amounting in all to
eighty-one books. The Act required him to
display these books once each year before the
court, so they could see how well he kept them.

August Term.—David Maple was allowed
the following hands on his road: John Mortimer,
Thomas Himes, Robt. M. Himes, John H. Himes,
Thomas Gillespie, Joseph Gillespie, Fleming
Jones, Wm. Starky, and Thomas Weaver.

Joseph Toncray was appointed overseer
some place along the State Road.

October Term.—William Yancy is mentioned
as a member of a commission to set apart the
dower of Catharine (Davis) Elson.

The Court of Claims allowed debits against
the county to the amount of $246.83, and levied
a tax on 945 tithes at $37\frac{1}{2}$ cents, amounting
to $352.87\frac{1}{2}$.

Andrew Zorns was overseer on the road on
Kinny, from Shain's to Stratton's, and Stephen
Lewis is named as one of the hands.

December Term.—The last will of James Laird was presented, and Nathan Halbert appointed executor, with will annexed.

January Term of Court of 1827.—The death of Marmaduke Swearingin is noted, and Polly, his widow, appointed as his administratrix. James Swearingin and Alfred, children over fifteen years, chose Aaron Stratton as their guardian.

William McEldowney was commissioned justice of the peace October 30, 1826.

Alexander Bruce's wife, Amanda Bragg, daughter of Thomas Bragg, who died intestate, moved the court for commissioners to assign her interest in his estate.

Thos. Shain was commissioned sheriff October 30, 1826, and John and Daniel Halbert were appointed his deputies.

February Term.—Robt. B. Garland was released as overseer on the Spy Run Road, and Nathaniel R. Garland appointed.

The children and heirs of Anderson Garland, *viz.:* Robt. B., Cynthia Ann, and Anderson N. Garland chose G. W. Bruce as their guardian.

April Term.—On petition of Ann W. Calvert, Seth Porter, Jesse Carrington, Wm. Campbell and Robert Shepherd were appointed commissioners to change the road through her lands on Salt Lick. (See Dudley Calvert's letter, "Early Settlements on Salt Lick.")

Daniel J. Carrington, overseer on the State Road from John McDaniel's (now Valley) to Thomas Parker's house (now the Mefford farm), was discharged, and William Hamlin was appointed in his stead.

Solomon Thomas, on account of age, was released as overseer on the Kinny Road, from mouth of Grassy (T. B. Harrison's farm) up to Holly, and up said Holly to the head, and David Arthur was appointed in his stead.

William Heath, overseer from mouth of Holly to Bear Branch, on Kinny Road, was released, and Hesekiah Griffin was appointed.

John Bell, overseer on the road from Benjamin Plummer's to North Fork, was released on account of age, and Joshua Powers appointed in his stead. Of those named to work under the overseer were the following: Benjamin Plummer, who lived at the top of the hill above the head of that branch of Kinny which turns westward from Petersville; Jeremiah Beckett lived farther out on the same ridge toward the head of Mudlick; Reason Beckett's farm was on Mudlick, just where the road came down the hill; John Hammond, when his apprenticeship was over, settled on North Fork at the mouth of Mudlick, and adjoining his master, Mr.

Powers, who lived where the road first came to North Fork, and perhaps half a mile from the crossing; Thomas West's farm was on the hill on the west side of Mudlick. The turnpike road from Petersville to Mt. Carmel is on almost the same ground, except some changes on the hillsides, that was traversed by the road worked by Mr. Powers and his hands in 1827.

A new constable district, called the Kinniconnick District, was laid off with the following boundary: Beginning at the mouth of Laurel, and passing up Kinny to the Lewis and Fleming line, and with the same to the Greenup or Carter line to the head of Grassy Fork of Laurel, so as to include all the waters of Kinny and Laurel. William Heath was appointed constable in the new district. He gave bond of two thousand dollars, with Wm. McEldowney and Henry Halbert securities.

John G. McDowell was appointed constable in District No. 1, vice Green H. Smith, resigned.

Peter D. January was still at this time "holding the fort" at the White Sulphur Hotel (Esculapia), as is shown by his motion for an order to change the Salt Lick Road.

Hugh McIlvaine was appointed trustee in the town of Clarksburg in the stead of Thomas Bragg, deceased.

It was ordered that W. B. Parker and John

Carter go to the house of William Fink and examine into the situation of said Fink and family, and ascertain if they stand in need of any provisions, etc., and furnish them what will be necessary for their use till the next court, and make report of the same to the court. "That's how they did it then!" said an old citizen, "and that's how humanity manifested itself toward a suffering or unfortunate member of society, in our grandfathers' days."

John Wallingford was made overseer of road on Kinny, from James Silvey's house to Benjamin Plummer's, on the ridge above the head of Kinny.

Joshua Power produced a commission as magistrate and took his seat in the court.

Rowland T. Parker, James Carr, George Swingle, Joseph N. Ralston, and Ben T. Holton were appointed trustees for the town of Vanceburg, according to an Act of the Legislature, approved January 24, 1827, establishing the said town of Vanceburg.

Jonathan M. Grover emancipated a colored woman who was his slave, and gave bond for her maintenance, should she ever become a charge on the county.

Henry Biven and Jas. H. Biven are mentioned as hands on the road from Quick's Run across Martin's Gap to the Ohio River.

Marmaduke Swearingin's administrators listed his property as 100 acres of land, on Salt Lick, and 2 horses—total value $350.

June Term.—Charles Wood, overseer of the road from Quick's Run to head of Sycamore, had the following additional hands allotted to him: John Irwin, James Calhoun, and Andrew Sherdine.

Mr. Wood lived on what is known as the John Wood farm, just at the top of the hill at the head of Quick's Run. Messrs. Calhoun and Sherdine both lived on the farm where Mrs. Brunette Secrest now lives. Mr. Wood had a tanyard, the remains of which are still to be seen. He was the father of John Wood, who lost his life on the same farm by being gored by a vicious bull, in 1872. Mrs. John Wood, nee Sarah Bell Stout, daughter of James Stout, later moved to Vanceburg. Her son, James Wood, who was deputy county clerk under R. D. Wilson, became paying teller in the Metropolitan National Bank, at Kansas City, Mo., and was a model young man of strictly correct habits.

The Deatley family first come on the record at this session of the court. Austin Deatley and Guffin Deatley are named as living in the bounds of a road from James Boyd's blacksmith shop, on Cabin Creek, up the branch, and over the hill to Mason County line.

July Term.—John Thompson was commissioned justice of the peace April 30, 1827.

There appeared only two magistrates in August, and no court was held.

September Term.—A road was made down Brown's Run, on Cabin Creek, on a route known as Tolle's path. George Rea, John Ginn, and Jose Tolle were the hands living on it.

Daniel Swearingin, on account of old age, was released from being road overseer on Little East Fork of Cabin Creek.

The Mudlick constable precinct was laid off, with the following bounds: Beginning at Robert's old mill, on North Fork; thence with the county road to the top of the mountain above Esculapia; thence with the dividing ridge between the waters of Salt Lick, Kinny, and North Fork to the Fleming County line; and with said line down North Fork to the place of beginning.

The claims allowed this year against the county amounted to $281.16. The levy on 970 tithes, at 50 cents, amounted to $485.

John H. Reganstine was found by the sheriff as a taxpayer not listed by the assessor. Mr. Reganstine lived near the head of East Fork of Cabin Creek, near McKenzie post-office. His son, Henry, lived in that locality until his death, a few years ago, a model citizen, respected by all. His children were teachers in the county, possessing the best grade certificates. Omar attended the Bible College of the Kentucky University, at Lexington, with the intent of becoming a minister of the gospel. He actually began to preach, and gave promise of much ability; but an attack of phthisis so affected his delivery that he has been compelled to desist from public speaking for some years, but recovered. He was married to Miss Ida Wellman, daughter of Jeremiah Wellman, some time in 1895.

December Term brought in a settlement with the sheriff, showing him indebted to the county in the sum of thirty-nine dollars.

Robert Smith was awarded a contract to repair the court-house in Clarksburg.

H. C. Bedinger gave in lands and slaves valued at $5,636.50.

January Term of Court of 1828.—On motion of Andrew May, it was ordered that Ezra Toncray, Baily Bryant, Daniel Thomas, and William Easham, Sr., were appointed commissioners to view a road beginning on the State Road at Cordingley's path; thence the nearest route to intersect the Salt Lick or Gunpowder Gap Road, near the house of Daniel Thomas.

Peter M. Cox, a regularly ordained minister of the "New Light" Church, was granted license to celebrate the rites of matrimony.

Some years after this Mr. Cox became a little daft in mind, and was attending a meeting and baptizing under the ministry of Elder Hathaway, on the farm now owned by James Hampton, on Henderson's Fork of East Fork. After the candidates had all been baptized, Rev. Cox appeared on the bank of the creek at a place still known as "Hathaway's hole," where the baptizing occurred, and demanded that Elder Hathaway baptize him. The minister protested, saying, "You have been baptized, Brother Cox." But he said "That John the Baptist at first refused the Savior, but He said suffer it to be so, for it becometh us to fulfill all righteousness, and, Brother Hathaway, you must baptize me."

Hathaway got away from Brother Cox, who was still standing on the creek bank, and seeing that he was not likely to succeed in getting baptized, called out, "If you won't baptize me I will do it myself," and throwing up his hands, made a plunge into the water, and came out on the other side of the creek, much to the amusement of the spectators, some of whom are yet living in the county.

On motion of the trustees and inhabitants

of Clarksburg, leave was granted them to build a schoolhouse on the public square for use of town.

February Term.—The name of Charles Caines appears on the road list, from Clarksburg to Vanceburg. This is the first mention of the Caines family in the court record; but Mr. Caines afterward took a prominent part in the county's history, being a sheriff, accumulating quite a fortune, and rearing a large and influential family. His old homestead is still standing, about two miles from the river at Vanceburg, on the S. L. T. & M. Turnpike Road. It is now in possession of his son, C. G. Caines, whose daughter, Mrs. Morgan, and son Charles, are residing on it.

The last will of David Looney was produced and proven by John Boyd and John Wiley. Mr. Looney was one of the earlier settlers on Crooked Creek, having probably settled there as early as 1800. There are none of his descendants now in the county. The family removed to Rush County, Ind., and carried some of Lewis County apple trees with them. In 1877 one of the family presented some of these apples, known as "Little Milam," to the editor of the Rushville *Republican* newspaper, who comments on Mr. Looney having brought them with him from Kentucky. But Mr. Looney did not bring them from Virginia. Mr. Israel Thomas did that by tying a few scions to a saddle and riding through from Virginia to Lewis County with them. In 1840 to 1850 the "Milam" was the apple of Lewis County, a majority of all orchards being made up of that variety. There are many of these apples yet, and as a general good keeper none are better.

French Martin was relieved as overseer of the road on the "left hand fork of Salt Lick," and James McCormick is appointed in his stead.

April Term.—Edward Wallace was appointed the first constable in the Mudlick District.

Robt. Parker was appointed overseer of the road above Clarksburg to Cottingham's bridge.

On motion of the heirs of George Wilson, deceased, it is ordered that the ferry at the upper end of Wilson's bottom be discontinued.

Mathias Tolle, Daniel Fetters, Charles Himes, and Peter Hoover were appointed commissioners to view and mark a roadway from the Ohio River, opposite Manchester, O., the nearest and best way over the hill to intersect the Crooked Creek Road, near Irwin's mill.

Aaron Stratton granted tavern license at Kinny Crossing on the Ohio River Road, and W. B. Parker the same at Clarksburg.

June Term.—On motion of William Watkins and John P. Savage, leave was given them to build a mill dam on land they owned, embracing the stream of Indian Run, a branch of Cabin Creek.

September Term.—The last will and testament of George Wilson, on account of the death and removal of the subscribing witnesses, was proven by the oaths of Samuel Wilson, Andrew Wilson, and William Hendrickson.

Chancy B. Shepherd gave in a list of property for taxation embracing 13 blacks over 16 years of age, and 11 others, a total of 24 blacks and 26 horses and mules, at a total value of $6,000.

The claims allowed this year amounted to $617.11, and the taxes assessed on 994 tithes, at $1 each, to $994.

January Term of Court of 1829.—The last will of Francis Henderson was admitted to probate and proven by Joseph Taylor and James Dickson.

James McClain, who had been commissioned sheriff November 11, 1828, resigned his seat as justice of the peace in the court. John and Daniel Halbert were appointed his deputies.

February Term.—There was no court held in February nor March.

April Term.—G. "Washington" Bruce got permission to build a mill above the first island in Kinny above the mouth.

William Fletcher Mavity, a minister of the gospel in the Christian Church, on Cabin Creek, was granted a license to celebrate the rites of matrimony. He gave bond with Daniel Halbert and John Irwin securities.

The settlement of Motley M. Morrison's estate was ordered.

John G. McDowell renewed his bond as constable.

Lewis G. Fry was made a constable in District No. 3.

The last will of Susanna Thomas was proven by James McClain and William McEldowney.

James McCormick was discharged and Jacob Strode appointed overseer on Salt Lick Road. Woodford Roberts made overseer on the road above Clarksburg to Cottingham's bridge, and Laban Tolle on the Three Island Road, to Brown's Run, on Cabin Creek.

Jonathan Corns had moved from Ohio to the river bottom above Concord, and he was given an order on the sheriff for six dollars as per an account filed with the court.

May Term.—David Polly died intestate, and his wife, Elizabeth, and his father, David Polly, were granted administration.

July Term.—Andrew Wilson resigned as a magistrate, and Alexander Young having removed from the county, did the same.

Barton Palmer was appointed one of the commissioners to examine and settle the estate of Thomas Bragg; but he was afterward released and another appointed in his stead.

William Barkley was appointed guardian for the children of John Hendrickson.

August Term.—James Fyffe died intestate, and administration was granted his wife, Nancy, with Wm. Watkins, J. P. Savage, and Thomas Grover as her securities on a bond of five thousand dollars. In November Nancy married Joseph Watkins, and her securities moved the court for counter securities.

September Term.—Thomas Marshall resigned as justice of the peace in Lewis County.

John Stalcup was appointed overseer of the lower Quick's Run Road, vice John Voiers, resigned.

October Term.—On a proposed road up the river from Wilson's old ferry to Concord, the commissioners found the lands of George Wilson, deceased, David Davis, John Stephenson, heirs of Thomas Forman, but occupied by John Purcell, Littleberry Bedford, Michael and John Doyle, Ben. Bedford, John Stephenson, Esq., a Mr. Tolle, Tavenor Moore, and Edward Stephenson. Above Ed. Stephenson's the road was to strike a street in the town of Concord, and follow the same to the crossing of Sycamore

20

Creek. John Wilson was ordered to open said road.

John Fry resigned as constable, and Wm. McEldowney as justice of the peace.

Five new justices were recommended by this court to the governor, Thos. Metcalf, for his appointment.

Caleb Richards was appointed by the court as constable in stead of John Fry, resigned.

Larkin Liles, the first of that family mentioned, is named as a hand on John Thompson's road, on Kinny.

Curtis Launtz, overseer on the Three Island Road in the stead of Samuel Wilson, and John appointed on the Quick's Run Road, from the forks to the dividing ridge toward Cabin Creek.

Joseph Robb, County Court and Circuit Court clerk, produced commission from the governor as notary public.

The claims this year were $534.91; levy on 1,017 tithes, at $1, $1,017.

Robert Grant died intestate, and F. R. Singleton was appointed administrator.

George Warner was allowed a fee as a guard over criminals.

November Term.—Daniel K. Putman, a minister in the Methodist Episcopal Church of the United States, was granted a license to celebrate the rites of matrimony.

Fred R. Singleton and John Johnson were commissioned as justices October 24, 1829, and took their seats in court.

December Term.—John Fry was commissioned as a justice of the peace October 24, 1829.

Charles Cox got tavern license at Clarksburg this year.

John Patterson lived on Reed's Run, near the forks of Sycamore, and Edward Stephenson owned the tanyard at Concord, as shown by a road order from the house of Patterson to the Ohio River, passing by the tannery. That road was probably on the exact ground now occupied by the C. & T. Turnpike.

February Term of Court of 1830.—Henry Halbert being about to remove from the county, resigned his commission as justice of the peace.

Robert Bagby, Jr., chose Mathew Thompson as his guardian.

March Term.—Edward and John Stephenson petitioned the court for the establishment of a town on their lands at the mouth of Sycamore. They had complied the law in such cases made and provided by advertising on the courthouse door and by notice in the Maysville *Eagle* newspaper, and "On due consideration of the application of the proprietors and petitioners hath been granted them by the court agreeable to their petition and notice, a town established, called Concord." The following are the recorded metes and bounds of the said town: "Beginning at the stone on the bank of the Ohio River, North 52° West from the mouth of Sycamore and 42 poles below the mouth of said creek. Then from said stone, South 36° West 72 poles to another stone as a corner, and from thence North 54° West 100 poles to a stone, and from thence North 36° East 76 poles to a stone on the bank of the Ohio River, and from thence up the same and binding thereon to the beginning, containing forty-six and one-quarter acres, more or less."

A ferry was also granted to John Stephenson, and the rates established as follows: "For wagon, team, and driver, $1; for carriage, Dearborn or phaeton, horses, and driver, 50 cents; man and horse, 25 cents; single or led horse, 12½ cents; every head of horned or neat cattle, 6¼ cents; every sheep, hog, or goat, 3 cents; all other property in proportion to these rates."

Hugh McIlvaine removed from the county, and W. B. Parker was appointed in his stead as trustee for the town of Clarksburg.

April Term.—George McCreary had been commissioned as justice of the peace, and took his seat in court.

G. Washington Parker was appointed deputy county clerk.

Abednego Hunt made counter claim against Thomas Marshall for the maintenance of John Dredden and wife, for whom the court had granted Marshall an order on the sheriff, and it was ordered the sheriff retain said money in his hands till a settlement was effected with Mr. Marshall. The money was afterward paid to Mr. Hunt.

The court refused to adopt as the road law an Act of the Legislature relating to roads.

The Rev. Thomas Gibbons, minister of the Methodist Episcopal Church, was granted a license to unite persons in the bonds of matrimony.

Caleb Richards resigned as constable, and William Hamlin was appointed in his stead.

William Lloyd bought the dower of Mary Kennard in the estate of William Kennard and prayed for a division of the property.

Thomas J. Walker was appointed assessor of that half of the county lying northwest of the State Road from Vanceburg to the North Fork, and William Heath of that portion lying southeast of the same road.

William Norwood had been commissioned as justice of the peace, but refused to qualify, and court recommended James Boyd and John

Tolle to the governor, one of which was to be appointed. The court then made Mr. Norwood overseer of the road from the Mason County line, up Cabin Creek to Swearingin's horsemill— they seemed determined that he should have an office.

Abel Burris was appointed road overseer from Thomas Parker's to Jonathan Hayden's, and Jacob Applegate from Swearingin's mill over to Widow McKenzie's, on East Fork.

Preparations for the first alms or "poor-house" was begun at this court. Aaron Owens, John McDaniel, Mathew Thompson, and Arch. Frizzell were appointed commissioners to find a site and contract for land for the same. In about a year afterward they reported that they had bought of Daniel and William Hendrickson thirty acres on Indian Run, a tributary to Cabin Creek, at two dollars per acre. The court accepted this, and the poor-house was established there, where it remained till 1881.

July Term.—Willis Bagby was appointed guardian for William and John Bagby, infant heirs of Robt. Bagby, deceased.

August Term.—Last will of Ruth Burris was proven by Jno. P. Savage and Barton Lee, subscribing witnesses. Richard Taylor, Nesbet Taylor, William Watkins, and Thomas Boggs, appraisers.

September Term.—Rev. John Thompson, a "New Light" minister, was granted a license to marry people.

October Term.—Edward Wallace resigned as constable in the Mudlick District.

The levy on 1,050 polls was $657.50.

Alexander Bruce was ordered to take care of Anges Ruffner, who was sick at his house, and mentally deranged, and to employ medical aid for him; and if no friends came to pay his bills, to report the same to the court.

November Term. — John Fry resigned as justice of the peace. Mr. Fry seemed fond of resigning. He had twice before resigned as constable and once as road overseer before he resigned as magistrate.

December Term.—The last will of Thomas Kukins was probated, with Thos. Y. Payne and John M. Roulston witnesses.

January Term of Court of 1831.—G. "Washington" Bruce built two more mills on Lower Kinny.

Joseph G. Ward, a minister of the Methodist Episcopal Church, was granted a license to "practice matrimony on other people."

Wm. P. Ball was commissioned sheriff November 6, 1830.

William Taylor admitted as an attorney at the Lewis County bar.

February Term.—Archibald Frizzell renewed his bond as coroner.

March Term.—James W. Singleton was appointed a justice January 24, 1831.

April Term.—Robert Means was appointed constable in District No. 4, to fill the place of James Singleton, promoted to justice of the peace; and Mathias Tolle also in District No. 2, while W. C. Logan and William Heath renewed their bonds as constables in other districts.

A new constable precinct was formed, beginning at Samuel Cummings' farm; thence down the river to the mouth of Blockhouse Run; thence up the same to the dividing ridge between the waters of Crooked and Sycamore, and with said ridge around and including all the waters of Sycamore to the place of beginning. Mathew Hanning was appointed constable in the new district.

Thomas Mitchell, who had been acting jailer since 1819, but who had failed, through neglect, to give bond at proper times, had a special Act in his favor passed by the Legsilature under which he renewed his bond in this court.

Abednego Hunt was allowed fifty dollars for keeping his mother-in-law, Mrs. Dredden.

Ambrose D. Parker was appointed assessor in the South District, and Thos. J. Walker in the North District.

At this court an excellent plat of the town of Concord was presented to the court and was recorded in the order book. It shows all the streets and alleys as first laid out. Water Street and the lots in front of it, and also about one-third of the width of those back of it, are now gone down the Ohio River. The next street parallel to the river is "Madison." It is now the roadbed of the C. & O. R. R. The first street next to Sycamore, and running back from the river, is Washington, and then in order following are "Jackson," "Main," "Adams," and "Jefferson." The "public spring" at the northeast corner of the lot included by Main and Madison, is shown, and it still exists in the corner of Mrs. W. H. Coxe's yard.

George F. Fox was appointed overseer of the Three Island Road from near Donovan's to Phillipp's Creek, and Thomas Essex was appointed on the road from Quick's Run to Salt Lick, called Hance's Trace.

Reason Beckett on the road from Benjamin Plummers to North Fork.

The court authorized commissioners to build a permanent bridge across Salt Lick, at the "Sycamore Ford." At a future court it was found that the contract had been awarded to James Cooper, at $250, of which $18.25 had been subscribed by citizens, and the remainder was appropriated by the court out of money in the hands of the sheriff.

Wm. H. Taylor was appointed Commonwealth attorney by the court, and his salary fixed at fifty dollars for one year. He was also allowed to read that "Little's Digest," for which reading Benj. Aills served the county one year as attorney.

The settlement with the late sheriff, James McClain, for two years showed the county indebted to him by overdrawn orders during the first year of eighty-six dollars, and that he owed the county for the second year $15.68.

June Term.—William Watkins was commissioned surveyor April 26, 1831.

John G. McDowell was appointed constable in District No. 1, with Rowland T. Parker, Alexander Bruce, and John Halbert, securities.

John Aills was granted permission to build a mill-dam on Quick's Run.

July Term.—Nicholas Elson was commissioned justice of the peace June 25, 1831, and received the books of Thos. Marshall.

John Strode was granted tavern license at Vanceburg.

August Term.—Elijah H. Thomas, overseer on the Kinny Road, is ordered to begin Ben. Cole's (T. B. Harrison's) and work up to Bear Branch.

September Term.—The first road from Ben. Cole's to Vanceburg was laid off at this time, and passed up the right hand fork of Grassy to the top of the hill, and then turned to the left to the point leading into Dry Run Branch; and thence down said branch to the Ohio Lick, and thence to the river, at Vanceburg. Ambrose D. McDaniel, overseer and hands; John W. Johnson, overseer and hands; Ben Cole, overseer and hands; Elijah H. Thomas, overseer and hands; Cole Redden, overseer and hands, were ordered to assist John Thomas, who was overseer of the new road, in opening the same.

October Term.—The clerk, Joseph Robb, reported seventy deeds as recorded by him from October, 1830, to October, 1831. Quite a large number of them were for lots in Concord, and one of these was to John Lovel, father of Hon. R. B. Lovell, now of Maysville.

The claims allowed this year amounted to $321.08½, and the tithables were 1,128, at 62½ cents each, amounting to $705; fines, etc., collected, $16.69, making a total amount of $721.69.

Commissioners were appointed to build a poorhouse at Poplar Flat, on the land purchased of Messrs. Hendrickson.

The sheriff found Johnson Littleton as a taxpayer who had not been assessed.

November Term.—The sheriff, after having advertised in the Maysville *Eagle* and on the court-house door, according to law, proceeded to sell the lands on which taxes had not been paid. No bids were offered, and the lands were "knocked down" to the State as purchaser.

W. S. Parker was paid $17 for a stove for the county clerk's office.

January Term of Court of 1832.—The last will of Thomas Mackey was probated, and Thomas Mackey and William Kelly were executors.

March Term.—Wm. D. Lyons, of Quick's Run, made a motion to have the road changed from the upper corner of Wm. Pell's field to the upper corner of his own field.

John Hilles was appointed a commissioner to view a road from the mouth of Clear Creek, a tributary to Cabin Creek, across the hill to Robt. Rea's, on East Fork.

April Term.—There is a meeting house mentioned as being on Sycamore in April, 1832, and a place on the Ohio, above Pond Run, called "The Deadening." It seems to be on the land of Geo. G. Graham.

Joseph Tolle was appointed overseer from Widow McKenzie's, on East Fork, over the ridge and down Crooked Creek to Wilson's sand fields.

On the Quick's Run Road, from Moses Ormes' place, to intersect the Salt Lick and Washington Road at a schoolhouse on the top of the hill, between Parker's and Everett's, James Price was appointed overseer and Thomas Pool, Andrew Pool, David Irwin, Wm. McCann, and John McCann were allotted as hands. Alexander Irwin, overseer, over age, was released from this road.

James Pollitt was made overseer from Swearingin's mill to where the Salt Lick Road crosses the Three Island Road; one of his hands not hitherto mentioned was William Hillis, an uncle to Lewis County's present county judge.

William Cropper was overseer on Salt Lick from Daniel Thomas' house to Gunpowder Gap. He had, as hands, William Esham, Allen Martin, Dudley Martin, Solomon Cropper, James McCormick, Jno. B. McDaniel, Elias Spurgin, George Johnson, James Ruark, and John Esham.

King D. McClain was appointed deputy county clerk.

W. H. Taylor refused the appointment of county attorney, and he was also fined one dollar for contempt concerning an order of the court appointing road commissioners.

Henry C. Bedinger is charged with having the Ohio Salt Works this year (1832).

June Term.—Jacob, Myer, overseer from Sycamore over to Crooked Creek, had John Myers, Robert Myers, Jacob Slaton, Richard Kellum, Joseph D. Smith, Jos. Moore, John Patterson, Samuel and Ezekiel Doyle, Jos. Huffman, John, James, and Charles Stevenson, Brice Virgin, and John Moore as hands on his road.

Tavernor Moore, overseer on road from the bottom below Concord up Sycamore, had, as hands, Ezekiel Reed, Jas. Reed, Samuel Cogan, John Pasahal, John Robb, Edward Parks, Sheldon Riggs, Arthur Stevenson, Michael Spawn, Wm. Wade, John Hayslip, John Morris, Thos. Tacker, Jos. Davis, Allen Williams, John Greenlee, Thomas, Isaac, and Joseph Linley, Samuel Stevenson, George Rea, James Stephenson, John Munford, Edward Stephenson, D. B. Morgan, Jesse Mathiny, John Lovel, John L. Boyd, Eli Bilyen, Samuel Bilyen, and Paul Bilyen.

The older citizens in the Concord vicinity, and some of the younger ones, will remember most every man named in this list as citizens of that little town, or adjacent to it. The Reeds and Cogans are still residents of that vicinity. John Greenlee went to Iowa; the Rea, Stevenson, and Bilyen families still have representatives on the old camping grounds of their fathers.

John Lovel and John L. Boyd died in Concord, but the Boyd family is still living there.

July Term.—Charles Himes, Ferdinand Fry, Mike Fetters, Joshua Graham, Wm. Fry, Lewis G. Fry, Daniel Fetters, James Kennard, John Hoover, Wm. and Jacob Mowery are all mentioned as hands on the Chalk ridge and McKenzie Road.

Elijah H. Thomas was appointed clerk of the election on Kinny.

Henry Bivan was made overseer from Kennedy's bottom, over Martin's Gap to Quick's Run.

John Hunter chose Elijah H. Thomas as his guardian.

Elijah H. Thomas, above mentioned, was the father of Judge G. M. Thomas, of Vanceburg.

September Term.—Clayton Bane, John and Madison Osburn are new hands on John Walker's road.

Harrison Ball was appointed deputy sheriff under Wm. P. Ball.

October Term.—Joseph Robb, county court clerk, made his annual settlement with court of the taxes received by him. The amount due the State was $145.82½.

Tavern license and license for clock peddlers cost ten dollars each. There was a great rage in clock peddling about this time. The clocks were sold on credit at about thirty dollars each, and many of them are still to be found as heirlooms in the families of the descendants of that generation.

Thomas Meglassen is named as a hand on the "Three Island Road."

The name of Uriah McKellup, who was afterward a representative of Lewis County in the Legislature, first appears in the record of this court as a hand on the Cabin Creek Road, under the supervisorship of Eli Vaughn.

John Thomas renewed his bond as constable in the Mudlick District.

Charles Caines got the job on the courthouse repairs at forty-three dollars, of which sum the county clerk assumed five dollars and the county the remainder.

In those days those magistrates were selected by the court each year to grant injunctions, writs of ne exeat, restraining orders, writs of habeas corpus, etc. This year Alex. Bruce, F. R. Singleton, and W. B. Parker were selected.

Claims allowed amounted to $268.25. The tithes were taken at 1,128, per 62½ cents each, amounting to $705.

The Legislature had changed the law in regard to assessing, and no assessment had been made. The estimate was made on the previous year.

Jefferson Evans was appointed county attorney.

The poorhouse was received of the contractor, Stephen Halbert.

December Term.—The Rev. David Hathaway, of the Christian or "New Light Church," was licensed to perform the marriage service for people in Lewis County.

The first mention of Socrates Holbrook, who was ever after a conspicuous figure in the Lewis County Court till his death, at Vanceburg, in 1885, and whose picture, life-size, now hangs in the court-room, appears in this session of the court in a bastardy case between William Hamlin and Mary Swearingin. Mr. Holbrook won the case for his client, and the court, on his motion, proceeded to recommend him as a young man of honesty, probity, and good demeanor to the judges of the Circuit Court.

It was ordered that a set of rules for the observance of everybody connected with the court be drafted, and Joseph Robb and two of the magistrates were appointed to do the work.

January Term of Court of 1833.—Samuel Ezekiel Forman was appointed overseer to cut out the new road from Wilson's old ferry, opposite Manchester, O., to widow Lewis' land, in Doyle's bottom.

Aaron Stratton was commissioned sheriff October 26, 1832.

Robt. Means was appointed assessor in the "North District" and John G. McDowell in the South.

February Term.—Aaron Stratton died, and a court was called to qualify a new sheriff. It was found that Thompson N. Stratton had been commissioned by the governor, and he was therefore qualified.

Henry C. Bedinger had removed and John Carter was appointed road overseer in his stead on the road from Quick's Run to Rocky Ford of Salt Lick, near Vanceburg.

March Term.—The order book for 1832-33 was the first that had ruled paper, and the clerk did some artistic work in colored inks in marking the headings of the different monthly courts. It must be seen to be appreciated.

Abner Brightman was commissioned justice February 22, 1833, and was seated in this session.

On the road from the top of the mountain above Esculapia, to North Fork below Robert's old mill, lived William Mackey. Thos. J. Sabins, John West, Henry Luman, Jesse Luman, Thomas Osburn, George Sanders, Wm. Rayburn, Louder Pollitt, Thomas Pollitt, James Pollitt, James Warren, Benjamin Williams, Lander

Hurst, Nimrod Thomas, Henry Morrison, Staten West, George Johnson, and John Flord.

Daniel Cupp is noted as a citizen on the road from the lower end of Wilson's bottom to James West's, on the hill near the Lewis and Mason County line.

April Term.—Isaac Eads was road overseer up Brown's Run to Wilson's old farm, near the Mason County line, and William Tully and Jackson Tully were hands on his road.

On the Salt Lick and Washington Road John Hayden was overseer, and Abraham Carr, Jonathan Hayden, Jesse Truesdale, Charles Taylor, Harrison Everett, Abel Burris, and Alex. Menix were hands to work under him.

Silas Wallingford is an additional hand on Coleman Riddle's road, on Kinny.

Mathias Tolle received his bond as constable in Lewis County.

John A. Clark and Curtis Smulling, ministers of the Methodist Episcopal Church, were granted' licenses to marry people.

Jesse Hamrick, also of the same Church, granted the same privilege.

June Term. — Rowland T. Parker, Alex. Bruce, George Swingle, Jeremiah Snyder, and Thos. E. Redden were appointed trustees of the town of Vanceburg.

Constable District No. 2 was divided into

two sections for the upper end of the whirlpool, at Vanceburg, back with State Road to the line. of District No. 1. The upper side to be called Kinny, and the lower or down-river side to be called Vanceburg District.

Wm. Frizzell was allowed to keep tavern in Vanceburg one year by depositing ten dollars with the clerk as license fee.

John G. McDowell renewed his bond as constable in District No. 1.

July Term.—John Doyle proved in court, in order to get a pension under certain Act of Congress, that he was a Revolutionary soldier. The record further on shows others doing the same, and we hope to be able to show thereby the names of all Lewis County's soldiers of the Revolution.

John and George Hoobler were citizens living on the river road above Vanceburg, and in the neighborhood of Pleasant M. Savage.

August Term.—Richard Bane is also proven a soldier of the Revolution.

The court ordered that Alex. and John McKenzie, John G. Piper, Ambrose Thompson, William Thompson, Ellis Owens, Amos Means, Willoughby Flinn, Isaac Dickson, Geo. F. Elijah, and John Hendrickson, Francis Fagan, Raleigh Fagans, and Henry Fagans work under John Piper, and keep the road from McKenzie's, toward Concord, in repair.

September Term.—Benj. Henness was appointed trustee in Vanceburg instead of Geo. Swingle, removed from the town, and Thos. N. Davis in place of Alex. Bruce, who refused to qualify. George Swingle and Thomas Williams were two more of the soldiers of the Revolution.

October Term.—John Means produced a commission as paymaster of the 69th Regiment of Kentucky Militia.

The claims allowed this year amounted to $374.89. Fines and taxes collected to $36.33, and the levy on 1,154 tithables, at 50 cents, to $577.

There was nothing of importance in the January term of court of 1834.

February Term of Court of 1834.—Thomas Marshall, road overseer, had Henry Lucas, William King, and Mr. W. Brittam as hands to work under him.

The following rather peculiar, though perhaps valuable, record was made in the order book of the Lewis County Court: "The following persons are the only heirs of James P. Savage, deceased: Pleasant M. Savage, James Savage, John P. Savage, Francis Asbury Savage, Samuel P. Savage, William P. Savage, Mary Jane Johnson, late Mary Stout, the daughter and only child of Sally Stout, who, previous to her marriage, was Sally Savage and the daughter of the above-named James Savage, deceased;

and James A. Frizzell, Alexander Frizzell, and Margaret Frizzell, children of Polly W. Frizzell, deceased, who was, previous to her marriage, Polly W. Savage and the daughter of the above-named James P. Savage, deceased."

April Term.—Rowland T. Parker resigned as constable in Vanceburg.

Thos. J. Bunn, overseer of road near Clarksburg; Henry Pell above the forks of Quick's Run; Samuel Pollitt on the Clarksburg and Williamsburg Road; Thomas Sanders on the Spy Run Road; James Ruark on the Salt Lick and Flemingsburg Road; Daniel Thomas on the left fork of Salt Lick; and George Moss on road from Quick's Run to Vanceburg.

On motion of Rowland Parker a road was ordered viewed from State Creek, over the hill to Kinny, at the mouth of Trace, and thence up the same to Greenup County line.

George McCreary Wilson, Esq., was granted license to celebrate the rites of matrimony.

May Term.—King D. McClain was appointed justice April, 1834. He lived in Concord.

Samuel and Andrew Manuel were hands on the Quick's Run Road to the top of the hill, at Joseph Taylor's.

Jacob Staily died intestate, and his widow, Susan Staily, was granted the administration.

A commission to settle accounts of guardians, administrators, and executors was appointed, according to an Act of the Legislature, and Wm. Mitchell, W. S. Parker, and Joseph Robb were the appointees. Thus slowly the business affairs of the court was developing toward that period where a county judge should be elected and take charge of these several side issues in the court.

The following gentlemen seem to have lived on the Spy Run Road: Jason and Elias Miller, Henry Liles, James Clark, Thomas Zornes, John and William Royster, Levi Royster, Thomas Bruce, Thomas Williams, Constantine Bruce, Thomas and Edward Campbell.

The last will of David Davis was proven by John Kelly and Samuel Spencer.

A road from Buck Lick to Fleming County passed through the lands of Thomas West, Henry Morrison, Bullock's heirs, Harmon Hurst, William Rayburn, James Duke, Nicholas Wallingford, Jordon Ruark, and Milton Grigsby.

September Term.—The last will of James Graham was proven in part by Joshua Graham, and laid over for further proof.

October Term.—The commissioners appointed to let the poor-house had not succeeded in finding anybody who wanted it, and the court authorized to offer for bids again, and to let the public know that the county would pay seventy dollars per annum for the keeping of each pauper.

John Thompson was made constable in the Mudlick District.

George Conway was granted the administration of the estate of Richard Conway.

Claims allowed amount to $344.83; 1,183 tithes, at 62½ cents, amount to $739.37½.

Alfred Frizzell admitted as an attorney at the Lewis County bar.

Willis Bagby was appointed road overseer from Montgomery Run, up the river toward Portsmouth to John Thompson's.

November Term.—Benjamin Aills had been commissioned justice of the peace, and took his seat in the court.

December Term.—John Stockholm was registered in court as a Revolutionary soldier.

Joseph Foxworthy, Dudley Calvert, Wm. Winsor, and Isaac Ginn are hands on William Campbell's road.

William P. Savage was appointed as deputy county clerk.

January Term of Court of 1835.—Thompson N. Stratton got a ferry privilege across Kinny, near the mouth. He also was granted tavern license at his house on the bank of Kinny.

William B. Parker was made sheriff of Lewis County November 1, 1834.

George Means was appointed constable in District No. 4.

Robt. W. Robb got license to keep tavern in the house once occupied by Rowland T. Parker, in Vanceburg.

William S. Parker and Harry Willim were recommended for justices.

Wm. Mitchell, John Kendrick, and Leroy Preston Parker were appointed deputies to the high sheriff.

The court appointed commissioners to improve the State Road, and took their bonds, as required by an Act of the Legislature. (See Chapter of Acts.)

John Purcell, through his attorney, Horatio Bruce, moved the court for a change in the road through Doyle's bottom.

Nathaniel Kirk wanted the Gun Powder Gap and Flemingsburg Road changed, somewhere near Kirk Springs.

Larkin Liles, of Lower Kinny, died between the December term of 1834 and the January term of 1835, as is evidenced by an account brought into the latter term in relation to him.

February Term.—William S. Parker, justice of the peace, appointed in the room of W. B. Parker, promoted to sheriff.

March Term.—This term was principally taken up by suits against Thompson N. Stratton, administrator of the estate of Aaron Stratton, deceased; but it seems that Mr. Stratton got out "on top" in most of the cases, even if "Socrates Holbrook was against him."

The last will of John Means was admitted to probate with Amos Means as executor.

Henry Halbert's property was administered by John Halbert.

Elijah H. Thomas was appointed constable in the Kinny District.

May Term.—William Kellum was granted the administration of the intestate property of Richard Kellum.

King D. McClain took the administration of the estate of William Mackaboy, upon the refusal of Francis Feagans and Willoughby Flinn, his nearest of kin, to qualify.

Jacob Stricklett was overseer of the road from Kennedy's bottom over to Martin's Fork of Quick's Run, in the room of Henry Bivan, discharged.

For thirty years we have given you, in the succession of offices, the doings of the courts as well; but feel we must call a halt for lack of space and only give you from here to the conclusion of this chapter simply the succession of officers.

Officers from 1833 to 1835.—Joseph Robb, clerk County Court; William Watkins, county surveyor; Archibald Frizzell, coroner; Thos. Mitchell, jailer; Jefferson Evans, county attorney; Aaron Stratton, sheriff, deceased; Thompson N. Stratton appointed sheriff February, 1833.

Justices.—Thomas Parker, Edward Stephenson, Joshua Power, Fred R. Singleton, John Johnson, George McC. Wilson, Alexander Bruce, James Boyd, James McClain, Chas. C. Marshall, Abnor Brightman, King J. McClain, Benjamin Aills, William S. Parker, Robert Means.

Constables.—Jno. G. McDowell, No. 1; Mathias Tolle, No. 3; William Hamlin, No. 5; John Thomas, Mudlick; Joseph H. Davis, Concord; James H. Cooper, No. 2; Jacob Frizzell, Vanceburg; Elijah H. Thomas, Kinniconnick; George Means, No. 4.

Officers from 1835 to 1838.—Joseph Robb, county clerk; Thos. Parker, sheriff; William Watkins, surveyor; Thos. Mitchell, jailer; Socrates Holbrook, county attorney.

Justices.—Joshua Powers, Fred Singleton, John Johnson, George McC. Wilson, Alex. Bruce, James Boyd, James McClain, Chas. C. Marshall, King D. McClain, William S. Parker, Robt. Means, John T. Waddle, John Hampton, Jonathan Ruggles, Harvey Griffith, Chancy B. Shepard.

Constables.—John Laech, No. 1; Jas. H

Cooper (resigned), No. 2; Mathias Tolle, No. 3; Geo. Means (resigned), No. 4; William Hamlin (dead), No. 5; John Thomas (resigned), Mudlick; Jas. H. Davis (out), Concord; Jacob Frizzell (out), Vanceburg; Elijah H. Thomas (out), Kinny; Humphrey Beckett, Mudlick; Chas. T. Apperson, Kinny; Richard W. Davis (out), Concord; Robt. Robb (resigned), Vanceburg; Harry Parker (resigned), No. 2.

Officers from 1838 to 1842: Charles Caines, sheriff (resigned); Alexander Bruce, appointed sheriff; William Watkins, surveyor; Thos. Mitchell, jailer; Socrates Holbrook, county attorney; Robt. W. Robb, treasurer; Joseph Robb, clerk.

Justices.—Joshua Power (resigned), Geo. McC. Wilson (dead), James Boyd, James McClain, Chas. C. Marshall, King D. McClain, William Parker, Robert Means, John T. Waddle, Jonathan Ruggles, Stephen V. Bliss, Joshua Power (reappointed), Geo. F. Hendrickson, John Thompson, Geo. W. Collins, Richard Nash, Robt. W. Robb, Alfred H. Frizzell.

Constables.—John Leach, No. 1; James Dickson, No. 2; Asa McNeal, No. 3; Wm. H. Thompson, No. 4; James Hoover, No. 5; Jno. R. Duke, Concord; William F. Hamrick, Mudlick; Jos. M. Montgomery, Clarksburg; John Stone, Laurel Fork; Jeremiah Snyder, Vanceburg.

Officers of 1844.—John W. Mitchell, coroner;

John P. Pell, surveyor; Thomas Mitchell, jailer; Larkin J. Proctor, county attorney; vice S. Holle; Robt. W. Robb, treasurer vacant land warrants; Joseph Robb, county clerk, notary, and treasurer jury fund; James McClain, sheriff.

Magistrates.—King D. McClain, Wm. S. Parker, Robert Means, John Waddell, John P. Hampton, Jonathan Ruggles, Stephen V. Bliss, Joshua Power, John Thompson, Geo. W. Collins, Richard Nash, Robt. D. Taylor, Nathaniel R. Garland, James Boyd, Robt. G. Carter, Nathan B. Webster, John W. Veach.

Officers from 1842 to 1849.—John Mitchell, coroner; John Pell, county surveyor; Larkin J. Proctor, county attorney; Robt. W. Robb, county clerk; James McClain, sheriff.

Justices.—King D. McClain, Wm. S. Parker, Robt. Means, John Waddle, John P. Hampton, Jonathan Ruggles, Stephen V. Bliss, Joshua Power, John Thompson, Geo. W. Collins, Richard Nash, Robt. D. Taylor, Nathaniel Garland, James Boyd, Robt. C. Carter, Nathan B. Webster, John Veach.

Constables.—John W. Leach, No. 1; William F. Hamrick, Mudlick; James H. Garrett, No. 3; Wyatt S. Owens, No. 5; Thos. D. Dickey, Vanceburg.

Officers from 1849 to 1851.—Joseph Robb, county clerk; John Pell, surveyor; John W.

Mitchell, coroner and jailer; Robt. Robb, treasurer; King D. McClain, sheriff.

Justices.—John T. Waddle, Jonathan Ruggles, Joshua Power, John Thompson, Geo. W. Collins, Richard Nash, Nat. G. Garland, James Boyd, Nathan B. Webster, John W. Veach, Stephen Bliss.

Constables.—Jno. W. Leach, Jos. G. Garertt, Francis M. Owens, William Hamrick, Jno. W. Stevenson.

Officers from 1851 to 1855.—Joseph Robb, clerk; Jno. Pell, surveyor; John Mitchell, coroner; Socrates Holbrook, county attorney; Lewis C. Stricklett, Keeper of Stray-pen and jailer; Robt. Robb, Treasurer; John Waddell, sheriff; William C. Ireland, police judge.

Justices.—Jonathan Ruggles, Joshua Power, John Thompson, Geo. W. Collins, Richard Nash, Nat. R. Garland, James Boyd, Nathan B. Webster, Stephen V. Bliss.

Constables.—John V. Leach, Leroy P. Parker, Robt. McEldowney, Thos. G. Wallingford, Milton Evans, John Fry, Uriah B. McKellup.

"An election having been held (under the New Constitution) on Monday, the 12th day of May, 1851, for the purpose of electing county and district officers, in pursuance of the Constitution and laws on that subject. And it appearing from the returns and certificates of the election, filed in the clerk's office of Lewis County Court, that the following persons were duly elected by the qualified voters of Lewis County, as county and district officers in and for said County of Lewis agreeable to the Constitution and the Acts of the Assembly in such case made and provided: Order Book, page 26.

Thomas Henderson, county judge; Joseph Robb, county clerk; James M. Todd, sheriff; Thos. O. Mershan, coroner; John Pell, surveyor; Socrates Holbrook, county attorney; Lewis C. Stricklett, jailer; Leroy P. Parker, assessor.

Justices.—Asa McNeal and Jacob Mower, No. 1; Edwin F. McFarland and Jonathan Ruggles, No. 2; Wm. B. Ruggles and Stephen V. Bliss, No. 3; Mathias Meredith and Patrick H. C. Bruce, No. 4; George W. Stamper and Edward Roe, No. 5; Josiah Burriss and Austin B. DeAtley, No. 6; John B. Fenley and Numan Glasscock, No. 7; John Thompson and Dempsey Power, No. 8.

Constables.—John Fry, constable in District No. 1; Thos. G. Wallingford, District No. 2; James Cottingham, District No. 3; John W. Leach, District No. 4; Benjamin Rayborn, District No. 5; Nesbit Taylor, District No. 6; Gabriel Bane, District No. 7; Robert McEldowney, District No. 8.

Officers from 1855 to 1858.—At the October

term of the County Court of 1855 the following new names as justices of the peace are found: Samuel B. Pugh, P. H. Clark, David W. Fearis, John R. Duke, William Blankenship, and Samuel Ellis.

Special Term, September, 1854. — Thomas Henderson was shown to be re-elected as county judge in an election August, 1854; and James R. Garland elected sheriff, Alfred Harrison, surveyor; George T. Halbert, county clerk.

August, 1858.—James R. Garland elected county judge; John Mitchell elected assessor; James D. Secrest coroner; Seth Parker, sheriff; James Rowland, jailer; Alfred Harrison, surveyor; Geo. T. Halbert, county clerk; Socrates Holbrook, county attorney; R. B. Case, justice of peace; G. M. Thomas, school commissioner; George Hughes, constable.

Officers from 1858 to 1864.—James Ruark elected constable; Robt. Voiers appointed constable District No. 3.

Officers 1862.—Socrates Holbrook elected county judge; Dr. R. G. Barber, coroner; James S. Pollitt, school commissioner; Angus V. Wilson, county clerk; John W. Mitchell, assessor; Seth Parker, sheriff; Wm. R. Hendrickson, jailer; J. B. Fitch, 1861, sheriff; John T. Parker, appointed county clerk at special term, September 1, 1863, on account of the death of

Angus V. Wilson; Alfred Harmon, surveyor; W. C. Halbert, county attorney.

In 1863 David Fearis, David M. Dunbar, Wm. S. Parker, Robert Richards, N. R. Garland, Edward Roe, Peter Duzan, A. H. Seatley, Samuel McEldowney, Jesse Markland, Peter Mawk, Lewis C. Stricklett, Dudley Calvert, and W. T. Jones were elected justices of the peace.

List of County Officers, October, 1865.—James S. Pollitt, judge; Lewis C. Stricklett, Samuel Ellis, Jesse Markland, Samuel McEldowney, Peter C. Mawk, Nicholas Moore, Edward Roe, W. D. Parker, Wm. Ruggles, N. R. Garland, A. H. Deatley, Peter Duzan, Dudley Calvert, magistrates.

Manley Trussell, county attorney; J. B. Fitch, sheriff; Wm. R. Hendrickson, jailer; Alfred Harrison, surveyor; Thomas W. Mitchell, county clerk.

Officers from 1864 to 1869.—First court held in Vanceburg, on Monday, March 21, 1864, Hon. S. Holbrook, county judge.

Thos. W. Mitchell appointed as deputy county clerk May 17, 1864; and, upon the death of John T. Parker, he was appointed county clerk at a special term, July 4, 1864. His certificate as clerk of the Circuit was signed by L. W. Andrews.

1865.—James S. Pollitt, county judge; Thos.

22

W. Mitchell, county clerk; Mandley Trussel, county attorney; J. B. Fitch, sheriff; R. G. Barber, coroner; James McDermott, assessor; Wm. R. Hendrickson, jailer; Geo. M. Thomas, 1868, county judge, on resignation of J. S. Pollitt; Mandley Trussell, county attorney; Thos. W. Mitchell, county clerk; Wm. R. Hendrickson, jailer; James McDermott, school commissioner; R. G. Barber, coroner; Smauel Ellis, sheriff; Alfred Harrison, surveyor.

Officers, 1870.—Geo. M. Thomas, county judge; Mandley Trussell, county attorney; W. R. Hendrickson, jailer; Thos. W. Mitchell, county clerk; Alf. Harrison, surveyor; John Woodworth, assessor; R. G. Barber, coroner; Samuel Ellis, sheriff; James McDermott, school commissioner.

August, 1870, to 1871.—James R. Garland, county judge; Joseph A. Spark, county clerk; Thos. W. Mitchell, County Court clerk; Lewis Plummer, jailer; Samuel Ellis, sheriff; Henry C. Bruce, treasurer; Robt. B. Lovell, 1871, sheriff; Thos. W. Mitchell, school commissioner; W. C. Halbert, county attorney; Alfred Harrison, surveyor.

Officers from 1871 to 1878.—Justices of the peace: D. W. Fearis, D. H. Brightman, L. C. Stricklett, W. W. Moore, Wm. Ruggles, Samuel W. Williams, Thos. J. Walker, Jesse Markland, D. M. Dunbar, J. J. Fitch, Wm. S. Parker,

Dudley Calvert, Henry McKee, and Peter D. Lykins. Joseph D. Secrest later elected; also R. R. Hines, John Hackworth, Peter C. Mawk, N. R. Garland, Lewis Dickson, D. H. Boyd, Wm. P. O'Doherty, Joshua D. Fitch, Richard P. Thomas, Dudley Calvert (re-elected), Samuel McEldowney, R. R. Williams, Samuel W. Williams (re-elected), J. J. Fitch, Thos. J. Walker (re-elected), James R. Gidding.

August, 1874-1878.—M. P. Lewis, county judge; W. L. Fitch, county attorney; Thos. A. Mitchell, county clerk; Jos. A. Spark, County Court clerk; H. F. Warder, 1872, sheriff; A. J. Harrison, 1874, sheriff; Willis Hisey, jailer; Peter C. Mawk, surveyor; A. Dud. Pollitt, assessor.

Officers from 1878 to 1882.—A. W. Fryer, county judge; Thos. A. Mitchell; Jos. A. Sparks, deputy county clerk; S. J. Pugh, county attorney; Thos. C. Wilson, W. G. Bullock, deputy sheriffs; Willis Hisey, jailer; Peter C. Mawk, surveyor; R. G. Barber, coroner.

Magistrates. — James M. Dunbar, Isaiah Grigsby, D. H. Boyd, D. W. Fearis, Geo. W. Herrin, John W. Keyser, Alexander Plummer, Benj. F. Branham, B. W. Parker, Henry McKee, Isaac W. Lykins, Wm. M. Parker, E. G. Rayborn, F. M. Taylor, J. J. Fitch, Jas. Nolen, B. D. Pollett, W. E. Reed, Jas. M. Fults, Jesse

Markland, Ammon Cooper, Isaac Conley, Wm. Sharks.

Officers from 1882 to 1886.—A. W. Foyce, county judge; R. D. Wilson, county clerk; S. I. Pugh, county attorney; Samuel L. Hall, 1882, S. H. Parker, 1884, sheriff; J. W. Cottingham, jailer; W. G. Bullock, assessor; Dr. W. H. Campbell, coroner; Peter C. Mawk, surveyor; T. B. Bullock, superintendent schools.

Magistrates of 1884.—Henry McKee, S. I. Dodd, G. H. Harrison, D. H. Boyd, J. E. Lang, W. B. Parker, Geo. W. Heselton, A. J. Armstrong, G. H. Gilbert, H. I. Bell, R. H. Fisher, Geo. W. Herrin, B. D. Pollett, G. H. Bane, Jesse Markland, W. E. Reed, A. N. Coofer.

Officers from 1886 to 1890.—Samuel J. Pugh, county judge; E. H. Fitch, county attorney; Thos. A. Mitchell, county clerk; J. C. Willim, sheriff; Joseph W. Cottingham, jailer, 1890-94; Henry C. Myers, assessor; T. J. Adam, J. M. Wells, coroner; Wm. H. George, school commissioner; Alfred Harmon, surveyor; S. A. Agnew, treasurer.

Magistrates 1889.—R. W. Higgins, E. R. Hays, W. H. Wright, L. N. Rayborn, J. W. Lykins, W. B. Cooper, Isaiah Grigsby.

Officers from 1890 to 1894.—A. W. Fryer, county judge; Thos. A. Mitchell, county clerk; W. C. Halbert, county attorney; J. C. Willim,

1890, Ed. Willim, 1892, sheriffs; Joseph W.
Cottingham, jailer; Jack Hendrickson, assessor;
G. E. Dunbar, school commissioner; A. Harrison,
surveyor.

January Term, 1890-93.—Magistrates: R. H.
Fisher, H. L. Bilyen, W. D. Gully, Jas. M. Lee,
Thos. W. Irwin, B. F. Branham, Wm. Sparks,.
John T. Dodd, G. W. Hamilton, Isaiah Grigsby,
B. D. Pollett, R. W. Higgins, Wm. E. Reed,
R. M. Parker, J. T. Bowman, Ralph Stafford,.
E. W. Hackworth, W. K. Hampton.

1893 to 1894.—S. G. Hillis, county judge;
Thos. A. Mitchell, county clerk; W. C. Halbert,
county attorney; Ed. Willim, sheriff; Geo. W.
Dale, jailer; W. H. Hamrick, assessor; Dr. G.
M. Will, coroner; E. C. Rowland, surveyor;
Geo. E. Dunbar, school commissioner; E. A.
Jones, treasurer.

1897, New Constitution.—Ed. Willim, county
judge; O. P. Pollett, county clerk; W. C. Halbert, county attorney; Marshall Bertram, sheriff,
Thomas Cooper, assessor; E. C. Rowland, surveyor; Geo. E. Dunbar, school commissioner;
E. A. Jones, treasurer; C. A. Tamnam, jailer.

Officers of 1903: Magistrates.—E. W. Mc-
Clain, W E. Darragh, W. H. Wright, Joshua
Stampa,   W. Lykins, W. B. Cropper, Isaiah
Grigsby.

Officers from 1901 to 1905.—J. M. Lee, county

judge; O. P. Pollett, county clerk; W. C. Thoroughman, county attorney; T. M. Bowman, sheriff; David Smith, assessor; Ernest H. Staley, surveyor; J. T. Burchart, coroner; W. Rich. Henderson, school commissioner; C. L. Tamnam, jailer; Geo. E. Dunbar, treasurer.

Officers from 1905 to 1909.—J. M. Lee, county judge; O. P. Pollett, county clerk; W. C. Thoroughman, county attorney; M. Bertram, sheriff; Thos. Cooper, assessor; Dr. J. T. Owry, coroner; W. R. Henderson, school commissioner; G. P. Adams, jailer.

Officers, 1909.—Same officers, except G. W. Lykins was elected sheriff, H. F. Sullivan, jailer, and Dr. J. M. Wells, coroner.

Officers of 1911: Magistrates.—W. H. McClain, No. 1; A. R. Campbell, No. 2; Theo. Bagby, No. 3; H. L. Walters, No. 4; O. L. Lee, No. 5; R. M. Parker, No. 6; P. C. Henderson, No. 7.

List of county judges and county clerks:

1856 Thos. Henderson, Judge.			
1860 J. R. Garland,	"	Geo. T. Halbert, Clerk.	
1865 Socrates Holbrook,	"	Thos. W. Mitchell,	"
1866 J. S. Pollett,	"	"	"
1870 J. R. Garland,	"	"	"
1874 W. S. Lewis,	"	Jos. A. Sharks,	"
1878 A. W. Fryer,	"	Thos. A. Mitchell,	"
1882 *same*	"	"	"
1886 S. J. Pugh,	"	"	"

1890	S. J. Pugh, Judge.	Thos. A. Mitchell, Clerk.
1894	A. W. Fryer, "	" "
1894	S. G. Hillis, "	" "
1898	Ed. Willim, "	O. P. Pollett, "
1902	J. M. Lee, "	" "
1906	" "	" "
1910	" "	" "

REPRESENTATIVES.—The following are Lewis County's list of Representatives.

STATE SENATE

W. C. Halbert.....................1866-1870
R. B. Lovell......................1873-1877
H. C. Bruce.......................1880-1884
S. J. Pugh........................1894-1895
J. D. Rummans.....................1895-1899
W. H. Cox.........................1900-1906
B. C. Grigsby.....................1907-1910
T. F. Bagby.......................1912

HOUSE OF REPRESENTATIVES

Aaron Owens.......................1810-1813
Samuel Cox........................1813-1816
Thos. Marshall....................1817
Aaron Stratton....................1818
Samuel Cox........................1819
Wm. B. Parker.....................1820
Alex. Bruce.......................1821
F. R. Singleton...................1822-1823
C. B. Shepherd....................1824
Alex. Bruce.......................1825
C. B. Shepherd....................1826
John Bruce........................1827
Thos. Marshall....................1828

John Bruce........................1829
Thos. Henderson..................1830
C. B. Shepherd...................1831-1832
Thos. Henderson..................1833
Chas. H. Marshall................1834
Israel B. Donaldson..............1835
Thos. Marshall...................1836
W. B. Parker.....................1837
T. J. Walker.....................1838
Thos. Marshall...................1839
Manley Trussell..................1840
Socrates Holbrook................1841
Thos. Marshall...................1842
Benj. Given......................1843
Thos. Marshall...................1844
U. B. McKellup...................1845
L. J. Proctor....................1846
James Bilderback.................1847
N. R. Garland....................1848
John L. Fitch....................1849
John Thompson....................1850
Cleaton Bane.....................1851-1853
Joshua Given.....................1853-1855
F. M. Wood.......................1855-1857
T. H. C. Bruce...................1857-1859
G. M. Thomas.....................1859-1861
Same (resigned August 16, 1862)....1861
P. S. Layton.....................1862-1865
P. H. C. Bruce...................1865-1867
J. B. Fitch (declared ineligible).....1867-1869
Alex. Bruce......................1867-1869
A. J. Hendrickson................1869-1871
Thomas J. Walker.................1871
(Seat contested and declared vacant, 1872)

G. M. Thomas...................1872-1875
Rufus Emmons..................1875-1877
J. D. Thompson................1877-1879
Isaiah Grigsby................1879-1881
F. H. Hull....................1881-1883
Wm. Bowman....................1883-1887
S. G. Hillis..................1887-1891
G. T. Halbert.................1891-1893
Wm. Bowman....................1893-1895
A. Dud. Pollitt...............1895-1897
D. D. Lykins..................1898-1900
Jas. Cooper...................1900-1902
R. C. Hanna...................1902-1904
W. C. Halbert.................1904-1906
J. D. Lowder..................1906-1908
T. M. Bertram.................1910-1912

Before 1810 Lewis and Greenup were represented together, by Plummer Thomas, in 1809, and other gentlemen of Greenup County.

GENERAL ELECTIONS.—The issues before the people in 1798, at the time delegates were elected to form a new Constitution, were the slavery question and the election by the people of the office holders. The famous "Resolutions of '98," probably from the molding hand of John Breckinridge, came into existence in the Legislature of 1798. But this was before our county was born—a few years; yet the Constitution then framed was that under which she came into existence, and under which her course was guided for nearly fifty years.

The subjects for discussion before the people in 1849-1850 Convention were:

"First.—The relation of the State to slavery.

"Second.—The election of all officers by the people.

Third.—The inhibition of the use of the credit of the State for internal improvements.

"Fourth.—The Constitution of the several courts of the State.

"Fifth.—The introduction of a clause for the prevention of dueling.

"Sixth.—The distribution of representation in the State Legislature.

"Seventh.—A common school system."

(From "History and Texts of the Constitutions of Kentucky," by Bennett H. Young, 1890.)

This Constitution went into effect in June, 1850, and was the supreme law of the State for about forty-one years. Under it Lewis County elected her officers, fought in the great Civil War, builded her present county seat, organized her macadam road system, helped build a railroad, went through a tobacco growing mania, saw the rise and fall of the Farmer's Alliance, discussed at various times the temperance question, promulgated the gospel; built churches and schoolhouses in every section of the county, and now, under another "New Constitution," she is moving smoothly and each year marks a change for the better in some of the abuses of the county's administration.

Chapter V

Common School System: Commissioner—Superin-
tendents—Boards of Education—Teachers—
Growth of the School System in the County—
Districts and Schoolhouses.

"The Common School! O, may its light
    Shine through our country's story;
Here lies her wealth, her strength, her might;
    Here rests her future glory."

The "Free School Fund" of Kentucky orig-
inated from money distributed by the General
Government before and up to 1836, to those
States that had no land grants for educational
objects. By that time Kentucky had received
$1,433,757; but the subject of the schools and
of education, by the Constitution of 1799, had
been left to the tender mercies (?) of the Legislature, and by 1837 the fund had been reduced
to $1,000,000, and, in 1838, to $850,000. In
1845 an Act passed the Legislature authorizing
the school bonds to be burned in the presence of
the auditor and treasurer. This was actually
done, and the enemies of free thought seemed
to have triumphed by wiping out the last obligation of the State to educate its citizens.

But this spirit of injustice aroused the friends of common schools, and a set of representatives were returned to the Capital in 1847 who passed an Act requiring the governor to reissue the bond, or rather, issue a new bond, and also providing for submission to the vote of the people of an additional tax of two cents on the one hundred dollars for schools. The people ratified the tax by a majority of 36,000 votes.

By the time the Constitutional Convention of 1849-50 had met there was due the school fund from the State $1,276,391.71.

It was upon this condition of affairs that the Convention began to discuss the proposition of placing a school clause in the New Constitution.

The discussion was opened by Benjamin Hardin, delegate from Nelson County, in which he made a roaring speech against the proposition, wherein he ridiculed the "free school," stigmatized its teachers as a set of low, brutalized ignoramuses, and said that they were a "miserable set of humbugs." He declared his county never had, nor ever would have, a free school. He had "no opinion of free schools—none in the world."

He thought it would take forty-five hundred schools to accommodate the children of the State, and that the expense would be more than she could raise. He was sending all the time five or six children, beside his own, to the Methodist and Catholic Colleges, and he seemed to think that was the better way to educate the future citizens of the State.

All this tirade of abuse put the friends of education on their mettle, and Larkin J. Proctor, of Lewis County, threw down the gauntlet to Mr. Hardin in defense of the education of the masses. "He not only contended that the adoption of this provision of the Constitution for the permanent security of the school fund was demanded by the people, but was demanded by all lovers of free government and intelligence and virtue; that the members of the Convention were engaged in making a Constitution which was to be thoroughly democratic in all its operation; that they were throwing back into the hands of the people all political power, and that it was essential now to secure to these people and their posterity the means of giving their children the blessings of an education in order that they might be qualified to discharge the duties that might devolve upon them." He said: "While, however, these great and important truths are recognized and admitted by all, it is to be feared that gentlemen are not practically alive to the important influence of these truths on the operation of our government. The gradual extension of the privilege of free suffrage in the provisions of the Constitution which we are about to adopt, and which is to place in the hands of the people the selection of every officer of the government, imposes on the members of this Convention the solemn duty of making a corresponding effort to extend the great privileges, the light of knowledge, and the means of cultivating the minds of those who are to come after us. For, sir, if we mean to preserve our free institutions, we must watch over them; we must learn to know and number our great political rights; we must study the tenure by which we hold them, and must also qualify ourselves to discern from afar off the dangers that threaten us—for the rights and liberties of man are always in danger from some quarter."

That the children who are now basking in the beams of the sunshine of education vouchsafed to them by the Constitution may know what a valiant fight its friends in the Convention made for it, we copy a few of the speeches made in its favor. Mr. Taylor, Chairman of the Committee on Education, made a grand speech. He said: "There are in Kentucky (1849) ninety-one thousand children whose parents are mostly unable to educate them, and yet we are besought not to interfere. Great God! Can it be possible that we shall be non-combatants in the great battle of life—for knowledge is life.

I ask if gentlemen can look upon this barren and unproductive field and not desire to plant and nurture within it the tree of knowledge (perhaps of life also), to lead through it those fountains of living water which slake not, but rather increase the thirst of him who drinketh? Who does not desire to cast upon this still and unfruitful pool bread, with the cheering assurance that it shall indeed be gathered after many days? To sow broadcast over this land the seeds of knowledge which shall germinate and produce for ever? With the startling facts presented in this report of the second auditor how can gentlemen hesitate about the absolute necessity of a constitutional provision for some system of general education? It can not be that this convention will adjourn without the expression of some solicitude on this great matter. We have been told by the gentleman from Nelson (Mr. Hardin) that the Catholics are opposed to this system of common schools, and that if we put it in the Constitution they will oppose its adoption. Sir, I do not believe it. I will not do them the injustice to believe this imputation upon their patriotism and intelligence. They will not send their children, as said, to free schools. Be it so. Let them educate their own children; they have the right to do so, and the ability, too. Is that any reason why the friends of education should neglect to provide for such a system of public instruction as will hang up at every man's fireside the lamp of knowledge? We have erected the lamp—if I may use the figure—like the brazen serpent in the wilderness, and invited every man to look and live, and if he will not, we have the consolation that it is not our fault or our neglect."

William B. Machen, afterwards United States Senator, took grounds against this constitutional provision.

Dr. William K. Bolling, from Logan County, made a magnificent oration for the common school clause. He says:

"But the gentleman from Caldwell (Mr. Machen) would not force the State to pay the interest on this National gift, made sacred by a solemn Act of the Legislature for ever, to educational purposes. He thinks it might be inconvenient. That is her concern, not mine. It will not be denied that she justly owes the money, for she has, through her Legislature, ordered the evidences of the debt to be listed. A listed debt, I understand from the lawyers, is not assignable, and therefore does not require the baptismal fire to stave off its payment until a more convenient season. But, sir, let these hundred chosen delegates go home and tell the anxious thousands that will greet their return

23

that a part of our labors here insures to the descendants of this land of heroes and song the keys to the temple of knowledge; that henceforth, under the new organization, schools are to spring up in every neighborhood, and to be as free as the gush of waters from the mountain rock.

"Tell them that the mountains and the valleys and the plains of this heavenly heritage are to be studded with schoolhouses, which, like the temples of the living God, are to be free to all, without money and without price. Tell the children of the poor and unfortunate that hope, heretofore that mystic shadow of good which receded as they advanced, and whose home was fabled terminus of the rainbow, has been made to receive substantive proportions and become a smiling reality. Tell them that the fountains of living water have been opened up, in which the budding desire for knowledge may slake its thirst, and where all are invited to come and partake freely. Let this be told them, sir, and a voice redolent of thanksgiving and benediction will go up from half a million of the best of our people to the God of the widow and the fatherless."

T. J. Hood, of Carter County, also made a speech in favor of the schools. He said:

"We are also admonished by that same

gentlemen (Mr. Hardin) and others upon this floor to leave the school fund and the proceeds of the school tax to the guardian care and tender mercies of the Legislature. Sir, the experiences of some eleven years have demonstrated to the people of Kentucky the necessity of placing that fund upon more elevated ground, and securing it against that rapacious spirit of legislation which has not hesitated to lay violent hands upon it whenever an emergency seemed to require a prostitution of its means. The general principles of this report, as I before remarked, meet my cordial approbation. It consecrates and forever establishes the school fund, and places its principal beyond the reach of legislative abuse, while, at the same time, it secures the faithful application of the interest to the education of the children of all classes of society.

"Under the benign auspices of these extended means for intellectual development we shall see loom out from every city and country, from lowland and mountain, many an intellectual giant, with names gilded with no phosphoretic aureola borrowed from a distinguished ancestry, but with minds swelling with energies; fresh, free, native, and vigorous, and owing their attractions and power alone to their own masculine proportions.

"Then, indeed, will Kentucky become what I would have her as distinguished for virtue and intelligence of her citizens as for the chivalry of her sons and the beauty of her daughters."

The outgrowth of all this oratory and logic was the admission into the late Constitution of Article XI, on Education.

It has been preserved in the New Constitution of 1890, and is to-day the bulwark of defense against the enemies to the common school, who, thank Providence, are growing fewer every day as the system becomes more and more perfect.

There might have been some excuse for Ben Hardin's reproach of the ancient pedagogue, but it was the fault of a faulty system which had not thrown around it those safeguards which now prevent ignoramuses from taking the chair of the teacher.

In 1839 a change was made in the school law, reducing the county commissioners from five to three. There seems to have been more officers than schools up to 1851.

As well as I can determine, although there were five districts laid off in Lewis County in 1822, the common schools went into operation in Lewis County about 1853. The first free school was taught on Mudlick by John S. May, who died only a few years ago, in that same locality. He was followed by Artensia Everett, now Mrs. Hardin Shaw. Next came Mr. Joshua T. Harry, who died on Upper Kinny a few years ago; and after him came Mathew Mitchell, who was an excellent teacher and far above the average of his day in educational attainment. Under his management our log schoolhouse, with its split log branches, received its first blackboard, and he also introduced the study of grammar, geography, history, and organized a Friday evening debating club. The subjects for discussion were such as would require historic research, and to stimulate the boys to do their best the good-looking girls were put on the stand as judges to decide which side produced the best argument. I will never forget how I studied my speech and then spread myself in its delivery, when Lavinia Virginia Martin, Mary Louise Evans, and Emily M. Beckett, or either of them, might have been on the judge's stand.

The history of the school on Mudlick is parallel to that of almost every school in the county. It was slow but gradual development toward a better order of things. The payment of money by the State served to draw teachers from the Eastern States, who were generally poor, pecuniarily, but shrewd, erudite Yankees, well qualified to teach and excite the pupils to seek a broader field of research for knowledge.

The War of 1861 affected the schools to considerable extent, preventing any noted improvement during its continuance; but after its close, and its passion began to subside, the schools started on again toward a better system.

Step by step the coils have fastened, by legislation, around the teacher, the trustee, and the patron, till now the teacher must be an educated person and the common school curriculum contains all the elements of a good English education. The teacher must not only know science, but he must be examined in theory and practice as well. He must show ability to teach as well as knowledge of the subjects to be taught. Then, again, the "Reading Circle" and "County Teachers' Library" are widening the scope of his mental horizon and giving him an introduction to classic literature, to the works of the ancient masters in his own art, and to the mythology of the primitive ages. Indeed, to be a teacher in the common school now requires character, erudition, ability to command and to impart instructions to others. Instead of the "miserable humbug" which Ben Hardin pictured in the Convention of 1849-50, the teacher is the peer of the foremost statesman in that Convention. His moral character, scholastic

attainments, and respectability place him on a
place far above the trickster politician who has
sought, through legislative enactment, to put
out the lamp of knowledge among the masses.

The "commissioner," with his "examiners"
scattered over the county and "holding examinations on the top of a rail fence," has given
away to the superintendent, who must himself
possess a first-class certificate, and a Board of
three examiners, also possessing certificates of
the highest grade, and examinations held at
regular intervals at the county seat upon a list
of questions on eleven different subjects, prepared by the State Board of Education. In
these examinations the strictest rules of order
are observed, and any attempt at fraud is pun-
ished by failure to pass, "for reasons."

The Teachers' Institute is another worthy
feature of the common school system, for it
brings together all the persons in the county
engaged in teaching and places them under the
instruction of a normal school graduate. It
also gives opportunity to compare experiences,
discuss difficulties, and discover means to over-
come them. It also brings about a spirit of
fraternity which tends to make the teacher feel
that teaching is a profession, and, like others,
he must have his associations and teachers'
meetings to further his interests and advance

his cause. He must also have his "organ," the *School Journal*, that he may keep to the front in educational ethics.

All these demands on the teacher require that he keep ever learning, and thus he patronizes the "Normal Schools" to expand his information and to get better methods of teaching.

These conditions make the teachers grow intellectually, and this influence is felt in the schools and disseminated in the community.

The more advanced teachers have felt that some more potent means than persuasion has been needed to reach a certain class of should-be school patrons, and, therefore, they have urged the Legislature to pass some compulsory bill. At last they have been heard, and a mild, but, we hope, effective law has just passed and become a law, requiring at least eight weeks attendance each year of all children in the school age.

Since 1865 several distinguished gentlemen have held the office of commissioner or superintendent: Rev. Alfred Harrison, Joseph A. Sparks, E. A. Jones, A. Harvey Parker, Thos. B. Bullock, Prof. W. N. George, Prof. G. E. Dunbar, and Prof. R. C. Henderson, the present incumbent. Each of these gentlemen, as a school officer, has borne well his part and performed his duty as he had been given light to see it; but much of the progress in material interest as well as intellectual advancement is due to the untiring effort and progressive spirit of these men, who, with the law as their guide, can square up to their duty without fear or favor. They may have made a few enemies and mistakes in their performance of duty, but their friends are a solid phalanx of the true friends of education.

With the Nation's flag, "Old Glory," floating over the schoolhouse, and the young patriots within breathing the free air of heaven as they study the history of the "Declaration" and of Washington, we may well say the common school is the "wealth, strength, and might" of our country, and therein "rests her future glory."

CHAPTER VI

WAR PERIODS: INDIANS—SOLDIERS OF 1812 AND 1861
—COMPANIES ORGANIZED—OFFICERS—NUMBER OF
ENLISTED MEN—THOSE KILLED IN ACTION—G. A. R.
POSTS—MONUMENTS.

WAR OF 1812.—The War of 1812 produced a great commotion in Lewis County, and the inherent patriotism of the true Kentuckian manifested itself by sending about three-fourths of the men to the Canada battlefields.

MILITIA OF 1832.—69th Regiment: John Tolle, colonel; A. D. McDowell, lieutenant-colonel; James Boyd, judge advocate; Robt. Means, adjutant; John Cutcher, quartermaster; Nesbit Taylor, surgeon; Thos. Lindley, assistant surgeon; John Walker, color bearer; John C. Barkley, sergeant major; George Saulsberry, fife major; Geo. W. Himes, drum major.

APPOINTMENTS, MAY 19, 1832.—Thos. J. Walker, captain; Jas. W. Singleton, first lieutenant; Joseph Hampton, second lieutenant; Samuel Pollitt, captain; Elijah H. Thomas, captain; Nelson Plummer, lieutenant; John Staggs, ensign; Robt. Jack, captain.

DELEGATES TO CONVENTION.—Hon. S. J. Pugh, 1894.

INDIANS.—There are no Indian records in Lewis County, except those already told in this History.

There is no record of the names of the soldiers of 1812 Militia.

Lewis County had the 69th Regiment of 7th Brigade Kentucky Militia, 1849. Captain, L. B. Ruggles, R. R. Williams, Amos Means, D. W. Fearis, Joseph Sparks (Kinny).

W. R. McKellup, judge advocate.

Wm. J. Taylor, colonel; and Wm. Carr, lieutenant colonel.

Wm. J. Tully, colonel; and Geo. W. Reeder, major, 1851.

James R. Garland, captain, 1852.

Joshua D. Fitch, captain, 1852.

James P. Stricklett, captain, 1852.

Geo. M. Thomas, sergeant major, 1852.

James M. Lee, sergeant major, 1852.

Robt. T. Voier and Henry Gilespie, ensigns.

Austin Dudley, lieutenant.

John S. Edwards, ensign.

William Fitch, captain.

George Conway, ensign.

John T. Carrington, captain.

Wm. Swearingen, lieutenant.

Moses Ruggles, ensign.

Wm. Boyd, captain.

Samuel Hampton, lieutenant.

Wm. Sparks, ensign.

Wm. Wade, captain of Light Infantry.

Wm. Corns, lieutenant of Light Infantry.

Jno. M. Greenlee, ensign Light Infantry.

MARCH OF 1861:

Company I, 4th Regiment Kentucky Veteran Volunteer Infantry. James B. Brewer.

Company G, 10th Kentucky Cavalry. Captain Milton Evans.

Company K, 16th Regiment Kentucky Volunteer Infantry. Jas. A. Lee, captain.

Company E, 22d Regiment Kentucky Veteran Volunteer Infantry. Alexander Bruce, captain.

Company K, 23d Regiment Kentucky Veteran Volunteer Infantry. Ephraim P. Mavity, captain; Thos. M. Hamrick, major.

Company A, 45th Regiment Mounted Infantry. Jos. W. Cottingham, captain.

Company C, 54th Regiment Kentucky Mounted Infantry. Dexter B. Gray, captain; Jas. W. Stewart, first lieutenant.

Besides these companies, organized wholly in the county, there were perhaps a hundred men, belonging to Lewis County, who enlisted in outside organizations.

There were also a company of Confederate troops organized mostly from this county, and commanded by Captain Geo. Seaman, whose family lived on and owned the farm which is now the county infirmary.

The monument in the court-house yard, erected by Lewis County citizens, contains the names of Lewis County soldiers killed in action during the war, as follows: (See page 93.)

COMPANY I, 4TH REGIMENT KENTUCKY VOLUN-TEERS.—J. Maffeth, T. J. Barard, J. W. Blaunt, J. O. Carter, J. W. Dunning, G. W. Ford, N. R. Bennett, J. H. Falkner, J. E. Fetters, G. H. Himes, H. G. Kauffman, J. R. Himes, W. E. Himes, W. D. Himes, W. H. Himes, J. Hilterbrand, G. R. Hughes, J. D. Hollenger, H. G. Boyd, C. A. Thompson, J. Witty, G. Kellum, A. Kellum, R. Penrod, W. W. Fry, H. G. Logan.

10TH KENTUCKY CAVALRY.—J. Bryant, T. Hughes, J. S. Holland, Jno. McDaniel, A. Plummer, J. Spurgeon, Alex. Staggs.

COMPANY K, 16TH REGIMENT.—Wm. H. Rowland, Sylvester Blankenship, T. M. Dunnegan, D. Featherkyle, Wm. R. Wallingford, Harrison Fetters, M. V. Simer, S. Cox, Geo. Fry, F. Roe, S. A. Nolen, G. Redman, S. Spillman, D. D. Reed, W. H. Knapp, G. W. Smith.

COMPANY E, 22D REGIMENT.—W. C. Stewart, Simon Clark, E. G. Faber, S. L. Winter, Robt. Petitt, R. A. P. Riggs, S. M. Bruce, Jabez Truitt.

COMPANY K, 23D REGIMENT.—Major Thos. H. Hamrick, Captain E. P. Mavity, D. O. Swearingin, Ambrose Shain, S. T. Ruggles, Hiram Hamlin, John Tearin, E. V. McGinnis, Wm. Parker, Wm. Ruby, G. S. Ginn, J. T. Busby, B. Jones, W. R. Gully.

COMPANY I, 41ST KENTUCKY INFANTRY.—R. S. Davenport, A. B. Burris.

COMPANY A, 45TH REGIMENT.—A. V. Wilson, W. H. Bailey, T. M. Clark, O. S. Crane, T. A. Hicks, Ira Yates, J. Gillespie, J. Sparks, R. T. Walker, H. Hoover.

COMPANY C, 54TH REGIMENT.—M. D. Moore, J. W. Webster, W. D. Spurgin, O. C. Poe, G. W. Hendrickson, S. R. Johnson.

SPANISH-AMERICAN WAR VETERANS OF 1898-99.

Company M. 3d Regiment Kentucky Infantry, Captain A. W. Brewer. 117 men.

G. A. R. POSTS

E. P. Mavity Post. Petersville.
Craxton Post, Fearis.
John T. Parker Post, Vanceburg.
No. 57. G. H. Reeder, commander; J. S. Mavity, adjutant.

There are over five hundred pensioners now in Lewis County.

(We discover, as we are about to go to press, that the numbers, commanders, adjutants of E. P. Mavity and Craxton Posts have not been submitted to us.—O. G. R.)

CHAPTER VII

PUBLIC ROAD SYSTEM—MACADAMIZED ROADS—ORIGIN-
ATORS OF IN THE COUNTY—THE FIRST BUILT—
NUMBER NOW IN THE COUNTY, AND LOCATION—
COST OF CONSTRUCTION—COUNTY SUBSCRIPTION—
PRESENT ROAD SYSTEM.

IN the beginning the roads were authorized
by the County Court, and were "cut out" and
worked by overseers and hands living along the
route. These roads were first viewed by commissioners, who reported to the court whether
the road was needed, if it could be built over
such route, and whose lands it would pass
through and whether the owner was willing.
If he was not, a jury was summoned and the
damages assessed. If the amount was not too
much, in the opinion of the court, it was paid
and the road ordered opened; but if the court decided the allowance of the jury to be "enormous,"
they quashed the order for the road and let the
fellow who wanted damages get to market the
best way he could until he became satisfied that
a road was necessary.

The following are some of the roads laid out
and opened in 1807-8-9. In 1807 a road from
Lewis to Mason; from Sutherlains', on Quick's

Run, to the Ohio River; from Swearingin's mill,
on Cabin Creek, to the Salt Lick Road where it
crosses to Williamsburg; from Salt Lick to
Oharrow's mill; from Gunpowder Gap to Salt
Lick, below McDaniel's; from East Fork to
Main Cabin Creek; from Wilson's bottom to
East Fork; from Swearingin's mill to Mason
County line; from the forks of Quick's Run to
the head of the same creek; from Sycamore up
the river to Salt Lick. In 1808 from Cabin
Creek to Tollesboro; from Tollesboro to North
Fork. In 1809 a road from Vanceburg, up the
river, to Greenup County line.

About the time the county seat had been
well established at Clarksburg a road was made
across the mountain to Grassy Fork of Kinny—
this was probably not till 1819. In 1820 a road
up Holly Fork of Kinny to Salt Lick, near
Valley. Previous to this a road had been established from upper Kinny to Spurgeon's mill,
on Salt Lick, and in 1819 a road over the mountain from Esculapia to some place on North
Fork.

Some time before 1812 the State had a
system of roads known as State Roads; two of
these passed through Lewis County. In 1833
the Legislature passed an Act appropriating the
proceeds from the sale of public lands to the
aid of these roads. A road from the North Fork,

by way of Clarksburg and Vanceburg, to the Greenup line, was the recipient of some of these land warrants. John McDaniel, James Hannah, and Pleasant M. Savage were appointed commissioners to attend to this road. On a State road from Barton Lee's to Concord, Joseph Cox and Samuel Stephenson were appointed commissioners. Three hundred and fifty dollars worth of land warrants were issued to the former of these roads and one hundred and fifty to the latter.

In 1849 the Legislature, by an Act, authorized the Esculapia Springs Company to build a turnpike road from Maysville, via Esculapia, to Vanceburg. It is needless to say it was not built.

In 1856 the Legislature passed an Act authorizing a "Mud turnpike" to be built from Vanceburg, up Kinny, to Mt. Carmel, or to the county line at North Fork, near William White's residence. This road was built by a capitation tax on the citizens, and several Acts giving more time to collect the taxes were granted by legislation. The writer can remember the building of this road through his father's land on the ridge between Kinny and Mudlick. This was a well-graded road, and only needed stone to have made it a first-class road.

In 1863-64 Colonel W. S. Rand built an

24

"air line" railroad, by the aid of the Legislature, from Kinny to Vanceburg. The Colonel and his associates were unable to determine whether they desired steam or horse power as a means of locomotion, and as it has never been determined, the road is still resting on the charter.

In 1867 the Vanceburg, Salt Lick, Tollesboro, and Maysville Turnpike Road Company was chartered. (Said charter can be found in Acts of the Legislature in this volume—See Act, 1867.) This was the real beginning of the macadam roads in the county. But Mr. A. Dud. Tolle claims to have held the first turnpike meeting at his house. We give from the Vanceburg *Courier* of December 30, 1879, his story:

"The first turnpike meeting held in Lewis County, and looking to the building of the Lewis and Mason Turnpike Road, was held in the house of A. Dud. Tolle, in the southwestern corner of the county, and greatly surprised his lady, who, returning home from Illinois without previous knowledge of the turnpike meeting, found some forty men gathered at her home, and supposed that "there was a funeral;" but just such a funeral as that gave the ball its impetus, and put in motion the scheme that gave Lewis County all the turnpike roads she has."

The charter of the V. S. L. T. & M. Road has

had the following amendments by legislation: An Act in 1870 amends the law in regard to stockholders paying taxes—it makes them pay. In 1872-73 an amendment changes the limit of lands taxed in aid of said road. In 1884 a tax was levied to build bridge approaches at the Caines' farm, on Salt Lick. This Act was repealed in 1885. The Act of 1888 divides the road into two sections, and allows two sets of officers thereon. This Act is amended in 1890, properly naming the divisions of the road. This road is nineteen miles in length, and has had $21,000 worth of county bonds issued to it. In 1877 it has cost over $64,000 to build it. It has never paid a cent of dividend on its stock, and was, in 1880-81, in the hands of a receiver. It has since managed to keep in tolerable repair from the money received from tolls.

The other roads chartered are: Salt Lick, Esculapia, & Mt. Carmel, in 1868; The Cabin Creek, Sand Hill, and Manchester, in 1869; The Vanceburg, Dry Run, and Kinniconnick, in 1869; The Vanceburg, Quick's Run, and Stout's Lane, 1869; The Cabin Creek Road, 1869; The Mason and Lewis Road, 1869; Concord and Tollesboro, in 1867; The Fleming and Lewis Road, in 1869; The Kinny Creek Road, in 1881; Vanceburg and Concord, in 1881; Vanceburg, Quick's Run, and Stout's

Lane, rechartered in 1881; Tollesboro and Mt. Carmel, in 1881; Tollesboro and Esculapia, in 1881 (never built); Poplar Flat and Indian Run, in 1881; Vanceburg, Quincy, and Springville, in 1883; Cabin Creek, East Fork, and Concord, in 1888; Quick's Run and Ohio River, in 1890; Vanceburg and Stout's Lane, rechartered in 1890; Kinny and Laurel, in 1894.

Most of these roads have been built, and one of them, the Concord and Tollesboro, has surrendered its charter and is now a county road. The county has aided, by its bonds, or otherwise, the construction of every bridge in the county. We name the following: Bridge over Crooked Creek, near Sand Hill; bridge over Cabin Creek, near Cottageville, and over same on C. & T. Road; over same on V. S. L. T. & M. Road; over Salt Lick, at Valley; over same at Caines' farm; over same at Vanceburg; over Kinniconnick at mouth of Montgomery; over same at mouth of Trace; over same at Blankenship's; over Scaffold Lick; and over Quick's Run, near its mouth. These bridges are either solid iron structures or they are covered wooden bridges of the most approved pattern. They have cost the county quite a large sum of money, which has been raised by a tax set apart as a bridge fund.

In 1881 a long Act was passed by the Legislature entitled a General Road Law. It seems to have been a "Grand Muddle," as nothing was ever accomplished under it in Lewis County.

In 1893-94 another Act was passed authorizing the counties to be laid off into road districts, permitting delinquent taxpayers to work out their taxes, and appropriating some money to hire labor on the roads. Under this system Lewis County is now laid off and the date fixed to begin work. We append the report of Judge Hillis to the county paper:

"LEWIS COUNTY COURT

"(S. G. Hillis, presiding judge; T. A. Mitchell, clerk.) 1896.

"*February Term.*—Order establishing 99 road precincts and fixing boundaries for same, as per provision of Section 4309, Chapter 110 amended road law.

"Order allotting all the able-bodied male citizens to work six days in the year on said road, viz: between the ages of 18 and 50. The delinquent tax list will be listed, and same to be worked out on the roads at the rate of $1.50 per day.

"The pro rata per mile is $8. There is 320 miles of road established, and the county attorney and judge have fixed April 9th as the day to commence road work, and the wages will be 60 cents per day for team and hand, and in no instance is there to be expended more than the amount allotted to each road. Each supervisor will be furnished with a blank payroll and ledger account book when they qualify."

There has been a law passed by the late session of the General Assembly (1896) looking to the purchase or surrender of all the turnpike charters, and to changing them into free roads to be maintained by taxation. The Act is rather a "bungled" affair, and seems to have been drawn with malice aforethought against the roads or the people who want them free; but it is hard to tell which. It may have been that the author of the bill was scared at Bradley's Militia, and was unable to do his best—in a literary effort. But jokes aside, Lewis County means to have some free macadam roads and some good ones of the ordinary kind before the new century dawns.

January 20, 1899.—The turnpike roads have, at this date, all surrendered their charters to the county and are now all free roads. Some little mob violence occurred to accomplish this, but the mob did not hurt anybody or get hurt by anybody—only the long poles across the road felt the power of the mob. Our county judge and the turnpike officers took a sensible view of affairs and turned over the turnpike investments which never had paid any dividend to the county, to be maintained as public roads.

CHAPTER VIII

BIOGRAPHY OF IMPORTANT MEN: THE BAR—THE PUL-
PIT—THE FORUM—TEACHER—THE DOCTOR.

THE history of the Nation is the acts of the
men composing that Nation. The following
sketches represent a few of Lewis County's citizens:

BRUCE, John, whose wife was Elizabeth
Clay, came from Virginia and settled in Garrard
County, Kentucky, late in the eighteenth cen-
tury. From this marriage the following sons
were born: General George W. Bruce, H. C.
Bruce, Alexander Bruce, Constantine Bruce,
Horatio Bruce, John Bruce, and Richard P.
Bruce.

BRUCE, General Geo. W., came to Lewis
County in 1804 or 1805. He married a widow
Garland in Virginia, in 1815. His sons were
Thomas H. Clay, who married Susan Crawford.
Their children were Perry G., who married
Isabel Bruce, and Horatio, who died unmarried.
Colonel Geo. W., who married Della Stratton,
daughter of Thompson N. Stratton, and resided
on Kinniconnick, near the mouth of Spy Run.

BRUCE, John, the son of John Bruce, of Garrard County, Ky., came to Lewis County in 1804 and engaged for a short time in the manufacture of salt on Dry Run, near Vanceburg. The following are his children: Thomas Bruce, Mahala, who married a Mr. Jamison and went to Missouri; Therese, who married Mr. Gaw, and died without issue; Aristides, who was drowned; Patrick H. Clay, who is still living in Clay County, Kan.; Aaron B., Margaret, Andrew J., Alexander, who was the late Captain Alexander Bruce, of Forman's Bottom, in Lewis County; and Robert, who died without issue.

BRUCE, John, was a representative of Lewis County in the General Assembly of Kentucky in 1823.

BRUCE, Henry Clay, came to Lewis County about the time of the arrival of his brother John, and, in partnership with Horatio Bruce and Joseph Morgan, operated the Ohio Salt Works, in 1809. On April 8, 1813, he was commissioned as one of the justices of the county. He married a Miss Mary Price, of Bourbon County, and died in 1815 without heirs. It was the estate of H. C. and Horatio Bruce which was given in the Lewis County Court at $77,600, as shown in another chapter in this volume.

BRUCE, Horatio, also came with his brother from Garrard County, and continued for some time in the manufacture of salt after the death of his brother, Henry Clay Bruce. He married Eliza Beasley, of Mason County. There was born to them the following children: Elizabeth, who married a Mr. Weathers, but soon afterwards died; Horatio, who went to Johnson County, Texas; Henry, who was a "'49er," and died in California; Richard, who was an attorney-at-law in Mason County for a while, but finally went to Garrard County, where he died.

BRUCE, Constantine, the twin brother of Alexander, was the "Daniel Boone" of the family. He cared only for the dog and gun, and loved the chase more than the business pursuits of men.

BRUCE, Richard P., married in Garrard County, and then moved to Indiana. His wife and children all died of fever and ague, and in 1830 he returned to Vanceburg, Ky. He married Sallie Cofrin, by whom he had two children: Horatio, who is dead, and Robert, who lived in Forman's Bottom. Richard Bruce had a small farm on Cabin Creek, where he died.

BRUCE, Alexander, the father of Hon. H. C. Bruce, of Vanceburg, came to Lewis County with his other brothers and studied law. He was admitted to the bar in Lewis County Court in February, 1818.

BRUCE, Washington, engaged in the sawmill and lumber business on Kinny. He was at one time justice of the peace in Lewis County, also sheriff, and was twice elected to represent the county in the Legislature in the sessions of 1821 and 1825. In canvassing the county in 1850, as a candidate for county judge, he contracted pleurisy, of which he died before the election was held.

BRUCE, Thomas J. M., one of the sons of Alexander Bruce, lived in Stout's Bottom until his death, March 18, 1896.

BRUCE, John L., brother of Thos. J., also owns an adjoining farm in Stout's Bottom, where he resided until the death of his wife, a few years ago. He now lives with his daughter, in Vanceburg. His children are: Alice, who married John Brooks and moved to Kansas, where she still resides; and Minnie, who is the wife of John Cox, one of the leading merchants in Vanceburg.

BRUCE, Henry C., the second son of Alexander Bruce, is in business in Vanceburg, having been continuously so since 1869. Before that time he was connected with steamboating, having gone on board Captain Thos. Redden's boat, "Hunter," as clerk, in 1836. He was on the river about thirty-three years before he settled in Vanceburg and became one of its merchants.

BRUCE, Samuel E., who is now the trusted cashier of the Deposit Bank, whose photograph is found elsewhere in this volume. He was united in marriage to Josephine Smith, of Bourbon County, Ky.

BRUCE, Doctor Wm. E., who married Pauline Jones, of Vanceburg, and is now practicing his profession in Silver Cliff, Nevada.

BRUCE, John L., married Martha W. Smith, of Bourbon County, and is a prosperous attorney in one of the best legal firms in St. Louis, Mo.

KLINE, Eliza Bruce, is the wife of John Kline, of Garrison, Ky.

BRUCE, Thomas H. Clay, son of General Geo. W. Bruce, married Susan Crawford, and to them was born the following children: Thos. H. C. Bruce, who married Nancy J. Alley; Perry G., whose wife was Mary Logan; Nancy, the wife of Elias Sellards; Virginia, wife of Frank Staggs; Brunette, the wife of Professor John Keyser; and Susan, wife of Ralph Stone.

BRUCE, Captain Alexander, son of John Bruce, was born in Lewis County, Ky. He was a farmer and lived in Forman's Bottom, above Quincy, until his death. During the war of 1861-65 he was captain in a company of a regiment of Kentucky Volunteer Infantry, and did good service for his country. After the war, 1869, he was elected representative of Lewis County, and served until 1871.

BELYEW.—This family introduces itself to the Lewis County Court from the Sycamore neighborhood. Its first representatives are Abraham Belyew and his wife, Anna. Paul Belyew seems to be one of his children, but others may have and may have not existed. Certain it is, however, that Paul made up any lack of progeny in his parents. His wife was Sallie Snider, and his children are: Eli, who married Betsy Patterson and lived on Brush Creek, in Ohio; Samuel, who also married a Miss Patterson; William, who married Susan Watson; Hiram, who went to Iowa; Nancy, who married John Greenlee, and moved to Iowa; Betsy, who lives in Concord; Harriet, who married John Taylor, of Concord, famous as a mill and steamboat owner, but now residing at Higginsport, O.; Margaret, who married William Vance.

EASHAM, William, who came to Lewis County in 1806 and settled on the farm known as the

Pugh farm, on Salt Lick, married Martha Ruark, and died in 1850. The following are their children: Peggy, Joshua, Nancy, John Handly, William, Lucretia, Harriet, Rebecca, and Arthur.

EASHAM, John Handly, was born in 1804, and died 1877. His children are William, John, Nancy, Robert,' and Betty.

EASHAM, William, married Lucy Thomas, and now lives on Indian Fork on Kinniconnick. His children are Betty, who married William Jordan; Richard, who is married and lives with his father; Frederick, Nancy, Parma, William, Clay, Lucy, and Clark, still children at home.

EASHAM, Elisha, was born 1802 and died 1868; married his cousin, Lucretia Easham, and settled on Kinniconnick, near Crum Post-office. To them were born the following children: Jonathan, who still lives on Kinniconnick; Edward, who lives on Paint Lick; Eliza, Elizabeth, Martha Jane, and Nancy, who is the wife of Marion Meadows; George, Mary, and Sarah.

EASHAM, George, married Virginia Meadows, and lives on the old Ben Plummer farm, at the top of the hill on the road from Petersville to Mudlick and Mt. Carmel. He has four children: Charles, Crosby, Marion, Ora.

WILLIAMS, Zachariah, was born in Maryland in 1787, and died in Lewis County, Ky., in 1863. He was married to Sarah Hoover, in 1806, near Frederick, Va. She was born in 1789 and died in 1882. They are buried in the Beech Chapel Cemetery, in Fleming County, Ky. Zachariah Williams came to Fleming County in 1818, and removed to Leiws County in 1820, settling in the neighborhood between North Fork and Burtonville, where he lived until his death. In the latter part of his life he became a minister of the gospel. Seven children were born to this union, as follows: John W., Benjamin, Robert, Thomas, who lives near Poplar Plains, Ky., and Sallie Ann, who lived in Johnson County, Mo.; and Washington, who lives near Burtonville.

WILLIAM'S, John, wife was Mary Wallingford, of Kinniconnick, Lewis County. They were married in 1828. The following are their children: Lucinda, who was the wife of Andrew Jackson, of Quick's Run; James, who married Kate Rigdon, daughter of Clayborn Rigdon, in 1860. Their children are Lorenza, Joseph, Cora, wife of Samuel Moone; William, Robert, Mary, who is dead; and John. The above-named families have and still live in Lewis County, near Valley.

TONCRAY, Ezra, was born in Duchess County, N. Y., and emigrated to Rockbridge County, Va. He married Hannah Mitchell, and came to Kentucky in 1804. He came by way of Lexington, and settled in Lewis County where the old homestead now stands, on the old State Road. There was then neither road nor path by which he could travel farther on his journey, so he built him a shanty in the woods, near the blazed trail, and settled his family as comfortably as he could until he could move on farther. But he concluded later to stay, and bought the land where he was camped and immediately set about to make a home in the wilderness.

PARKER, William, of Virginia, was the father of Harry and Thomas Parker, who were citizens of Lewis County at its organization, in 1807. Just in what year they came to Lewis County is not definitely known, but perhaps about the year 1800.

PARKER, Harry, married Joanna Thomas, and they were the parents of Charles, whose wife was Jane Cooper. They had no children, and he died in Vanceburg.

PARKER, John F., who married his cousin, Nancy Parker, and he married at Fairview, and the following are their children: William, who is dead; James, a cigarmaker, now dead;

and Robert H., commonly called "Kitty," and who lives on Black Jack Branch, near Vanceburg. Robert, the third son, married Elizabeth Parker, December 19, 1823, and died July 27, 1859, near Clarksburg. The following are his children: Harry Thomas, died in Greenup, November 30, 1859; Melvina Ann, married W. W. Winter in June, 1848; Benjamin W., once a saddler in Vanceburg; Harriet Lucy, wife of W. T. Swearingin, now living in Ashland, Ky.; Mary Jane, wife of Joseph W. Cottingham, of Vanceburg, both deceased; John Grant, who married Sarah E. Thomas in March, 1860, died in Vanceburg in June, 1871; Martha Ellen, born July, 1837, and died November, 1847; Georgia Ann, born June, 1840, and was married to P. M. Stricklett December 21, 1860; Mary Eliza, born April, 1842, and was married to J. M. Ruggles in December, 1869, and now lives in Saybrook, Ill. Mason Brown, the tenth child, was born November, 1844, and died in September, 1873. Harry, the fourth son of Harvey Parker, married Elizabeth Mitchell, by whom he had a son, Edwin, who now lives in Vanceburg. Mr. Harvey Parker afterward married a second wife, and later moved to Missouri.

We now take up the history of the Thomas Parker branch of the family. Thomas Parker was twice married—first to Betsy Smith, of

Fayette County, Ky., and secondly to Miss Botts, of Fleming County. His eldest son, Garland S., was born in April, 1794, and died near the mouth of Kinniconnick. His wife was Patsy Voiers. Their children were Rebecca, John, Robert, Plummer, Sallie, and Seth. Besides these there were several girls whose names we were not able to obtain.

PARKER, William S., was born May, 1799, and died in May, 1880. His wife was Theresa Mitchell, daughter of Captain Thomas Mitchell. Their children are: Granville S., living in Black Oak Bottom; Thomas, who died at Fairview; Anna Maria, late wife of Dr. John White; Elizabeth, who married a Mr. McCall; Harriet Lucy, wife of Fred Savage; Susan, who married John Frizzell; and Eliza Preston, who lives with her sister Harriet, near Fairview.

PARKER, Ambrose Dudley, is represented at Vanceburg by the families. Thomas Parker, who was scalded to death in a mill vat, in this city, in the year 1807. His widow and son Jesse are living on a farm near the city, and their daughter Lizzie, now Mrs. Marion McGill, lives on a farm two miles west of Vanceburg.

PARKER, Fred H., his second son, also lives in this city, and has four children: Emma, William, John, and Priscilla. Robert, the third

25

son, went to the war of 1861, and has never been heard of since. There were also three daughters, one of whom is Mrs. John Sullivan, another Mrs. Abraham Sullivan, and the last first married Thomas Moore, and, after his death, married J. Cole Redden, of Valley, Ky.

Rowley.—This family came to Vanceburg in 1838. It consisted of Charles Rowley, Amanda, his wife, and seven children: Hiram T., George W., Benjamin F., Edwin S., Charlotte S., James H., and Eliza J. Mr. Rowley was born on Long Island, N. Y., and his wife was born in Connecticut; but her parents moved to Canandagua Lake, in Lew York, when she was a child. After leaving New York the family went to Indiana. From there they moved to Brandenburg, Meade County, Ky. From this place they moved to Washington County, O., and thence to Vanceburg, Ky., in 1838, as above noted. They have lived here since that time, except George, who married James Carr's daughter, and moved away, making his home elsewhere. Hiram and Ben never married. James H., who is known as one of the best steamboat pilots on the Ohio, married Miss A. J. Ingram, and lives on Second Street, in Vanceburg. His children are James H., also a pilot, who married Miss Anna Carter, daughter of Thomas Carter, of Vanceburg; and Millie J., who married Mr. James Gardner, of the Vanceburg Flouring Mill Company.

MOWER, Samuel D., the son of Jacob P. Mower, was born in 1842, and is a citizen of the county precinct that bears his name. Mr. Mower is a business man of marked ability, and has a wide acquaintance in business circles. His farming interests are extensive, and he sustains a large tentantry. He was united in marriage to Rebecca Cox. To this union were born twelve children, nine of whom are living.

MEANS, John.—About one mile west of the Covedale Post-office John Means settled in 1846. He was born in Miflin County, Pa., February 21, 1744. In 1794 he came to Kentucky, settling at Maysville. He was the father of six children, three sons and three daughters, as follows: John, Robert, Amos, Phoebe, Nancy, and Margaret.

JACKSON, Jesse W., was born in Mason County in 1788. He fought in the War of 1812, and was wounded in the battle of Lundy's Lane. He married three times, and to these unions twenty-one children were born. He built and operated a water-mill on Quick's Run, in 1842. He died in 1875.

HERBERT, Dr. William, was born in New Jersey about 1796, and came to Kentucky, with his parents, in 1802, and settled at Poplar Flats. He later became a physician, and practiced medicine for sixty years. He was married three times, and raised thirteen children. Most of his children are now dead. S. J. Herbert, one of his sons, still lives at Sand Hill, and is an old soldier of the Civil War, aged eighty years. One daughter lives in Maysville, Ky., the wife of Mr. S. McKellup. One daughter on Cabin Creek, the wife of John D. Tully. Another in New Richmond, O., the widow of Marion Bannister.

WILLIM, Harry, was born in England. He came to Kentucky at an early date, and married Mary Spurgeon. They then moved to Salt Lick, about 1824, and he operated a tanyard in Clarksburg. To this union were born six children, four boys and two girls, as follows: Ernest, William, John P., Sarah, Catherine, and Thomas H. Lewis Spurgeon and Mary Spurgeon are half brother and sister, older than the Willims.

ROBB, William, was born in July, 1775, in the city of Luxenburg, Germany. His wife, Elizabeth McGougin, was born in 1773, and they were married in 1800. David Robb was born October 13, 1801, in Pennsylvania. He was married to Martha McNutt in 1825, in Lewis County, Ky. Joseph Robb was born March 2, 1831, and was married to America Launtz in 1849, in Lewis County, Ky. Joseph Robb, now living, is eighty years of age. He is a cousin to the Joseph Robb who served forty-four years as a circuit clerk of Lewis County.

PARKER, William M., the grandfather of this sketch, was born in Philadelphia, Pa., in 1752. He served in the Revolutionary War, and came to Lewis County, Ky., in 1802. He was married to Miss Mary Lisson, and settled on Quick's Run. He died in 1850, aged ninety-eight. His son, Daniel Parker, was born at Marietta, O., in 1796, and moved to Lewis County and married Miss Margaret Knox. He died in 1869. The subject of this sketch, W. M. Parker, was born October 7, 1828. He served as justice of the peace for eight years, and was notary public for sixteen years, and now, at the age of eighty-three, is enjoying good health, lives at Concord, and has never lived out of the county.

MOWER, Jacob P., was born in Pennsylvania about 1811, and came to Lewis County in 1834, and was married to Frances Fry, in 1836. To this union ten children were born, eight boys and two girls. He was an honored citizen of the precinct, and served as justice of the peace sixteen years. Three of the sons are now living, viz: David S., Samuel D., and J. L. P., who all now reside in Lewis County and in this precinct.

STONE, Thomas, father of Ezekiel Stone, was born in Virginia and came to Kentucky early in the last century, and after living one year on Big Sandy River, moved to Kinniconnick, near the mouth of the Laurel Fork. He was the father of a numerous family, and most all the Stones in this part of Kentucky are descendants of his.

DOYLE, John A., was born in Maryland November 16, 1762. He came to Kentucky about 1790 as one of Simon Kenton's spies. (See Collins' History, page 553.) He was married to Christen Davis, daughter of Nicholas N. Davis, who lived on the farm now owned by William Kissick, March 18, 1796. To this union were born nine children, four sons and five daughters, viz: Edward, John, David, and Nichelson; Rebecca, Nancy, Elizabeth, Susan, and Ann. In the year 1798 he went to the Indian War and served four years. He also served in the War of 1812, and died December 8, 1845.

BEVIN, John F.—James H. Bevin, the grandfather of the subject of this sketch, was born in Charles County, Md., in 1775, of English parents. He taught school for a number of years in Maryland. He emigrated to Mason County, Ky., about 1803, where he married Miss Mary Evans, November 22, 1807. He taught school in that county until 1820. He then bought a farm on Martin's Fork of Quick's Run, Lewis County, and moved to it the same year. His father died in Maryland about this time, and he fell heir to sixteen slaves, which were shipped to him. With this force a farm was soon cleared in the wilderness. His family numbered seven children, four boys and three girls, as follows: Harry W., Chloe, Elizabeth, Catherine, Benjamin D., Charles A., James T., Benjamin D., the father of the subject of this sketch, married Miss Jane Henderson, November 28, 1839. To this union were born six children, as follows: John F., Lonzo J., Richard B., Mary E., who died in infancy; Albert R., Andrew C. John F., the subject of this sketch, married Miss Charity Hampton, daughter of Squire John Hampton, September 29, 1859. To this union were born four children, as follows: Elizabeth J., Paris C., Cora A., and Ben R. Lizzie and Paris C. died single. Benjamin R. married Miss Olive Irvin, daughter of Squire

T. M. Irvin, of Martin, Ky. She taught in our public schools for a number of years, and now owns a store in Carrs, Ky. Cora A. married James D. Jackson, and they now live on the old Bevin homestead, on Martin's Fork. John F. and wife are still living at a ripe old age, surrounded by many comforts of life.

FITCH, John L., son of Benjamin and Olive Fitch, was born January 3, 1821. Mr. Fitch was one of the early pioneers and legislators, having served in the State Legislature in the early days of the county's history. He died May 15, 1859.

MAY, John, son of Thomas May, came to this county from Pennsylvania in 1792, and settled in Lewis County about the same year. He lived to the ripe age of ninety-one, and died September, 1874. Thomas May, father of John May, came to Lewis County and lived with his son until his death, in 1811.

FREEMAN, Daniel, and wife moved from New Jersey to Dark County, O., in the latter part of the eighteenth century. The romance connected with this couple differs so widely from the romances of the twentieth century, I think it will bear relating. At that time it was contrary to law for the young man to steal the girl. But as wit and schemes prevailed in those days as they do now, the young lady overcame that difficulty by stealing the young man. As in the days of our Puritan fathers, we see two seated on one horse, but the young man riding behind.

To this couple were born eight children. A. E. Freeman, a farmer resident of Lewis County, Ky., being one. He was born February 7, 1810, in Dark County, O. At the age of twenty-three he was married to Elizabeth Hoover, whom he met while she was visiting her brother, who lived near him. They moved to Lewis County, Ky., in 1844, where he practiced his trade of shoe making, until he was about forty years old. He then began to cultivate the soil, and to clear out the forests which then covered a great part of Lewis County. Through the aid of his good wife, and his son's perseverance, he acquired a large farm and some other real estate. To this union were born nine children, three of whom still live in Lewis County.

Elizabeth Freeman died at her home, near Trinity, Ky., May 9, 1891. A. E. Freeman then went to Boone County, where he spent the remainder of his days, these being comparatively few after the death of his wife. He died December 1, 1891. He was then brought back to Lewis County and placed beside his wife in the old Mower Cemetery.

HALBERT, Judge William C. (taken from "Johnson's History of Kentucky and Kentuckians"), who is the present incumbent of the office of judge of the Circuit Court of the Twentieth Kentucky District, is a lawyer of prominence and influence in Lewis County, Ky. He was born on a farm fourteen miles west of Vanceburg on the 25th of February, 1856, but his parents removing to Vanceburg six weeks after his birth, he has since that time made his home in Vanceburg, and has seen it grow from a hamlet of twelve houses to its present size and importance. In this growth Judge Halbert has taken and contributed an active and generous part, and, like his father, has ever been one of the most public-spirited and important factors in the growth of his native city.

Judge Halbert is a son of William C. Halbert and Lavinia A. Halbert, who were cousins. They were both born and reared in Lewis County, Ky., their parents on each side having been born in Bourbon County, this State, and their parents on each side having come from Culpeper County, Va., in the early settlement of Kentucky, to the central part of the present State of Kentucky. Isaac Halbert, the great-grandfather of Judge Halbert, was a native of Scotland, born not far from the English border or boundary line, from whence he came to Virginia prior to the Revolutionary War, settling first near Alexandria, in Fairfax County, where he married Elizabeth O'Daniel, and then moved to Culpeper County, in that State, where he continued to reside until he removed to Kentucky, in March, 1785. He served as a private soldier from Culpeper County in a Virginia regiment during the War of the Revolution. In March, 1785, as stated, Isaac Halbert emigrated to Kentucky, moving his family and household goods by land from Culpeper County, up the waters of the Potomac, to Pittsburg, and then, by what was known as a family or houseboat, he made his slow journey to what was then called Limestone, now Maysville, where he landed and took the old buffalo trail or road to Boonesborough station, or fort, where he lived for the next three years, and in which his eldest daughter, Catharine, and perhaps one of his sons, was born in May, 1787. In April, 1785, Isaac Halbert located and surveyed various tracts of land, by virtue of treasury warrants obtained by him from the State of Virginia, aggregating about three thousand acres. These lands were situated in the vicinity of the station, where he then lived, and are now in Bourbon, Clark, and Jessamine Counties, this State, but then in Fayette County, Va. Daniel Boone, then deputy surveyor of Fayette County, Va., surveyed one of these tracts of land for him, and his survey and plat are now on file in the records of the land office at Frankfort, Ky. He was a friend of Boone and Simon Kenton, and bore his part in the struggle to wrest the new country of his adoption from the Indians and to make it a State. In 1799 he purchased four thousand nine hundred acres of land on Salt Lick Creek, in what is now Lewis County, but was then Mason County, in this State; and in the winter of 1800 he erected a dwelling house on this land, at the forks of Salt Lick Creek, seven miles west of Vanceburg, and in the spring of 1801 he moved into this house, which was the third house built in what is now Lewis County. He continued to reside on this land until his death, in 1825, and he is buried in sight of his home, where he died. He was a member of the first petit jury that was ever impaneled in the Lewis Circuit Court, in July, 1807. His wife was born in Virginia, of Irish stock on both sides, and she survived her husband twenty-two years, dying in 1847, in her eighty-seventh year. Isaac and Elizabeth Halbert became the parents of nine sons and three daughters, all of whom reached maturity, and six of their sons served as volunteer soldiers in the War of 1812 in various Kentucky regiments; three of them were at the battle of the Thames, and one served as a marine on board of Perry's fleet in the memorable battle of Lake Erie. Stephen Halbert, grandfather of Judge Halbert, was one of these sons who responded promptly to the call of Governor Shelby and marched with him to the Thames and helped to end the war with honor and victory in that section of the Northwest Territory. Another of their sons became a member of the colony that settled in Texas in 1828, and received a league of land on the Brazos River from the Spanish Government for settling on it. He afterward served in the war between Mexico and Texas, and subsequently served as circuit judge in his adopted State.

Stephen Halbert, the paternal grandfather of Judge Halbert, was born in Bourbon County, Ky., in March, 1793, and came, with his parents, to Lewis County in the spring of 1801. He married Mary Cottingham in that county in April, 1813, who died in 1829, at the early age of thirty-two. She was born also in Bourbon County, the daughter of William Cottingham and his wife, Mary Johnson, who emigrated from Snow Hill, Worcester County, Md., and settled in Bourbon County in an early day.

He came from Ireland, or his parents did, and his wife came from England, or was of English descent. To Stephen Halbert and his wife, Mary Cottingham, were born eight children—five boys and three girls—and of this number, William C. Halbert, father of the Judge, was the second in order of birth. He was born in Lewis County on February 20, 1817, and was there reared to maturity on a farm. When barely of age he served as deputy sheriff of St. Francis County, Ark., for three years. Resigning this position on account of ill-health, he returned to Kentucky, and shortly after his return he was appointed acting sheriff of Lewis County (all the county officers being then appointed and not elected), and he continued to discharge the duties of sheriff, and without any deputy, for six years to the entire satisfaction of the court and the people. It is said that he never returned a warrant not executed if the person named in the warrant was in Lewis County; that he never summoned any one to help him arrest a person for whom he had a warrant, and that he never carried a pistol while acting as sheriff; and that he promptly collected and accounted for all public taxes and moneys that came or should have come to his hands as collector.

He read law, and was admitted to the bar in

1856, and then removed from his farm to Vanceburg, where he made his home and engaged in the active practice of his profession until his death, in September, 1877. He was elected and served as county attorney of Lewis County in 1862, and again in 1870, and served eight years in all. He was nominated in 1852 for State senator by the Whig party from the Fleming and Lewis District, but declined the nomination on account of ill-health. In 1865 he was nominated by the Democratic party for State senator from the Mason and Lewis District, and was elected and served four years. He declined a renomination from that party in 1869, on account of ill-health, and the demands of his private business. He was the leader of the Whig party in Lewis County from the time he acted as sheriff of the county until the demise of that party. He then became a member of the Democratic party, and continued the leader of it in Lewis County until his decease. He had a talent and a liking for politics, and could lead and organize his party as but few men could in his day, or since then, in Lewis County. He never drank, used tobacco, or gambled, was a strict member and an elder in his Church, and his one diversion was playing politics; but he never sought office for himself, and when he made a race at all he was drafted to help out his party and lead a forlorn hope, he having always belonged to the minority party in Lewis County. He was never defeated when he did run for office.

He was a very successful lawyer and enjoyed a wide reputation and large practice in Lewis County, where he was on one side of every important case tried in that county for years prior to his death. He procured the passage of the law that secured the removal of the county seat from Clarksburg to Vanceburg, and to his efforts almost alone does Vanceburg now enjoy the honor of being the county seat. He was the father of the turnpike road system and the bridge law of Lewis County, under which more than one hundred miles of turnpike were built and many bridges erected over all the main streams in the county. He gave the site for the court-house and jail to the county. He also gave the site for the Christian Church, of which he was an elder, in Vanceburg. He was a charter member of Polar Star Lodge, No. 363, F. & A. M., and of Burns Chapter, No. 74, of Vanceburg. He built the flouring mill in Vanceburg and many of the dwelling houses therein, and took an active and intelligent interest in building up the town, of which at one time he owned practically half the land in it.

Judge William C. Halbert was the fifth in

order of birth in a family of nine children, and he was six weeks old at the time his parents settled in Vanceburg, in April, 1856. He attended the public schools of Vanceburg, and for two years attended the National Normal School, at Lebanon, O. When seventeen years of age he began reading law under his father, and in May, 1874, when slightly over eighteen years of age, was admitted to the bar. In the fall of 1874 he returned to school at Lebanon, O., and remained there until June, 1875, when he returned home and began the active practice of his profession as a partner of his father, with whom he continued to practice until the death of his father, in September, 1877. For three terms he served as city attorney of Vanceburg, and in August, 1890, was elected county attorney of Lewis County; was re-elected in November, 1894, and again in November, 1897, serving until January, 1901. In November, 1905, he was elected to the Legislature and served two years as a member from Lewis County. He was a member of the committees on judiciary, criminal law, and amendments to the Constitution while in the Legislature, and took an active part in the deliberations of that body while one of its members. He declined to accept a re-nomination for the Legislature on account of the demands of his law business. In

November, 1909, he was nominated and elected without opposition as circuit judge of the Twentieth Judicial District for a term of six years, and is now discharging the duties of that office. In June, 1910, he was commissioned by the governor as special judge for the State-at-large, under an Act of the Legislature passed in March, 1910, and held by the Court of Appeals as constitutional.

In politics Judge Halbert is a Republican, of which party he has been one of the most active and faithful of its workers in Lewis County, and on the stump and at the polls has fought its battles earnestly and with great zeal, fidelity, and ability; but on the bench he has endeavored to forget politics and mete out the law to all regardless of politics. He has so far succeeded in this effort that he decided against the candidates of his party in election contests involving the offices of county judge and sheriff in Boyd County, in which much feeling was involved. His decisions in these cases were subsequently approved by the Court of Appeals. It can be truthfully said of Judge Halbert that he is well-equipped both by nature and legal training for the position he now holds, and that he has given very general satisfaction both in his own district and as special judge when called to act outside of his district. He is strictly fair, courteous to and patient with the humblest member of the bar, and has untiring industry and energy to clear up the dockets and congested litigation in his district.

Judge Halbert is a member of the Masonic order, holding membership in Polar Star Lodge, No. 363, F. & A. M.; Burns Chapter, No. 74, Royal Arch Masons; and Maysville Commandery, No. 10, Knights Templar. He is also a member of the Junior Order United American Mechanics of Vanceburg.

In April, 1887, Judge Halbert was united in marriage to Miss Fannie Bate, who was born in Newport, Campbell County, Ky., and who was a daughter of Samuel Bate, a successful wholesale merchant in Cincinnati during and prior to the Civil War. He was born in Cheshire County, England, in 1818, and emigrated to this country in 1839, settling in Cincinnati, where he married a descendant of one of the first settlers of that city, and for whom one of the streets there is now named. To this union five children were born, of whom four are now living, whose names are: William C., Jr., John Bate, Harlan R., and Frances A., the eldest being twenty and the youngest nine. Judge Halbert and his wife are members of the Christian Church in Vanceburg, to which his grandparents adhered under the preaching of Alexander Campbell, the founder of that Church."

"ORVILLE P. POLLITT (taken from "Johnson's History of Kentucky and Kentuckians), the present popular and efficient incumbent of the office of county clerk of Lewis County, Ky., is now serving his fourth term in office, and in discharging the duties thereto is acquitting himself with all of honor and distinction. Mr. Pollitt was born at Portsmouth, O., on the 18th of September, 1871, and he is a son of James and Lucy C. (Parker) Pollitt, both natives of Lewis County and both members of old Kentucky families. Alexander H. Pollitt, paternal grandfather of the subject of this review, was born and reared in Maryland, whence he came, with his parents, to Lewis County in an early day, location being made on a farm. James Pollitt studied law as a youth, and became an eminent practitioner of his profession in Lewis County and in Portsmouth, O. He was summoned to the life eternal at the age of forty-seven, his death having occurred at Portsmouth, in 1885. He served as judge of Lewis County for several terms immediately after the close of the Civil War, and was very prominent in public affairs during his lifetime. His widow, who still survives him, now maintains her home at Vanceburg. Mr. and Mrs. James Pollitt became the parents of two children, of whom Orville P. is the only one living in 1911.

"Mr. Pollitt of this review was a lad of but

fourteen years of age at the time of his father's death. He was reared to maturity at Portsmouth, his education consisting of such advantages as were afforded in the public schools of that place. He also attended school at Vanceburg, and after leaving school he worked on a farm for a short time. In 1888 he was appointed deputy clerk of Lewis County, remaining in tenure of that office until the fall of 1897, at which time he was elected county clerk, of which latter office he has continued incumbent during the intervening years to the present time, this being his fourth term in office. His administration has been characterized by good judgment and stanch devotion to the duties at hand, and it is worthy of note here that in the last election he met with no opposition in either the primaries or in the election proper.

"In politics Mr. Pollitt is a stanch advocate of the principles and policies for which the Republican party stands sponsor, and he has ever been an ardent supporter of all measures and enterprises projected for the good of the community. In a fraternal way he is affiliated with the Independent Order of Odd Fellows and the Junior Order of the United American Mechanics. In his religious faith Mr. Pollitt is a devout member of the Methodist Episcopal Church. He is unmarried."

JUDGE JOSEPH M. LEE (taken from Johnson's "History of Kentucky and Kentuckians.") —"Lewis County figures as one of the most attractive, progressive, and prosperous divisions of the State of Kentucky, justly claiming a high order of citizenship and a spirit of enterprise which is certain to conserve consecutive development and marked advancement in the material upbuilding of this section. The county is signally favored in the class of men who control its affairs in official capacity, and in this connection the subject of this review demands representation, as he is serving his county faithfully and well in a position of distinct trust and responsibility, being the present county judge, to which office he was first elected in 1901, and in which he has continued to serve with efficiency during the long intervening years to the present time, in 1911. Judge Lee has long been known as an enterprising agriculturist, and he is a man whose business methods demonstrate the power of activity and honesty in the industrial world.

"Joseph Marion Lee, of Vanceburg, was born on a farm in Morgan County, Ky., on the 8th of August, 1856, and he is a son of James Harrison and Armilda Jane (Hunt) Lee, the former of whom was a native of Rowan County, Ky., and the latter of whom claimed Mont-

JOSEPH M. LEE.

gomery County, this State, as the place of her nativity. James Lee, the great-grandfather of him whose name initiates this review, was born and reared in Virginia, and he traces his ancestry back to stanch Scotch-Irish stock. Early in the nineteenth century James Lee, with his family, emigrated from the Old Dominion Commonwealth to Kentucky, locating on a tract of land in Rowan County, where he was identified with agricultural pursuits during the remainder of his life. He became the father of a large family of children, of whom six sons settled in various parts of the old Blue Grass State and in Indiana. Of those sons, Louis Lee, grandfather of Joseph M. Lee, was born in Virginia, and he was a mere child at the time of his parents' removal to Kentucky. He was reared in Rowan County, where was solemnized his marriage and where he reared to maturity twelve out of a family of thirteen children—ten daughters and three sons. Of those children James H. Lee became the father of Joseph M. Lee. He was reared on the old parental homestead, and after his marriage he established his home in Morgan County. In 1863, during the strenuous days of the Civil War, he removed, with his family, to Sangamon County, Ill., traveling overland and carrying all the portable goods in a covered wagon, drawn by an ox-team. At that time Joseph M. Lee was a child of but seven years of age, and he walked most of the way, driving before him three cows. While in Illinois Mr. Lee, who was an ardent Union sympathizer, organized a company for service in the war, but after being mustered into the army his entire family was taken suddenly sick with the smallpox, and he was compelled to remain at home in the capacity of nurse. After the close of the war he returned to Kentucky, where he soon made permanent residence in Lewis County, where his death occurred in 1906, at the venerable age of seventy-five years. His widow survives him, and now resides near Petersville, Lewis County, at the age of seventy-five years. Mrs. Armilda Jane (Hunt) Lee is a very wonderful old woman. During the early years in Kentucky there were no doctors in the neighborhood, and quickly recognizing the urgent need for medical attendance, she took up the study of medicine and became a practitioner, following the same with great success for many years. Although now quite advanced in years, she still retains in much of their pristine vigor the splendid mental and physical powers of her youth. She is a woman of most-gracious personality, and is dearly beloved by all who have come within the sphere of her gentle influence. She was a daughter of

Joseph Hunt, a native of Montgomery County, his parents having been born in North Carolina, whence they came to Kentucky in the early pioneer days. Mr. and Mrs. James Harrison Lee became the parents of seven children— five boys and two girls, four of whom are living at the present time.

"Joseph Marion Lee was the second in order of birth in the family of seven children, and he was twelve years old when his parents located permanently in Lewis County. As a result of the ravages of the Civil War the family was very poor, and as Joseph M. was the oldest son, many important responsibilities fell upon him while he was still quite young. The father was a trader and was obliged to be absent from home for long periods, during which Joseph M. had charge of the work and management of the home farm. As his early years were taken up with hard work, he had little time for schooling. His education consisted principally of such training as could be gleaned from reading and experience. When he had attained to the age of nineteen years he was married, and thereafter he was engaged in farming on his own account. Subsequently he engaged in the buying and selling of stock and in tobacco trading. In 1882 he was elected magistrate of Petersville, serving for one term in that office, at the expiration of which he declined re-election. In the fall of 1901 he was elected county judge of Lewis County, and through successive re-elections he has continued incumbent of that position to the present time, acquitting himself most creditably in the discharge of the duties incident to the office. In politics he is aligned as a stalwart in the ranks of the Republican party, in the local councils of which he has been an active factor for many years. In a fraternal way he is affiliated with the Knights of Pythias, the Junior Order of the United American Mechanics, and with other social organizations of a representative character.

"In the year 1875 was solemnized the marriage of Judge Lee to Miss Margaret Aldridge, who was born in Wayne County, W. Va., and who is a daughter of Frank Aldridge, a skilled mechanic, who built a number of large steamboats. To Judge and Mrs. Lee have been born six children, namedly—Nancy J., Mary E., James F., Lennie B., Rosie A., and Thomas R. In their religious faith the Lee family are devout members of the Methodist Episcopal Church, and they hold a high place in the confidence and esteem of their fellow citizens."

"JUDGE GEORGE MORGAN THOMAS (taken from 'Johnson's History of Kentucky and

Kentuckians'), of Vanceburg, Lewis County, Ky., who is now living practically retired from active participation in business and professional affairs, long held prestige as one of the most brilliant lawyers in the State and as a politician

GEORGE MORGAN THOMAS.

of the first rank. In the many and varied political offices of which he was incumbent, he served his State with the utmost proficiency and with all the ardor inspired by a good cause. He is a fine old man, and one who is eminently well worthy of representation in this publication, devoted to Kentucky and Kentuckians.

"Judge Thomas was born on Salt Lick Creek, Lewis County, Ky., on the 23d of November, 1828, and he is a son of Elijah and Araminta P. (Boggess) Thomas, the former of whom was a native of Lewis County, and the latter of whom claimed Loudoun County, Va., as the place of her birth. George Thomas, grandfather of the judge, was born in Culpeper County, Va., in 1770, a son of Michael Thomas, the latter of whom was likewise a native of the old Dominion State, and who traced his ancestry back to stanch Welsh extraction. Michael Thomas was twice married, and became the father of fifteen children by his first and ten children by his second marriage. He died in Virginia, in 1799, and his widow, who long survived him, came to Kentucky, with representatives of the Thomas family, and she passed away in Lewis County at an advanced age. Michael Thomas gave valiant service as a soldier in the War of the Revolution, and he was a man of influence and prominence in public affairs in the community in which he maintained his home. Of his children by his second marriage, George Thomas was the oldest in order of birth, was reared in Virginia, and soon after his father's death he emigrated, with other members of the family, to Kentucky, sojourning about one year in Clark County, where he married. In

1801 he and his wife came to Lewis County and settled on Salt Lick Creek, he being founder of this branch of the family in Kentucky. In those early days the country was new, and he lived the pioneer life of the day and died in 1834, at the age of sixty-four years. He was one of the founders of the Christian Church in Lewis County, to whose doctrine the Thomas family have long been faithful. He built the first log church of that denomination on his farm, and he now lies buried in its churchyard. This church weathered the storms of many years, and was but recently razed. The widow of George Thomas, whose maiden name was Levina Schull, was a native of Clark County, Ky. Her mother was born in North Carolina, whence she came to Kentucky, her death having there occurred, in 1848, at the patriarchal age of one hundred and one years of age. She emigrated to this State as a member of the colony headed by Daniel Boone, and was at Bryant Station when that stockade was under siege by the Indians. She was a woman of strong and noble character, and was of much assistance in those strenuous, pioneer days, even leaving the fort to go to the spring after water, as the Indians were supposed not to shoot at women. George and Levina (Schull) Thomas became the parents of three sons and eight daughters, all of whom were reared to adult age in Lewis County, where they married and had large families. George Thomas and his brother Israel were gallant soldiers in the War of 1812.

"Elijah Hart Thomas, father of him to whom this sketch is dedicated, was the second in order of birth of the children of George Thomas, and his birth occurred in Lewis County, in 1804. He was reared on the old homestead farm, and, being the oldest son, early became identified with his father in the work and management of the estate. He was engaged in agricultural pursuits during practically his entire business career, and his death took place in 1883, at the home of his son, the Judge. His wife was a daughter of Captain Thomas Boggess, a native of Loudoun County, Va., and a captain in a Virginia regiment in the Revolutionary War. He was captured by the English and held prisoner on one of the islands of the West Indies for some time. After the close of the war he returned to his home State, and there was married to a Miss Smith, of Culpeper County, one of whose ancestors was at one time governor of Virginia. Captain Thomas Boggess removed, with his family, to Nicholas County, Ky., in 1814, and two years later he established his home in Lewis County, where he was summoned to eternal rest in 1832. In those early days he and his wife frequently made trips on horseback across the mountains of Virginia to visit relatives and friends. Araminta P. (Boggess) Thomas was born in 1801, and was a child of eight years at the time of her parents' removal to Kentucky. Her marriage to Elijah Thomas was recorded in 1826, and they became the parents of four children—three sons and one daughter, of whom Judge Thomas, of this review, is the only one living at the present time, in 1911. The mother died in 1863.

"Judge George M. Thomas was reared to the invigorating influences of the home farm, and his early educational training consisted largely of private instruction. He remained under the parental roof until he had attained to his legal majority, at which time he went to Clarksburg, where he was engaged in the pedagogic profession for a period of two years, in the meantime studying law during his leisure time. He was admitted to the bar of the State in 1851, and concerning his subsequent career as laywer, jurist, politician, and statesman extracts are taken from a review of his life made by Hon. Robert D. Wilson, at a banquet given by Judge Thomas to members of the Lewis County Bar, on June 4, 1901, to celebrate his retirement from active practice.

"George M. Thomas was born on November

27

23, 1828, on Salt Lick Creek, near the valley in Lewis County, educated in the common schools in the county—taught school, read law, and was admitted to the bar in 1851. Elected school commissioner in 1850, and served nine years. Elected county attorney in 1854, and served four years. Elected a member of the Kentucky Legislature in 1859, and re-elected in 1861. In 1862 elected Commonwealth attorney in the Tenth Judicial District, and served six years. Elected county judge in 1868, to fill a vacancy, and served two years. In 1871 nominated for lieutenant-governor by the Republican convention, and made a joint canvass of the State with Hon. John G. Carlisle. In February, 1872, elected a member of the Legislature, to fill a vacancy, and re-elected in 1873. In 1874 elected circuit judge, and served six years. Defeated for circuit judge in 1880, and in the same year was a candidate for Congress in the Ninth Congressional District, receiving eight hundred more votes in the district than General Garfield, candidate for President, but was defeated by Judge Phister. Was appointed, in 1881, United States District Attroney for Kentucky by President Garfield, and served for four years. In 1886 elected a member of Congress in the Ninth District by two hundred and eighty-six majority. In May, 1897, was appointed solicitor of Internal Revenue by President McKinley, and served four years, at the expiration of which he returned to Lewis County, and, after fifty years of professional and official work, retired from active labors. Judge Thomas, as he is familiarly known to almost every citizen of this section of our State, and to every politician of any note in the State, is a man who has been eminently successful as a lawyer of recognized ability, a judge of strict integrity and sound judgment, and one who delivered the judicial ermine to his successor in office without spot or blemish. In every position of honor or trust to which he has been called he gave his time, his energy, his unceasing zeal, and almost unerring judgment to the work incident to the office. Although a man of delicate health, yet by his strong will in governing his appetite and in dieting himself, he has, no doubt, been able to accomplish a vast deal more than many men of rugged and robust health. One of his mottoes has been: 'Nothing succeeds like success.' How applicable this trite saying has been to his remarkable career!

"Teaching school, as nearly all our great men do in their early careers, reading law at odd times until, at the age of twenty-three, he was admitted to the bar, and, as heretofore shown, what a record is his from that day

until the present time! In all these years of
arduous toil his energy never lagged, his vigilance
for the welfare of his clients never ceased, and
he was a doer—not a dreamer. If one was
called to the court-house in the early morning
he would find the Judge there reading the orders
of the previous day. He would not rely on the
clerk to see that the orders were promptly entered, for he knew the clerk to be often over-
worked during the short time our courts are in
session. He has often said that his client was
paying him, and not the clerk, to see that the
work was properly and efficiently done. In
all the long years he was an active practitioner
no one who ever knew his unfaltering devotion
to his clients' interests ever whispered that he
wavered or faltered in doing all that the require-
ments of the profession demanded at his hands
to advance and protect the rights of his client.
He was never found occupying the anomalous
position of representing two clients whose interests were antagonistic. His career has demonstrated that one of the old ideas "that a
good lawyer could not be a good financier" is
untrue. For in this respect he has shown
himself to be a financier of no mean ability,
although not trying to become a Rockefeller
or a Pierpont Morgan. As a judge of human
nature it is conceded that he is not excelled by

many. This has been often demonstrated in the court-room, much to the discomfiture of opposing counsel. As a historian, I do not believe there is a man in Lewis County or Eastern Kentucky who has read more extensively, and retained what he read, better than the Judge. His memory at this late date is apparently as good as when he was in the prime of life, and then none possessed a better memory for facts or events. As a politician, it is conceded by those who know him, and who have suffered from the 'solar plexus blows' he was able to deliver, that he is unsurpassed by any members of either party in the State.

"On the 8th of July, 1850, was solemnized the marriage of Judge Thomas to Miss Catherine Willim, the ceremony having been performed at Clarksburg, this county. Mrs. Thomas is a native of Clarksburg, where she was born in 1831, and she is a daughter of Harry and Mary Wallace (Purnell) Willim, the former of whom was a native of Staffordshire, England, and the latter of whom was born near Snow Hill, Maryland. Mrs. Thomas' parents were married in Union County, Ky., in 1819, and in 1825 they removed to Lewis County, where they passed the residue of their lives and where their deaths occurred, in 1867. Mr. and Mrs. Thomas became the parents of three children, one of

whom died in infancy. Bruce Fraser was born
on the 20th of April, 1851, and died January 2,
1882. He studied law, was admitted to the bar,
and practiced his profession as a partner of his
father, until his death. He was graduated in
Miami University, at Oxford, O., and at the
time of his demise was survived by a wife and
two children. Walter William Thomas was
born September 1, 1853, and died September
25, 1854. The third and only living child is
Araminta, whose birth occurred on the 25th
of July, 1855. She is now the wife of Judge
Pugh, of this city. Judge and Mrs. Thomas
have five grandchildren and nine great-grand-
children.

"As already noted, Judge Thomas was active
in business and professional affairs for fully
half a century, during which time he has aided
materially in the upbuilding of his home city
and of the State at large. He is the owner of
considerable valuable property in Lewis County,
and has constructed several of the best business
blocks at Vanceburg. In addition to his other
interests, he is an extensive stockholder in the
Citizens' Bank of Vanceburg. In a fraternal
way he is affiliated with the Masonic order,
with which he has been connected since 1859.
Politically, he is a stanch Republican, and it
may be said without fear of contradiction that

no man in Kentucky has done more for the good of the party and more for the general welfare of the State than has Judge Thomas. He is a man of broad and generous thoughts, of high ideals and untarnished morals, a man whose entire life record will bear the searchlight of closest investigation, and one whose career may well serve as lesson and incentive to the younger generation. The splendid and almost unequaled record made by Judge Thomas in the service of his county, his district, his State, and the Nation is highly appreciated by all who are familiar with it."

"ROBERT DYE WILSON (taken from 'Johnson's History of Kentucky and Kentuckians') is an eminently successful and popular attorney at Vanceburg, Lewis County, Ky., where, through well-applied energy, unflagging determination and perseverance in the active affairs of life, he has won a high place for himself in the confidence and esteem of his fellow citizens. Mr. Wilson was born on a farm in the western part of Lewis County, the date of his nativity being September 18, 1855. He is a son of George F. and Sallie A. (Wells) Wilson, the former of whom was likewise a native of Lewis County and the latter of whom claimed Mason County, Ky., as the place of her birth. Representatives of the Wilson family were numbered among the pioneers of Kentucky, and they figured prominently in the history of the American Colonies, different ones having served as valiant soldiers in the War of the Revolution and in the War of 1812. John Wilson, great-grandfather of him whose name initiates this review, and George Wilson, his brother, were born in Washington County, Pa., whence they came to Kentucky, in 1795. They laid the first land warrant in the western part of Lewis County, on Crooked Creek, the same being for a tract of twelve square miles of land, extending three miles along the bank of the Ohio River and four miles back from the river. Soon after they had laid this warrant one Samuel Beal laid claim to the tract by right of a grant from King George III, of England. The controversy, however, was settled in favor of the Wilson brothers. The two oldest sons of John Wilson, Samuel and George, settled within one mile of each other on this tract, both becoming the fathers of large families and both being very prosperous and influential citizens in this section of the county. Of them, Samuel Wilson was the grandfather of Robert D., of this review. He had ten children, of whom George F. Wilson, father of Robert D., was the fifth in order of birth. George F. Wilson was identified with agricultural pursuits during the major portion of his active business career, was an active and devout member of the Christian Church, and he died on his home farm at the age of seventy-five years. His wife, who passed away about 1900, lived to the venerable age of eighty years. She was a daughter of John S. Wells, whose plantation was located four miles distant from Maysville. The Wells family were early settlers in Kentucky, the original progenitor of the name in this State having been a native of Pennsylvania. To George F. Wilson and his wife were born nine children, of whom but two are living in 1911. One son, John Samuel, was a member of the Fourth Kentucky Volunteer Mounted Cavalry in the Civil War, and he was one of the four or five who made their escape from capture in Georgia, all the rest of the company being taken prisoners.

"Robert Dye Wilson was the sixth in order of birth in the above-mentioned family of nine children, and he was reared on the home farm, his preliminary educational training consisting of such advantages as were afforded in the public schools of this county. Subsequently he attended Professor Smith's Academy, at Maysville, and he also pursued a course of study at Center College, at Danville, Ky. Prior to graduating from his collegiate course he was obliged to give up study on account of trouble with his eyes. In 1882, however, he was elected clerk of Lewis County on the Democratic ticket, he being the first Democratic county clerk to be elected after the war. In 1893 he was appointed master commissioner of the Circuit Court of Lewis County, remaining incumbent of that position for the ensuing fifteen years. In 1897 he was candidate on the Democratic ticket to represent his district in the State Legislature, but met defeat by a small vote in a largely Republican county. While county clerk he began the study of law, and he was admitted to the bar of the State in 1889, after which he immediately entered upon the active practice of his profession at Vanceburg. For three years he was a lay partner of W. C. Halbert, present circuit judge. He has been identified with the work of his chosen vocation for more than a score of years, and during that time has won for himself an enviable place as an eminently skilled lawyer and as a business man whose methods have ever been of the most honorable and straightforward order. In addition to his legal work, he is deeply interested in various industrial concerns in the vicinity of Vanceburg. He was largely responsible for the establishment of the button factory at Vanceburg, the same employing a force of sixty men at the present time, and he also helped to organize and is one-third owner of the spoke factory, which is doing a most prosperous business at Pikeville, Ky., employing fifty men.

"As already intimated, Mr. Wilson is a stanch Democrat in his political convictions, and he has ever manifested a deep and sincere interest in all matters projected for the good of the general public. He is an active politician and has done much to advance the interests of his party in this section of the State. Fraternally he has passed through the circle of York Rite Masonry, holding membership in Only Hope Lodge, No. 363, Free and Accepted Masons; Burns Chapter, No. 74, Royal Arch Masons; and Maysville Commandery, No. 10, Knights Templar. In his religious faith he is a devout member of the Christian Church, while his wife is a zealous Presbyterian.

"On the 23d of May, 1892, was recorded the marriage of Mr. Wilson to Miss Margaret M. Ingrim, who was born and reared at Vanceburg and who is a daughter of the late John C. Ingrim, long a prominent business man in this city. No children have been born to the union."

"MR. GEORGE T. WILLIM (taken from 'Johnson's History of Kentucky and Kentuckians') was born on a farm near Vanceburg, on the 4th of October, 1874, and he is a son of Thomas H. and Melissa R. (McKellep) Willim, both of whom were born and reared in Lewis County, Ky. Harry Willim, grandfather of him to whom this sketch is dedicated, was a native of England, whence he emigrated to the United States as a young man. He brought with him a large stock of queensware from England, intending to engage in business in New York City, but the ship on which he took passage was wrecked and everything on board was lost, the passengers being compelled to swim ashore. Traveling overland to Virginia, Harry Willim went down the Ohio River on a boat to Kentucky, and it was on this trip that he met his future wife. Subsequently he settled in Lewis County, at the old county seat of Clarksburg, where he operated a tannery for several years. Later he disposed of that business and purchased a tract of timber land, where he erected and operated a sawmill for many years. He died on his farm, near Clarksburg, in August, 1867. He and his wife, whose maiden name was Mary Wallace Bishop, became the parents of six children—four boys and two girls—of whom Thomas H., father of George T., was the fifth in order of birth. Thomas H. Willim was reared to adult age on the home farm, which he later inherited and on which he continued to reside during the residue of his life, his death having occurred in 1895. He married Melissa R. McKellup, who survives her honored husband, and who now maintains her home at Valley, Ky., and to this union were born nine children, seven of whom are living in 1911.

"Seventh in order of birth of his parents' nine children, George T. Willim grew up on the old paternal homestead and he received his preliminary educational training in the district schools, later supplementing that discipline by a course of study in Riverside Seminary, at Vanceburg, Ky., and by a commercial course at Nelson's Business College, at Cincinnati, O.

"When twenty years of age he secured a position as bookkeeper in the Deposit Bank at Vanceburg, and he continued incumbent of that position until the organization of the Citizens' Bank, in 1903, since which time he has been connected with the same, first as cashier and since 1907 as president, as previously noted. In politics Mr. Willim is aligned as a stalwart supporter of the principles of the Republican party. He is a former member of the Vanceburg city council, and in 1909 he was honored by the Fiscal Court with election to the office of treasurer of Lewis County. He is acquitting himself most creditably in discharging the duties

incident to his present office, and he is also
trustee of the jury fund. Mr. Willim is a man of
fine intelligence and extraordinary executive
and financial ability, and in all his business and
personal transactions he is widely known as a
man of honorable and straightforward conduct.
He is affiliated with various fraternal and social
organizations of representative character, and
his religious faith is in harmony with the teach-
ings of the Methodist Episcopal Church, while
his wife is a devout member of the Christian
Church.

"In July, 1898, Mr. Willim was united in
marriage to Miss Emma Jones, who is a native
of Lewis County and who is a daughter of Rufus
N. and Sallie (Voiers) Jones, the former of whom
was long a prominent business man at Vanceburg. No children have been born to Mr. and
Mrs. Willim."

"ULYSSES CRAVENS THOROUGHMAN (taken
from 'Johnson's History of Kentucky and Kentuckians') was born in Lewis County, Ky., on
the 12th of March, 1865, and he is a son of
George W. and Nancy (Bonham) Thoroughman,
the former of whom was likewise born in Lewis
County, and the latter of whom was a native
of Fleming County, Ky. The Thoroughman
family is one of old standing in the Blue Grass

State. It is said that three brothers of the name, natives of Virginia, in the latter part of the eighteenth or early nineteenth century, followed the tide of Westward emigration, two going to Ohio and one to Kentucky. The latter settled in the vicinity of May's Lick, Mason County, this State, and there made a home, was married, and reared a family. Of his offspring William Thoroughman, grandfather of him to whom this sketch is dedicated, was born near May's Lick about the year 1808. As a young man he came to Lewis County and established a home on Cabin Creek, eventually acquiring a large plantation, which he reclaimed from the wilderness, and he gained recognition as a man of prominence and influence in this section of the State. He married a Miss Ginn, a daughter of Isaac Ginn, an early settler in this county, and to them were born four sons and one daughter, who grew to maturity, and four children who died in infancy. After the death of his first wife Mr. Thoroughman married Miss Mary Blanton, by whom he had eight children—four boys and four girls. William Thoroughman was summoned to the life eternal in 1892, at the age of eighty-four years, and his widow, who still survives him, now maintains her home in Ribolt, Ky.

"Of the children by William Thoroughman's

first marriage, George W. was the third in order of birth, and he became the father of Ulysses C., of this review. George W. Thoroughman was reared to adult age on the homestead farm, where his birth occurred on the 1st of April, 1842. He continued as an inmate of the parental home until he had attained the age of nineteen years, at which time he was married, after which he located on a farm of his own in this county, to the conduct of which he devoted his attention for the remainder of his life. He died in 1905. His wife, who was called to her reward in April, 1885, in her thirty-seventh year, was a daughter of Nehemiah Bonham, who was for a number of years an expert cooper in Fleming County. When the Civil War was precipitated upon a divided Nation Mr. Bonham went to Ohio and enlisted in a Union regiment as a bugler. He was lost track of, and it is supposed that he lost his life while in service. Mr. and Mrs. George W. Thoroughman became the parents of three children, two of whom died in infancy, Ulysses C. being the only one to attain to years of maturity.

"Ulysses Cravens Thoroughman was reared to the invigorating influences of the home farm, in the work and management of which he early began to assist his father. He received but limited educational advantages in his youth, such training as he did receive consisting of attendance in a crude log schoolhouse, which was but meagerly furnished with mere slabs for seats. Later he gained some private instruction, for which he raised potatoes as tuition. Mr. Thoroughman himself states that much of his preliminary education was received under the old apple tree at home, where he used to read all the books which came into his possession. From earliest youth he was ambitious for an education, farming being particularly distasteful to him. Subsequently he had occasion to attend school for a short time at Tollesboro, and still later he pursued a course of study at the Vanceburg Normal School. In due time he secured a third-class teacher's certificate, and, armed with that, he began to teach, at the age of twenty years. He was most successfully engaged in the pedagogic profession in Lewis County for a period of fifteen years, in the meantime studying law with William Fitch, at Vanceburg. He was admitted to the bar of the State in 1891, but continued to teach school until the spring of 1902, at which time he became a candidate for nomination on the Republican ticket for the office of county attorney of Lewis County: After a closely contested primary, he received the nomination by a majority of sixty-seven votes in Lewis County. His opponent was the former county attorney and is, at present (1911), judge of the Circuit Court. Mr. Thoroughman has been twice re-elected to the position of county attorney, and he is now serving his third term in that office, his last election having occurred in the fall of 1909, without opposition for nomination or in election. In politics he endorses the cause of the Republican party, and he has ever manifested a keen interest in public affairs. He is an active politician, and has made many campaign canvasses for himself and friends in this section of the State. He is very popular and influential as a citizen, and no business man in Lewis County holds a higher place in the confidence and esteem of his fellowmen than does Mr. Thoroughman. He is a man of brilliant mental attainments, and is well-learned in the minutia of the law. He has participated in many important litigations in the State and Federal Courts, and holds distinctive prestige as an able and versatile trial lawyer and as a well-fortified counselor.

"Mr. Thoroughman has been twice married, his first union having been to Miss Hattie Shaw, in 1892. She was a native of Lewis County, where she was reared and educated and where she was a popular and successful teacher in the public schools prior to her marriage. She was a daughter of the late Richard H. Shaw, a farmer and tanner. No children were born to this union. After the death of his first wife, which occurred in 1903, Mr. Thorouhgman was united in marriage, in 1908, to Miss Tacie G. Jones, who was born in Ohio but who was reared in Lewis County, Ky. Mr. and Mrs. Thoroughman have one son, Walter Grave.

"Fraternally Mr. Thoroughman is affiliated with the time-honored Masonic order, in which he holds membership in Blue Lodge, No. 363, Free and Accepted Masons; and Burns Chapter, No. 73, Royal Arch Masons. He is also connected with the Woodmen of the World and the Junior Order of the United American Mechanics. In religious faith his wife is a devout member of the Christian Church at Vanceburg, and they are popular and prominent in connection with the best social activities of the community."

"GEORGE W. STAMPER (taken from 'Johnson's History of Kentucky and Kentuckians').— Vigor, enterprise, and persistency—these are the qualities which make for success and these are the characteristics which have dominated the career of George W. Stamper, who, through his own efforts, built the ladder by which he has climbed to affluence. He has been identified with farming, blacksmithing, merchandising, lumbering, and banking, and in each of these enterprises his success has been on a parity with his well-directed endeavors. He has also been an important factor in connection with public utilities, and as a citizen he holds a high place in the confidence and esteem of his fellowmen.

"George Washington Stamper was born on a farm in Lewis County, Ky., on the 26th of December, 1850, and he is a son of George W. and Catherine (Dyer) Stamper, the former of whom was a native of North Carolina and the latter of Morgan County, Ky. John Stamper, grandfather of him whose name initiates this review, was born, reared, and married in North Carolina, and in the early '20s he emigrated to Kentucky, locating on the Kentucky River, in Wolfe County, where he engaged in farming. He and his wife, whose maiden name was Sallie Stamper, and who was a cousin of her husband, raised a family of ten children, most of whom were born in Kentucky. The father of George W., Jr., was the first born, and he was an infant at the time of his parents' removal to the Blue Grass State. When he was fifteen years of age the family home was established in Carter County, and there he grew to manhood, married, and, in 1845, engaged in agricultural pursuits on a farm near Olive Hill, Lewis County. He was very industrious, an excellent farmer and business man, and in due time he accumulated a competency. About 1865 he opened a store on his farm, continuing to be identified with the general merchandise business for the ensuing twenty-five years. His death occurred on his old homestead in 1905, at the venerable age of eighty-two years. He was a stalwart Democrat in his political convictions, and he served for several years as justice of the peace. His wife was summoned to eternal rest in 1898, at the age of sixty-eight years. She was a daughter of Francis Dyer, of Morgan County, Ky. Mr. and Mrs. George W. Stamper became the parents of twelve children—five boys and seven girls— nine of whom are living in 1911, and of the number the subject of this review was the third in order of birth.

"George Washington Stamper, Jr., passed his youth in a manner similar to that of the farmer boy of that day, attending the district school during the winter months and working on the home farm during the summer seasons. When he had attained to the age of sixteen years he entered his father's store, where he learned the details of general merchandising, and he continued an inmate of the parental home until he had reached his legal majority. Thereafter he worked in a blacksmith shop for a time, and was engaged in farming on his own account for a couple of years, at the expiration of which he started a general store on a small scale on Grassy Creek. This store, which he still owns and operates, has been doing business for the past thirty-five years. For thirty-three years Mr. Stamper was the able incumbent of the office of postmaster at Head of Grassy, and he was one of the oldest postmasters, in point of continuous service, in this section of the State. He also became interested in the timber business while located on Grassy Creek, and he was for many years engaged in the stave business and in other enterprises most successfully. In 1888 he established his residence at Vanceburg, and in the following year he organized the Stamper Stave & Lumber Company, which carried on an extensive trade for nine years, at the expiration of which that firm was dissolved and Mr. Stamper continued in the lumber business in partnership with his brother, Joshua Stamper. Two years later, in 1900, he became a member of the firm of Johnson & Stamper, the same engaging in the railway tie business, getting out railway ties at various points in this section of the State. This business is now controlled by Johnson & Stamper, who are successors to the Elliott Tie Company, which conducts its operations on the Little Sandy River. The annual output of this concern is from two hundred thousand to five hundred thousand ties.

"In September, 1889, Mr. Stamper laid the foundation of his present large mercantile establishment at Vanceburg by opening a general store in one room. This concern has grown to such gigantic proportions that it now occupies space equivalent to nine ordinary storerooms, the stock consisting of everything found in a modern department store, except hardware. All Mr. Stamper's successes are due to his indefatigable energy and great business ability, and it is no exaggeration to say that he is one of the greatest hustlers in the State. In addition to his other interests he owns several fine farms in the Ohio valley, and he has extensive real estate holdings in Vanceburg, where he has constructed a number of residences and the majority of the business block he now occupies. He was one of the organizers of the Deposit Bank at Vanceburg, of which he is president at the present time and in which he is one of the heaviest stockholders. At the time of the building of the local electric plant he was elected president of that corporation, of which position he is still incumbent. He is a man of tremendous vitality and most extraordinary executive capacity. Beginning with practically nothing in the way of worldly goods, he grasped his opportunities as they appeared, and made of success not an incident, but a logical result. To-day he is recognized as one of the biggest financiers in Eastern Kentucky, and his fair and honorable methods in all his business dealings have gained to him the highest regard of his fellow-citizens.

"Mr. Stamper is a loyal Democrat in his political proclivities, but he has not had much time for political activity, having been a member of his first convention in 1910, at which time his influence was felt in no slight degree. In the Masonic order he has passed through the circle of the York Rite branch, holding membership in Polar Star Lodge, No. 363, Free and Accepted Masons; and Maysville Commandery, No. 10, Knights Templar. He and his wife are devout members of the Christian Church, to whose charities and benevolences he has ever been a liberal contributor and in whose faith his children have been reared.

"In 1862 was solemnized the marriage of Mr. Stamper to Miss Sophia W. Stafford, a native of Carter County, and a daughter of Sylvester Stafford, a farmer who served in the Union Army in the Civil War and who died in service. Mr. and Mrs. Stamper have eight children, namely—Rebecca, Cinda, William J., James E., Cora Mae, Julia, Bessie L., and Marie, all of whom were born in Lewis County and all of whom were afforded excellent educations."

SAMUEL POLLITT was born at Tollesboro, this county, in 1862, and spent his early life on the farm. At the age of seventeen he commenced to drive teams, and has been associated with the horse business ever since. At the age of twenty he commenced to drive an omnibus

SAMUEL POLLITT.

between Tollesboro and Maysville, which occupation he followed for fifteen years, having been in the same business between Germantown and Maysville for three years of this time. While in this business Mr. Pollitt made hundreds of friends, who will forget him only after they have answered the last roll call. In 1898 he

came to Vanceburg and has since been closely
identified with its business interests, and has
conducted his business in such a manner that
he enjoys the respect and esteem of all who
know him. Since coming to Vanceburg he has

A. J. STEIN.

been honored by election as school trustee and
city councilman, and many other offices in the
gift of the people of Vanceburg.

MR. A. J. STEIN was born and educated in
Germany, coming to this country in 1877 and
locating at Catlettsburg, where he learned the
tanner's trade and became associated with his

father in that business there, conducting successfully the largest plant in Catlettsburg for sixteen years. He came to Vanceburg in 1893 and took charge of the Buckhorn Tannery, and has built up a large circle of friends and an everincreasing business. He is the principal stockholder in our local telephone system, and the various telephone systems over the county, and the public can thank him alone for being instrumental in the development of that great convenience in our city and county.

That he is respected and honored by our people is shown by the fact that he was twice elected to the office of city council, in which office he showed so much ability in the management of municipal affairs that he has since been elected mayor of our city.

He is a member of the Masonic fraternity and has attained the Mystic Shriner Degree. He is director in the Deposit Bank, and is a prime mover in every movement which is made to benefit the business interests of Vanceburg.

J. LOUIS ROWSEY, the subject of this sketch, was born November 19, 1864, at Cedar Grove, Rockbridge County, Va. His work was in a construction crew on a railroad, and he worked in that capacity in several different sections of the country, being employed at one time on

the C. & O., between Augusta and Wellsburg.
He came to Vanceburg from Georgetown, Ky.,
on February 23, 1894, and was working life insurance at that time. He continued in the insurance business for about a year after he came
to Vanceburg, and then opened a photograph
gallery in the Alden Building, on the corner of
Third and Market Streets. He moved his
gallery to his present quarters, two doors north,
in 1903, and now has one of the nicest arranged
and best-equipped studios in the State. Mr.
Rowsey is a first-class artist in his line, and has
taken several freak pictures that have gained the
attention of the large city daily papers. There
is no class of work in the way of photography
which he is not prepared to do and do well.
He enjoys a fine business and has hard work
keeping up with his orders.

W. T. COOPER was born September 27,
1857, on Kinniconnick. His early life was spent
on the farm and in teaming. In 1890 he went to
Osgood, Ind., and engaged in the livery business.
He remained there about five months and then
returned to Vanceburg. He then went into the
business of logging for J. K. Valley, and then
hauling lumber and merchandise for Houghton
& Sweet and lumber and logs for John Bidell,
hauling one log for him from Salt Lick sixty

feet long and thirty inches at top with ten mules. After that he went into the livery business in the old Front Street stable, which was destroyed by fire several years ago. He is director in the Lewis County Fair Association, and is ever ready to take part in an undertaking for the betterment of Vanceburg.

DR. J. M. WELLS is one of twelve children born to Wm. W. and Matilda Wells, in Nicholas County, Ky., near the town of Mt. Olivet. There were two boys by a former marriage, which, added to the other twelve, makes fourteen children in all—seven boys and seven girls. Of the boys three became physicians and two ministers of the gospel. Dr. Wells received his education in Nicholas County, Ky., and Clermont County, O. He graduated from the Eclectic Medical Institute, of Cincinnati, February 23, 1877, and was married March 8, 1877. He located at Milford, Bracken County, Ky., where he practiced his profession for two and one-half years. Upon solicitation he moved to Vanceburg on November 10, 1879, and is to-day one of our most prosperous and successful physicians. He has always been prominent in Church and social circles, and enjoys the confidence of a host of friends. He is an elder of the Church of Christ, and has been a Christian

for many years. He is a member of the Kentucky Medical Association, the Cincinnati Eclectic Medical Society, the Alumni of the Eclectic Medical Institute, the National Eclectic
Medical Association, and honorary member of

J. M. WELLS.

the Wisconsin State Eclectic Medical Association, and secretary of the Board of Pensions of
Lewis County, and is coroner of Lewis County
at present.

He has contributed numerous articles to
the various medical journals which have given
him a national reputation among Eclectic phy-

sicians. It is said of Dr. Wells that "he is a man of strong convictions and stands firm for that he believes is right."

R. C. POLLITT was born at Rectorville, Mason County, Ky., May 10, 1869. He was raised on a farm until he reached the age of twenty, when he went into the music business in Maysville. After staying there six months he went to Ripley, O., and followed the same business for three years. He then went to Muncie, Ind., and remained the same length of time before coming to Vanceburg, in 1894. He has since made his headquarters here, and has sold a large number of pianos and organs in Lewis County and adjoining counties.

WIN PARKER BOWMAN, of Vanceburg, Ky., was born at Tollesboro, Lewis County, Ky., June 7, 1876. His father and mother, Dr. William Bowman and Maggie J. Bowman, both came from Brown County, O.

Win Bowman was educated at the common schools of Tollesboro, and at fifteen years of age was employed in the United States Consular Service, at Tientsen, China. Returned to Kentucky in 1893. He taught in the public schools of Lewis County till 1901, when he went to New York and served as a nurse in Bellevue

Hospital, but gave up the nursing business as too confining and returned to Lewis County, in 1902. Later he was employed by the Prudential Life Insurance Co., at Dayton, O. In June of 1904 he again located in Lewis County

WIN PARKER BOWMAN.

at Vanceburg, here he established an insurance office. He has put large energy into his work, and now enjoys the income of an extensive insurance business.

Mr. Bowman is not only a successful business man, but a Church man as well, holding

the position of local preacher in the Methodist
Episcopal Church, doing earnest, honest service
in the Church of his choice. His membership
is in First Methodist Episcopal Church, Vanceburg, Ky.

ELLSWORTH REGENSTEIN.—Among the sons
of Lewis County who in early manhood have
risen to distinction is Ellsworth Regenstein,
formerly State Superintendent of Public Instruction. He was born at McKenzie, near
the Mason County line, December 4, 1874. He
is the youngest of four brothers. His father,
John H. Regenstein, was the only son of John
H. Regenstein, Sr., who was of German blood,
but was born in London, England, in 1785, and
came to America with his parents in 1789. The
family settled in Virginia, near Mt. Vernon,
the home of Washington. At the age of twenty-
one John H. Regenstein, Sr., moved to Kentucky, and settled at Limestone, now Maysville. A few years later he moved to Lewis
County, purchased land and built the handsome
old country home where John H. Regenstein, Jr.,
and his children were born, and which is still
in the possession of the family. John H. Regenstein, Jr., was married in 1860, to Miss Susanna
Belle Moffett, a neighbor girl, who became
the mother of the subject of this sketch. She

29

was the daughter of a Virginia family of English blood, that crossed the Alleghenies in pioneer days and settled near Ripley, Brown County, O., but soon moved to Kentucky, the haven then for Virginia settlers. Of the six children

ELLSWORTH REGENSTEIN.

born to this couple, Henry L., Omar M., and Maurice E. are prosperous Lewis County farmers; Anna B. is a teacher in the schools at Ft. Thomas, Ky., and Clara, another daughter, died in her sixth year.

When Ellsworth was fourteen years of age his father died, and while the farm yielded a comfortable living for the family, there was not sufficient income to give the children an education beyond the country school. But in his boyhood Ellsworth determined on a professional career, and by means of the training he received at the little country school and by home study, he prepared himself to pass a teacher's examination, and at eighteen years of age taught his first school at Pence's Station, near Concord. He taught three years in Lewis County, and was then elected principal of the school at Helena, in Mason County. Within three more years he had established such a reputation as a teacher in Mason that the board of education of Maysville elected him principal of the first district school of that city. He held this position for three years with such success that the board promoted him to the principalship of the high school. He held this position two years, and was then elected to the principalship of the Newport high school. After serving two years in this capacity, the Newport board promoted him to the superintendency, which position he held four years. While he was superintendent of the Newport schools, State Superintendent of Public Instruction J. G. Crabbe appointed him to the State Board of Examiners, which position he filled during Superintendent Crabbe's term of office. At the close of the second year of his term, Superintendent Crabbe resigned to accept the presidency of the Eastern Kentucky Normal School, and Governor Willson appointed Mr. Regenstein to fill the office for the two years of the unexpired term.

By his own efforts Mr. Regenstein acquired the education which enabled him to fill the position which he has held. The money earned while teaching in the Lewis County schools was spent at the close of each five months' term in attending the County Normal School, at Vanceburg, and the State College, at Lexington. While teaching in Mason County and in Maysville he spent the summer months at the Northern Indiana Normal, the Northern Ohio University, and the University of Chicago. In 1903 the Northern Ohio University conferred on him the degree of Bachelor of Arts, and in 1905 this institution made him a Master of Arts. He passed a successful examination in 1899 for a State certificate, and in 1906 for a State diploma. At the annual Commencement, in June, 1911, the State University, at Lexington, conferred on him the degree of Doctor of Laws.

Although an eminently successful schoolman, Mr. Regenstein's great ambition from boyhood was to practice law. While a teacher in the country schools he purchased Blackstone and read both volumes through several times. While a teacher in Maysville he read law with L. W. Galbreath, a brilliant young attorney, who died in 1906. After locating in Newport he entered the McDonald Night Law School, took the complete course, and graduated with the degree of Bachelor of Laws. He was admitted to the bar in 1907. On retiring from the office of State Superintendent of Public Instruction, he engaged in the practice of law at Newport, and is one of the leading attorneys at the Campbell County bar.

In 1904, before leaving Maysville, Mr. Regenstein was married to Miss Marian Wormald, an attractive daughter of one of Mason County's oldest and best known families. She is a great-granddaughter of Judge Lewis Collins, the Kentucky historian. The couple immediately took up their residence in Newport. They have two children, Elizabeth and Ellsworth, Jr.

Mr. Regenstein is a vestryman in St. Paul's Episcopal Church, of Newport, and is a prominent member of the leading business and social organizations of his city. In politics he is a Republican, but liberal in his political views. As State Superintendent he appointed a nonpartisan board of examiners, and did much in many ways to remove the schools from politics.

He is a skillful debater, and has a State-wide reputation as a public speaker. While his father was a man of strong character and of high standing in his community, Mr. Regenstein attributes his success in life chiefly to the

JOHN S. MAVITY.

influence of his mother, a woman of high ideals, who gave careful attention to the rearing of her children.

MAVITY.—John S. Mavity, the subject of this sketch, was born in Bryantsburg, Ind., July 9, 1844. His father moved to Lewis County, Ky., when John Mavity was one year old. He settled on the hill between Petersville, on Kinniconnick Creek, and Mud Lick. His early training was, received on the farm and in the public schools of that day. Later he became a teacher in the county, having fitted himself at State University, at Lexington, Ky. At the age of seventeen he joined the army, in the War of the Rebellion, enlisting November 8, 1861, in Company G, 24th Regiment Kentucky Voluuteer Infantry, serving three years and eight months.

Mr. Mavity has been editor, teacher, and county servant in other capacities all the years since the war, and has ever proven himself a true citizen and business man, as he proved himself a soldier in the rebellion.

Mr. Mavity has been of invaluable service to us in the accumulation of facts for this work, due to his extensive knowledge of the county records and people.—[THE AUTHOR.]

McCANN.—John H. McCann was born January 31, 1855. He is of a family of twelve children—six boys and six girls. His father, Edward B. McCann, and his wife, Elizabeth Burriss McCann, bought a farm and settled on Nevill's Branch, a tributary to Quick's Run, in 1852. At this time Nevill's Branch was an almost unbroken wilderness. So the subject of this sketch early learned the use of the maul and wedge, the ax and the hoe. In fact, girls and boys alike, in this family, worked in the fields and woods to win a home from the forest and keep the wolf from the door.

Mr. McCann, like many another of our older citizens, obtained his larger education from "Red Brush College." However, he had advantage of the best school facilities his community afforded; the regular three months' term of public school in the old log schoolhouse accommodated, with split saplin seats, and he walked two miles and a half to get this advantage.

His parents were stanch Methodists, and trained their children in this faith.

John McCann was united in marriage to Miss Flora Marshall, daughter of Humphrey Marshall. To this union were born nine children, three of whom are now dead. On the sixth day of April, 1908, Mr. McCann buried his wife. He now lives on his farm, near Martin, Lewis County, Ky. His children are all single, and some of them live with him in the old home.

Mr. McCann has for thirty years been a close student of history, especially local history.

It was through Mr. McCann's solicitation that the author undertook this work, and many and generous have been the kindnesses of this man to us in this capacity.—[THE AUTHOR.]

PLUMMER, LOUIS P., was born near Mt. Carmel, Fleming County, Ky., December 15, 1815, being the first born to his father's second marriage.   William   Plummer, the father of

LOUIS P. PLUMMER.

Louis Plummer, came from Pennsylvania early in the century and settled at Mt. Carmel.

In the year 1828 the Plummer family moved to Lewis County, near the town of Burtonville. It was in this neighborhood Louis Plummer courted and married Sarah Luman. To this union were born fourteen children, six girls and eight boys, of which number three girls and six boys survive, as follows: H. F. Plummer, San Jose, Cal.; W. A. Plummer, Portsmouth, O.; Almedia Rourk, L. P. Plummer, M. L. Plummer, L. K. Plummer, A. M. Plummer, Cordelia Plummer, and Jennie Adams, of Vanceburg.

In 1865 Louis Plummer moved with his family to Vanceburg, and in 1870 was elected jailer of the county, filling this position during his encumbency with credit to himself and the county.

The descendants of Louis Plummer are honorable citizens of the county and stand for progress and purity of government, and take such active part in political affairs as will insure the betterment of the community.

Pugh.—Samuel Johnson Pugh was born in Greenup County, Ky., January 28, 1850. His father, Samuel B. Pugh, and his mother, Mary A. Pugh, moved to Lewis County in 1852, and the son has been a resident of the county ever since. He was educated in the common schools, Chandler's School of Vanceburg, for over five years a pupil of Rand's Select School, and finally graduated at Center College, Danville, Kentucky.

He studied law for about three years with

SAMUEL JOHNSON PUGH.

Judge George M. Thomas, and was admitted to practice in 1872, in which year, November 6, he was united in marriage with Mary R. Minta Thomas, only daughter of Judge Thomas. To this union were born three daughters and one son—Bessie H., now wife of Dr. F. A. Fitch, of Huntington, W. Va.; Nellie May, now wife of H. G. Hanford, of Washington, D. C.; Beulah L., now wife of Elder D. M. Walker, of Stanford, Ky.; and Bruce T. Pugh, now of Washington, D. C.

Judge S. J. Pugh served our State with credit to himself and his constituency in the State Senate of 1894-95. Judge Pugh has ever proven himself not only a stanch supporter of the political party he represents, but is alive with religious forces of his community under the direction of the Christian, or Disciples, Church. Mr. Pugh, among other offices tendered him in the gift of the people, now occupies the position as city attorney of Vanceburg. Mr. Pugh is not only interested in pure politics, but is a gentleman in his own community, honored and respected by all.

FULTZ, CHARLES H., M. D., was born near Wesleyville, Ky., March 3, 1876, and lived on a farm until fourteen years of age. At this time his mother died and his father, John Fultz, moved to Olive Hill, Ky. A few months later the subject of this sketch went to the country to work on the farm for an uncle, and never lived as a member of his father's family afterwards. However, after missing two full school years he managed to spend ten months in school,

CHARLES H. FULTZ.

and at the close of this term secured a first-class teacher's certificate in Carter County, Ky. Two years later he came to Lewis County and was here granted a first-class teacher's certificate. He taught three schools in this county and studied medicine in the intervals at St. Louis, Mo., and Louisville, Ky., graduating in Louisville, June, 1901. He then located at Garrison, Ky. Shortly after which he was married to Anna Cooper, daughter of James and Julia Cooper, of Ruggles, Ky.

After having practiced his profession at Garrison for four years he attended one term in medical college, Cincinnati, and then located in Vanceburg, November, 1905. He remained here ten months, then took a course of eight months' training at the College of Physicians and Surgeons at Baltimore, Md., graduating there June 3, 1907. He then returned to Vanceburg to resume his practice.

In the early fall of 1910 Dr. Fultz buried his wife. Mrs. Fultz was a true wife, and intensely interested in her husband's success.

Dr. Fultz occupies a place of distinction of being one of the most prominent physicians in his section of the State to-day. He is loved and honored by all who know him.

CHAPTER IX

WEALTH OF THE COUNTY—POPULATION: CENSUS OF
1810, 1820, 1830, 1840, 1850, 1860, 1870, 1880, 1890,
1900, 1910 — AREA — OCCUPATIONS: AGRICULTURE,
HORTICULTURE, MINING, MANUFACTURING—SOIL—
CLIMATE—SOCIETY—CHURCHES—SUNDAY SCHOOLS
—SECRET SOCIETIES—WATER TRANSPORTATIONS—
RAILROADS — POLITICAL PARTIES — NEWSPAPERS —
PUBLIC DEBT—CAPITATION AND PROPERTY TAXES—
DIVISION OF COUNTY FUND—MAGISTERIAL DIS-
TRICTS AND VOTING PLACES—MAP.

WEALTH OF COUNTY FROM 1876 TO 1911.—The
wealth of the county, as assessed by its officers,
embraces the lands, stones, animals, and all
other taxable property.

	RATES			
	State	County		
1876	$.45	$.90	$2,439,473	Thos. A. Mitchell, H. I. Mitchell.
1880	.45	.75	1,964,700	Thos. C. Wilson, R. D. Wilson.
1885	....	$1.27½	1,871,494	S. L. Hall, F. A. Mitchell.
1890	....	1.75	2,315,522	J. C. Willim, O. P. Pollitt.
1895	....	.....	2,239,215	O. P. Pollitt, Ed. Willim.
1900	....	.....	3,174,325	O. P. Pollitt. M. Bertram.

	RATES		
	State	County	
1905	....	.....	.... T. M. Bowman,
			O. P. Pollitt.
1909	....	....	2,406,803 M. Bertram.
			O. P. Pollitt.
1910	(3501 voters)	4,613,787	Geo. Lykins.

POPULATION.—The population of the county, as given by the census reports, are as follows: 1810, 2,357; 1820, 3,977; 1830, 5,229; 1840, 6,306; 1850, 7,292; 1860, 8,361; 1870, 9,115; 1880, 12,407; 1890, 14,803; 1900, 17,868; 1910, 16,887. There are about 200 colored people in the county.

AREA.—The county is about forty miles along the Ohio River front and about an average of twenty miles width, which would make it cover an area of four hundred square miles. But its shape is so irregular that without an actual survey it is hard to determine its exact area.

OCCUPATION.—Most all the people are engaged in agricultural pursuits, though of late years horticulture and market gardening have been receiving a share of attention. Mining has become one of the lost arts in Lewis County, though some little effort has been made of late years to locate zinc and lead mines that used to be worked, and if we are to believe the very creditable story of Mr. Battey, silver was, at

30

one time, plentiful on Kinny Creek, and mined by French and Indians, and also by others.

There have been, in times past, some manufactories in Lewis, but lately there is nothing except skiff oars, cooperage, railroad ties, flour, buttons, canned vegetables, and leather products. At one time Vanceburg boasted ten cooper shops, a hub and spoke factory, a planing mill, a furniture factory, and several other things.

Soil.—The soil of the county consists of almost every variety known to the United States. The western portion of the county is limestone, the valley of Quick's Run red rock or bastard limestone, and the remaining portion off the river is of sandstone formation. The river bottom lands are either sandy loam or limestone.

Climate.—The climate is in general healthful, though of recent years the winters have been quite variable, changing from heat to extreme cold very suddenly.

Society.—Lewis County, like every other place on earth, presents a stratum of society in which men and women of all stations in life may find their "kind;" but quite a large majority of her citizens are civilized and enlightened, are members of some religious body, and are endeavoring to educate their children.

Churches.—The Methodist, Baptist, Christian, Presbyterian, and perhaps several branches of these, are the Church organizations of the county.

SUNDAY SCHOOLS.—There were thirty-three Sunday schools reported last year. Vanceburg has four schools which have an enrollment of over three hundred and fifty pupils. The Christian Sunday school and the Methodist Episcopal Church, the Methodist Episcopal Church, South, and the Presbyterian.

SECRET SOCIETIES.—The Free Masons, the Independent Order of Odd Fellows, the Knights of Pythias, and the Junior Order United Workingmen are the orders represented in the county.

WATER TRANSPORTATION.—The only navigable stream in or near Lewis County is the Ohio River, running for forty miles along the northern boundary. A large amount of the county's products goes out and its imports come in by means of boats.

RAILROADS.—The C. & O. Railroad runs the entire length of the county along the river, and passes through Vanceburg on Third Street. The Kinny branch of the same passes up Kinny from its mouth to Trace Fork, thence up said fork to the Carter Avenue line. Lewis County gave ten thousand dollars in bonds to aid the building of the C. & O.

POLITICAL PARTIES.—The Republican party,

the Democratic party, the People's party, or Populists, and the Prohibition party are all represented in Lewis County.

NEWSPAPERS.—The first paper published in the county was the *Pioneer of Progress*, published in Concord in 1850, by E. Holderness. (For fuller description see History of Concord, in Chapter 2.) The second paper was the Vanceburg *Kentuckian*, established by Thos. Foster. It was afterward sold to the Republican Printing Company, and edited by Judge S. J. Pugh. The company sold it to W. S. Lewis and W. L. Fitch, who used it to political advantage and elected Lewis, a Democrat, county judge, and Fitch, a Republican, county attorney. Having no use for a paper and an office at the same time, they sold it to George B. Swap, who finally moved the plant away from Vanceburg.

The next man to be enveighed into the newspaper business was Jas. S. Mavity. He published the Vanceburg *Courier* from April, 1876 to October, 1880, at a loss of $2,200 besides his own labor. John B. Bradley, who had been the only successful sawmill man in the county, thought he might like the news business, and traded the proprietor some rock piles on Holly for his "elephant," but after a few weeks payment of expenses of five dollars above the income of the office, he rented it to Bullock and

Eaton for the consideration of "that they would not let the paper die." Messrs. Bullock and Eaton straddled the tripod and made paste in the sanctum for one year, when Mr. Bradley sold the outfit to A. L. McKay. Mr. McKay spent another fortune on the paper and office material, and made rather a better paper than any of his predecessors. But aggressive politics and financial trouble brought him to his back, and he left the office standing silent and alone in its hall, and, like the Arab, silently stole away. Somebody tried to run a religious journal from that office and with that material, but it was "no go." The old material lay around till 1888, when J. S. Mavity, feeling that "he hadn't had enough," launched the Vanceburg *Times*. Mavity, like the Farmer's Alliance, forgot that he was committed to the "non-political," and, with the Alliance, went through one of the hottest campaigns that was ever fought in Lewis County. A short time after he concluded "he had enough," and turned the paper over to J. W. Allen, who finally sold it to the Sun Publishing Company. The *Times* became extinct, and the *Sun* started off to light the citizens of Lewis. It made one annual revolution and suspended for a short time, when it was sold to Dr. J. P. Huff, who edited and published it for one year as a Republican paper. He sold it to D. J.

Drennan, who published a readable paper and made a living, both of which no other news-paper man had ever before done, in Vanceburg. At the present the Vanceburg *Sun* is owned and edited by Mr. M. O. Wilson, who has for four or five years published a paper that shows a healthy growth from the start. You will not find a more readable paper in any county in Kentucky. We trust Mr. Wilson will always prosper and for many years edit the *Sun*.

PUBLIC DEBT.—The county's first public debt of any magnitude, or when bonds were issued against the county, was contracted for building the present court-house, in 1864, and is described in Chapter 2.

The maximum amount of indebtedness was incurred in building the macadamized roads, and is shown by Public Debt Statement, issued and published in the Vanceburg *Courier* by Thos. A. Mitchell, county clerk, as follows:

BONDED DEBT, 1897

Statement of Eugene A. Jones, Treasurer of Lewis County, April 7, 1897:

COUNTY LEVY—

Amount received from all sources from April 6, 1896	$4,015.31
Amount disbursed	2,157.78
Balance on hand April 6, 1897	$1,857.53

COUNTY REVENUE—

    Amount received from all sources since
        April 6, 1896...................... $6,634.51
    Amount disbursed.................... 5,615.55

      Balance on hand April 6, 1897...... $1,018.96

INFIRMARY FUND—

    Amount received from all sources since
        April 6, 1896...................... $4,146.08
    Amount disbursed.................... 1,433.17

      Balance on hand April 6, 1897...... $2,712.91

GENERAL BRIDGE FUND—

    Amount received from all sources since
        April 6, 1896...................... $861.92
    Amount disbursed.................... 273.04

      Balance on hand April 6, 1897...... $588.88

RAILROAD—

    Amount received from all sources since
        April 6, 1896...................... $8,371.16
    Amount disbursed.................... 6,890.00

      Balance on hand April 6, 1897...... $1,481.16

QUICKS RUN BRIDGE—

    Amount received from all sources since
        April 6, 1896...................... $4,817.43
    Amount disbursed.................... 3,730.81

      Balance on hand April 6, 1897...... $1,086.62

FORFEITED LAND—

Amount received from all sources since
April 6, 1896...................... $291.76
Amount disbursed.................... 322.60

Deficit April 6, 1897............. $30.84

ROAD FUND—

Amount received from all sources since
April 6, 1896...................... $5,320.95
Amount disbursed.................... 3,172.76

Balance on hand April 6, 1897...... $2,148.19

BONDED DEBT—

Turnpike bonds outstanding............$32,150.00
Railroad bonds outstanding............ 6,000.00
Quicks Run Bridge bonds outstanding... 900.00

Total bonds outstanding...........$39,050.00
Paid on Bonded Debt during year 1896... $7,850.00

TAX LEVY

*The total levy for year 1897 is 70 cents per $100, and
is as follows:*

County Levy.....................12 cents per $100
County Revenue.................15   "   "   "
Road Tax.......................20   "   "   "
General Bridge.................. 5   "   "   "
Railroad....................... 5   "   "   "
Infirmary...................... 3   "   "   "
Turnpike....................... 5   "   "   "

Total 70

BONDED DEBT, 1899

Statement of Eugene A. Jones, County Treasurer of Lewis County, for year ending April 4, 1899:

COUNTY LEVY—
Amount received from all sources........ $4,286.02
Amount paid out..................... 3,007.92

Balance on hand April 4, 1899...... $1,278.10

COUNTY REVENUE—
Amount received from all sources........ $4,551.08
Amount paid out..................... 2,651.63

Balance on hand April 4, 1899...... $1,863.45

GENERAL BRIDGE—
Amount received from all sources........ $2,108.70
Amount paid out..................... 585.37

Balance on hand April 4, 1899...... $1,523.33

RAILROAD TAX—
Amount received from all sources........ $1,224.21
Amount paid out..................... 129.00

Balance on hand April 4, 1899...... $1,095.21

QUICKS RUN BRIDGE—
Amount received from all sources........ $1,202.34
Amount paid out..................... 1,051.29

Balance on hand April 4, 1899...... $151.05

FORFEITED LAND FUND—

    Amount received from all sources........ $139.11

    Amount paid out..................... 66.42

        Balance on hand April 4, 1899...... $72.69

INFIRMARY FUND—

    Amount received from all sources........ $3,188.90

    Amount paid out..................... 2,876.25

        Balance on hand April 4, 1899...... $312.65

TURNPIKE TAX—

    Amount received from all sources........ $2,134.46

    Amount paid out..................... 1,094.15

        Balance on hand April 4, 1899...... $1,040.31

ROAD FUND—

    Amount received from all sources........$10,764.23

    Amount paid out..................... 5,794.58

        Balance on hand April 4, 1899...... $4,969.65

INDEBTEDNESS PAID—

    County bonds........................ $1,755.00

    Note on Infirmary farm............... 888.30

    Turnpike............................ 969.15

        Total, 1899..................... $3,612.45

BONDED INDEBTEDNESS—

The following is a statement of the bonded indebtedness of Lewis County:

County bonds Nos. 471, 487, 489, 490, 491, 495, 496, 500, 501, 557, 558, 559, 560, 561, 562, 563, 564, 565, and 566, aggregating the sum of.................. $9,630.00

County refunding bonds Nos. 1 to 74, inclusive, aggregating the sum of...... 23,400.00

Railroad refunding bonds Nos. 5 to 16, inclusive, aggregating the sum of...... 3,600.00

Total bonded indebtedness, April 18, 1899.........................$36,630.00

The bonded debt was cleaned up in 1906.

The Vanceburg, Dry Run, and Kinniconnick had a small lot of bond issued to it in February, 1908.

CAPITATION AND PROPERTY TAXES.—The property tax rate for the State has ranged from forty-five cents on the one hundred dollars to fifty cents.

The poll tax on tithe runs from fifty cents to three dollars (1869) per head, and is now one dollar. The county tax is divided into the Road Fund, the Bridge Fund, the County Infirmary Fund.

Report of county clerk, 1878, to the presiding judge and justices of the peace composing the Lewis County Court of Claims.

The undersigned has learned, from various sources, that the people and taxpayers of Lewis County were desirous to know the exact financial condition of the county—the amount of its bonded debt at this time, and its resources to pay same. The records of my office contain all the information obtainable. The debt of the county now existing was contracted in aid of a system of internal improvements within its borders. The principal thoroughfares of the county are now macadamized turnpikes. In each and all of said roads the county is a stockholder to the extent of one thousand dollars per mile, and to pay the calls on said stock, subscribed by its officers, in obedience to law, the first bonds of the county were issued in October, 1868. From the records of my office, running through the terms of my mediate and immediate predecessors, I have coupled a statement showing the number, date, and amount of each bond issued; to what road issued and delivered; when due, and which bonds have been paid. From said statement it will be seen that the bonds of the county have been issued and delivered to the various turnpike roads in the county as follows:

To the V. S. L. T. & M. T. R.............$21.000.00
To the Concord and Tollesboro Turnpike.... 11,750.00
To the Mason and Lewis Turnpike.......... 4,200.00
To the C. C. S. H. & M. Turnpike.......... 7,800.00

To the S. L. E. & Mt. C. Turnpike......... $1,000.00
To the V. D. R. & K. Turnpike............ 5,781.25
To the Cabin Creek Turnpike............. 5,250.00
To the Vanceburg, Q. R. & C. Turnpike..... 3,000.00

Making a total of..................... $59,781.25
On the bonds so issued there has been paid,
    as shown by the statement referred to.. 29,991.18

Leaving due and unpaid the sum of....$29,790.07

To pay these bonds, or rather, $29,790.07 of them, we have a special county revenue tax of thirty cents on each one hundred dollars' worth of taxable property in the county, which, under an Act of the General Assembly, approved February 29, 1876, can not be used for any other purpose than paying the bonded debt and interest on same. (See Acts 1876, vol. I, Chapter 272, Section 3.) Said revenue tax yielded, for the year 1877, after deducting delinquents, costs of collection, etc., the sum of $5,470.80. Assuming that in the succeeding years the tax will yield the same amount, we can pay, in the year—

1878, after paying interest for said year...... $3,652.16
1879,   "   "   "   "   "   " 3,871.29
1880,   "   "   "   "   "   " 4,103.56
1881,   "   "   "   "   "   " 4,349.78
1882,   "   "   "   "   "   " 4,610.76
1883,   "   "   "   "   "   " 4,887.41

Total amount that will be paid in 6 years..$25,474.96

This leaves us only the sum of $1,315.11 and interest on that amount to pay out of the tax for 1884; therefore it is safe to say that the whole bonded debt and interest will be fully paid off in seven years.

The $3,000—amount of the bonds issued to the Vanceburg, Quicks Run, and Concord Turnpike—were issued for the purpose of building a bridge across Salt Lick Creek, at Vanceburg, and the amended charter of said company expressly provides that the $3,000 in bonds to be, and which were, issued to said company, shall be paid out of the bridge fund tax. (See Section 2 of Chapter 1021 Acts 1873, Vol. 2.) The bridge tax is five cents on each one hundred dollars' worth of taxable property in the county; and said tax yielded, for the year 1877, after deducting delinquents, exonerations, costs of collecting, etc., the sum of $875.14. Taking this as a basis, the said bonds and interest will be wholly discharged in four and a half years. These bonds, and also the bonds issued to the Vanceburg, Dry Run, and Kinniconnick Turnpike, were issued for ten per cent, and the interest is counted for each year ten per cent.

This labor has been undertaken and performed by the undersigned for the reasons herein before stated, and from a desire to inform those who are compelled to bear the burden, of the extent and probable duration of the debt, and hoping that it will prove beneficial to those for whose satisfaction and in whose interest it was prepared, it is respectfully submitted.

THOS. A. MITCHELL,
Clerk Lewis County Court.

STATISTICS 1879 vs. 1896

LEWIS COUNTY STATISTICS, 1879

Average value of land per acre, $5.07.

Number of acres cultivated, 289,658.

Value of land tilled, $1,507,164.

Number of horses and mares, 4,653.

Value of horses, $154,855.

Number of mules, 306.

Value of mules, $13,950.

Number of genets, 29.

Value of genets, $825.

Number of cattle, 4,487.

Value of cattle over $50, $34,637.

Number of stores, 60.

Valuation of stores, $45,325.

Value under Equalization law, $119,869.

Value of gold and silver plate, pianos, etc., $18,145.

Total valuation of taxable property, $2,149,099.

Tax at 40 cents on the $100, $8,580.20.

White males over 21 years old, 2,772.

Colored males over 21 years old, 42.

Legal white voters, 2,718.

Legal colored voters, 42.

White children between 6 and 20 years of age, 4,189.

Colored children between 6 and 20 years, 54.

Hogs over six months old, 4,165.

Studs, jacks, and bulls, 6.
Taverns licensed, 4.
Blind white persons, 5.
Deaf whites, 4.
Number of sheep killed by dogs, 48.
Value of same, $144.
Pounds of tobacco raised, 237,300.
Tons of hay raised, 496,700.
Bushels of wheat, 37,985.

TAX COMMISSIONERS' REPORT, 1896

To the Judge Lewis County Court:

We, the undersigned tax commissioners, year 1896, would respectfully report, on the completion of our labors, that we find the total amount of taxable property of Lewis County to be as, returned by the assessor, all told, $2,164,094 as against $2,191,305 for 1895. There are 3,725 voters, a gain over the return for 1895 by 222. In view of the depressed condition of business generally, and the very low prices of all farm stock and produce, and at the suggestion of our county judge and attorney, we adopted a rule at our first setting not to raise any list unless it was a very clear case of "too low in value" —our object from start to finish to hold up the assessment to 1895 as near as possible. The presence of the assessors was of great benefit to us, and will result in a much more correct tax book, and less annoyance to our taxpayers in having to come to the County Court to get errors corrected. All of which is respectfully sub-mitteR,

S. A. AGNEW,
E. C. SELLARDS,
GEO. M. DAVIS,
I. I. WALKER,
JAS. H. GARRETT,
Commissioners.

The total value of taxable property in Lewis County in 1865 was $2,471,269. White males over 21 years of age, 1,673. Enrolled in the militia, 848. The money paid for common schools out of the State fund was $2,722.50.

In 1896 the valuation of taxable property was $2,164,094, which is a decrease since 1865 of $307,175. This is perhaps one of the benefits of "resumption."

The number of voters in 1896 is 3,725, an increase of 2,052. The value of each voter's property, on a general average, in 1865, was $1,477.60; in 1896 it is $580.96, or a loss on each of $896.64. Counting the same number of voters in '65 as '96, the loss is $814.77 to each.

Expenses 1895-96

Statement of the receipts and expenditures from April 1, 1895, to April 1, 1896, of the taxes in hands of treasurer and collected for year 1895, as shown by settlements made with sheriff and treasurer for year 1895:

County Levy Tax Fund—

To amount in hands of treasurer, April, 1 1895...............................	$942.92
To amount transferred to the fund from Scaffold Lick Bridge fund, being surplus left in said fund after completing bridge...............................	945.08
To amount received from Lewis and Mason Turnpike. Dividend on stock held by Lewis County in said turnpike......	208.00

To net amount of county levy tax collected
for year 1895.................... 7,563.68

Total amount chargeable to the fund, $9,659.68

By amount drawn on this fund by Fiscal
Court, October term, 1894............ $2,729.43
By amount drawn on this fund by Fiscal
Court, April term, 1895............. 3,895.02
By amount drawn on this fund by the
County Court during the year 1895... 3,443.16

Total amount drawn on this fund...$10,067.61

Amount overdrawn.............. $407.93

COUNTY REVENUE FUND—
To amount in hands of treasurer, April 1,
1895.............................. $1,289.08
To net amouut of county revenue tax collected for year 1895................ 2,069.68

Total amount chargeable to this fund $3,358.76

By amount drawn on this fund for payment
of Lewis County Turnpike bonds and
interest during the year 1895......... $2,548.69

Balance in hands of treasurer, April
1, 1896...................... $810.69

QUICKS RUN BRIDGE FUND—
To amount in hands of treasurer, April 1,
1895.............................. $1,301.07
To net amount of Quicks Run Bridge, tax
collected for year 1895.............. 2,956.68

Total amount chargeable to this fund $4,257.75

By amount drawn on this fund for payment of bonds and interest, and to make fill and fencing to said bridge during year 1895........................ 2,360.83

Balance in hands of treasurer, April 1, 1896........................ $1,896.92

RAILROAD TAX FUND—

To amount in hands of treasurer, April 1, 1895............................ $1,197.65

To net amount railroad tax collected for year 1895........................ 1,065.61

Total amount chargeable to this fund $2,263.26

By amount drawn on this fund for payment of bonds and interests during 1895............................ $947.83

Balance in hands of treasurer, April 1, 1896........................ $1,315.43

INFIRMARY TAX FUND—

To amount in hands of treasurer, April 1, 1895............................ $2,990.66

To net amount Infirmary tax collected for year 1895........................ 887.09

Total amount chargeable to this fund $3,877.75

By amount drawn on this fund by the County Court during the year 1895.. $2,652.18

Balance in hands of treasurer, April 1, 1896........................ $1,225.57

ROAD TAX FUND—

To net amount road tax collected for year
1895.. $4,416.30
By amount drawn on this fund by County
Court during the year 1895.......... $1,515.83

Balance in hands of treasurer, April
1, 1896..$2.900.47

GENERAL BRIDGE TAX FUND—

To amount in hands of treasurer, April 1,
1895 (no tax levied for 1895)......... $667.66
By amount of orders drawn on this fund
by County Court during year 1895.... 535.86

Balance in hands of treasurer, April
1, 1896.. $131.80

FORFEITED LAND FUND—

To amount in hands of treasurer, April 1,
1895.. $44.70
To amount paid to treasurer by T. A.
Mitchell, county clerk, during year
1895.. 215.86

Total amount chargeable to this fund $260.56
By amount orders drawn on this fund by
County Court during year 1895...... $232.06

Balance in hands of treasurer, April
1, 1895.. $28.50

CLAIMS—

Claims allowed by the Fiscal Court payable out of
the County Levy Tax of 1896.

October Term 1895, viz.:

For aid to paupers outside of infirmary ... $1,324.98
"   work on roads 248.85
"   county officers' fees 432.05
"   justice of the peace fees 146.25
"   constable fees 34.65
"   miscellaneous claims 255.60
"   justices of the peace attending this
    court 42.00

    Total amount claims allowed, October, 1895 .... $2,484.38

April Term 1896, viz.:

For aid to paupers outside of infirmary ... $899.43
"   work on roads 515.63
"   county officers, fees 1,432.20
"   justice of the peace fees 57.95
"   constable fees 60.60
"   officers of election, 1895 .... 143.80
"   miscellaneous claims 126.02
"   rent of room to hold elections 31.00
"   justices of the peace attending this
    court 54.00

    Total claims allowed April term, 1896 .... $3,319.63

Total claims allowed by Fiscal Court, payable out of County Levy, 1896 .... $5,804.01

BONDED DEBT

The bonded debt of Lewis County is as follows:

Total amount turnpike bonds outstanding $33,578.84
Total amount railroad bonds 6,500.00
Total amount Quicks Run Bridge bonds .. 5,350.00

    Total amount of bonded debt of Lewis County $45,428.84

BONDS DUE 1896—

Turnpike bonds.......................... $3,750.00

Quicks Run Bridge bonds............... 4,450.00

Three of the railroad bonds will be paid off
in 1896, and the balance, $5,000, will
be refunded as per order of the Fiscal
Court, April term, 1896............ 1,500.00

Total amount bonds to be paid in
1896.......................... $9,700.00

TAX LEVY, 1896

*The taxes levied by the Fiscal Court for the year 1896
are as follows:*

County Revenue.................20 cents per $100

Quicks Run Bridge..............10 " " "

Infirmary......................10 " " "

Road...........................10 " " "

Railroad....................... 5 " " "

General Bridge.................. 2½ " " "

County Levy....................20 " " "

And $1.50 on each male over twenty-one years of age.

(Attest:)   THOS. A. MITCHELL,

April 23, 1886.   *Clerk Lewis County Court.*

The statements above are of previous years. Now, to get a more thorough understanding of the conditions of the county, we give you the following statements of 1911:

Statement of Geo. Willim, treasurer of Lewis County, term ending April 4, 1911:

COUNTY LEVY—

Amount received.....................$ 6,124.37

"   disbursed.................... 4,586.83

Balance on hand.................. $1,537.54

COUNTY REVENUE—
Amount received...................... $7,161.08
" disbursed..................... 3,357.14

Balance on hand................. $3,833.94

ROAD FUND—
Amount received......................$10,835.01
" disbursed..................... 6,706.11

Balance on hand................. $4,128.90

BRIDGE FUND—
Amount received...................... $3,769.68
" disbursed..................... 2,274.25

Balance on hand................. $1,495.43

McDANIEL BRIDGE FUND—
Amount received...................... $3,207.12
" disbursed..................... 2,632.00

Balance on hand................. $575.12

FORFEITED LAND FUND—
Amount received...................... $345.59
" disbursed..................... 142.75

Balance on hand................. $202.84

INFIRMARY—
Amount received...................... $2,910.08
" disbursed..................... 2,872.84

Balance on hand................. $36.24

BONDED DEBT—
McDaniel Bridge Fund................. $2,500.00

MAGISTERIAL DISTRICTS.—There are seven Magisterial Districts, numbered from one to seven, consecutively. They are fully shown on the accompanying map. In each district are two voting places, except in No. 3, Vanceburg District, there are four places to vote. The districts are also named—No. 1 being called Mowers; No. 2, Vanceburg; No. 3, Quincy; No. 4, Laurel; No. 5, Petersville; No. 6, Burtonville; No. 7, Tollesboro. The polling places are all known by names. In District No. 1 are Mowers and Concord; in No. 2 are Martin, Valley, Vanceburg No. 1 and No. 2; in No. 3 are Quincy and Tannery; in No. 4 are Laurel and Grassy; in No. 5 are Rands and Petersville; in No. 6 are Burtonville and Esculapia; in No. 7 are Tollesboro and Henderson, sometimes called Poplar Flat.

The law allows one magistrate and one constable in each of these districts, so that under the present law there are only seven magistrates instead of twenty-two, as under the old Constitution. This is quite a saving in expenses when the Court of Claims is in session and the justices are allowed three dollars per day. Three times 22 are 66, but 3 times 7 are 21, a difference of $45 in one day.

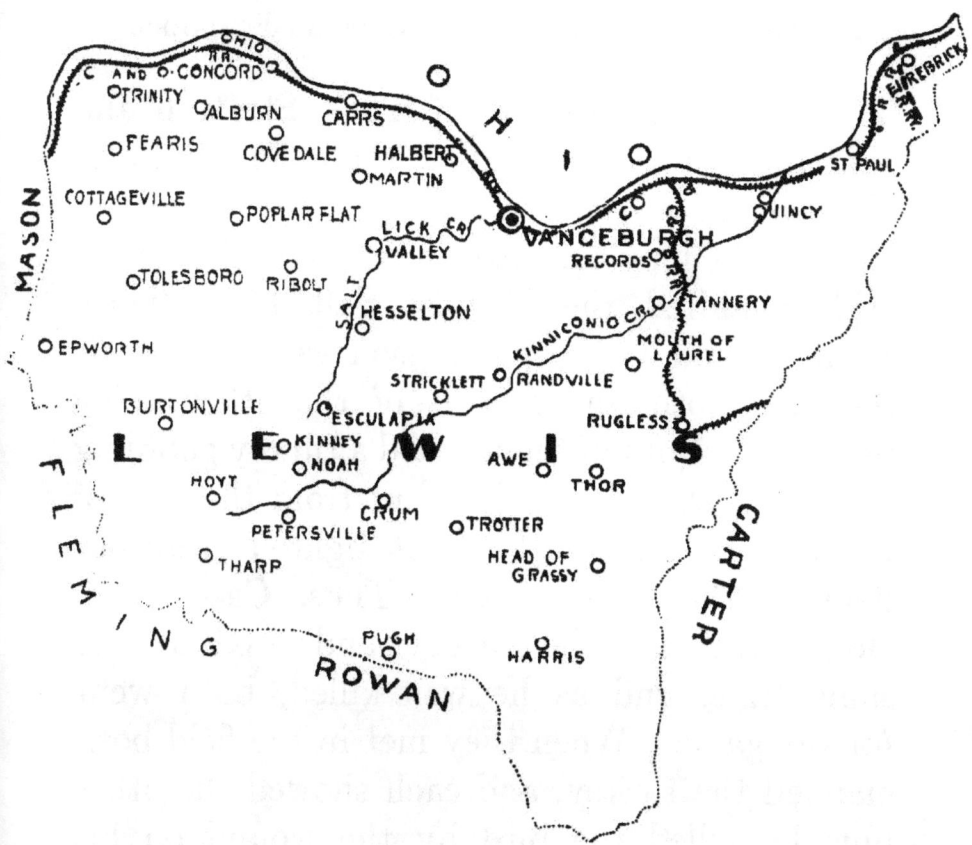

MASON

C AND O CONCORD
OHIO R.R.
TRINITY
ALBURN
CARRS
FEARIS
COVE DALE
HALBERT
MARTIN
COTTAGEVILLE
POPLAR FLAT
LICK CR.
VALLEY
OHIO
C AND O R.R.
FIREBRICK
ST PAUL
QUINCY
VANCEBURGH
RECORDS
TOLESBORO
RIBOLT
SALT
HESSELTON
TANNERY
EPWORTH
KINNICONIO CR.
MOUTH OF LAUREL
BURTONVILLE
STRICKLETT
RANDVILLE
ESCULAPIA
RUGLESS
KINNEY
NOAH
AWE
THOR
HOYT
CRUM
PETERSVILLE
TROTTER
THARP
HEAD OF GRASSY
FLEMING
LEWIS
CARTER
PUGH
HARRIS
ROWAN

Lewis County.

CHAPTER X

THE following anecdote of Thos. Stratton and William Sympson is told by the older people at Vanceburg:

"In the long time ago, when the wild turkey still inhabited the hills of Salt Lick, Thos. Stratton and William Sympson were out hunting, but both unconscious of the other being near him. Both of them heard a turkey gobbling and went in his direction, but from the side of opposite hills the turkey was sighted in an oat field in the hollow where Thos. Case lived. Both men saw the turkey and fired at the same time, and as he was killed, both went for the game. When they met in the field both claimed the turkey, and each showed the other how he killed the bird by the wound on his side which was toward him. They could not decide the matter, and agreed to take the turkey to Captain Mitchell, who lived near, and have it cooked for their dinner. In dressing the bird Mrs. Mitchell found two bullets welded together in the middle of its carcass. This revealed the mystery—both had hit it, and their

490

shots had met in its body, with the result above named."

A great deal of the unwritten history of a country can be picked up from the tales and traditions of the older inhabitants. Many times valuable secrets creep out in this way, which for some unaccountable reason the old inhabitant thought it was his duty to hold locked in his memory, and which, if divulged at the proper time, might have been of immense value to coming generations. The first two following are specimens of this class.

"About the year 1822 two men came, late in the evening, to the house of Robert Rea, on the East Fork of Cabin Creek, and at the same place where Thos. Rea now resides, and asked permission to stay all night. With the usual generosity of the Kentucky pioneer, Mr. Rea granted their request, and as the weather was warm, and they desired to sleep out on a porch, he also granted that request. In the morning he discovered that his two visitors had a haversack full of lead that they did not have the evening before, but they refused to tell him where they got it, though they intimated that they could not have gone far during the night.

Two old gentlemen who lived in that neighborhood always claimed that they knew where a lead mine was situated. Their names were

Wau and Miller, and they indicated that the mine was somewhere between Mr. Rea's and a roundtop, known as "Bald Knob." It is said that Mr. Wau once took a man by the name of Looney, who resided in the neighborhood, to a spot in the woods and showed him a large stone, with the remark that "this rock looks like one where I used to get lead," and pointing to an old handspike, he said, "That looks like the spike I used to lift rock with, and that cut limb on a dogwood looks like the place where I used to hang my powder horn when I came to get lead." Mr. Looney, whom it, seems, was well-named, did not think till he had been led away what the old man was really trying to disclose to him, but afterwards concluded that Wau was showing him the lead mine, and he spent many days vainly searching for the place again, and could not find it; because Wau had taken him such a circuitous route to and from the place that it was lost to him. The old settlers have always claimed that the Indians got lead in this vicinity. Mr. Peter Hoover attempted to locate the mine, but failed. In later years Messrs. Brady and Bassett spent months in excavating shafts and cutting trenches about Bald Knob, but to no purpose, as the mine is still as much a hidden mystery as it was before. But there seems, from the concurrent testimony

of old citizens, that there is no doubt of a pocket
of lead being hidden somewhere in the region
of the "Bald Knob."

SILVER MINES ON KINNY.—The following
letter is from the Portsmouth *Press,* the latter
part from the author of the *Press* letter direct
to the author:

A SILVER ARTICLE

Recently the *Press* contained a letter from a gentleman who knew the Waites, who used to make silver
money in Adams County. That letter stirred up Mr.
W. R. Beatty, Sr., of Sciotoville, who kindly contributes
the following interesting information relative to the
subject:

"EDITOR *Press.*—Having seen the articles in your
columns relative to the discovery of silver in Adams
County, O., and the mention of the family of Jonathan
Waite and the so-called 'Waite dollar,' I thought the
following would be of interest to your readers.

"The log cabin referred to by your former correspond-
ent was a veritable mint where thousands of silver dollars were coined, which passed as current as the coin of
the realm.

"But Waite could not work ore so impure as that
found in Adams County. The Waite dollar was made
from the ore just as found, without refining, and contained more silver than the American dollar.

"Waite procured his ore on Kinniconnick, in Lewis
County, Ky. My great uncle, Andrew Beatty, discovered the mine in 1812, and it was through the in-
timacy of his and my father's family that Waite
came to a knowledge of the mine.

"Andrew Beatty's prospecting extended from the head of main Kinny to within twelve miles of Boone Furnace. Here the ore became impure, and was not traced further. This territory embraces nearly the whole of Lewis and Carter Counties. My uncle, after many failures to open and work the mines, died upon the eve of success, and none of my ancestors ever made any further attempt in that direction.

"Waite was interested in the matter, and one day came to my grandfather's and told him that, as it appeared that they would never get to do anything with the mines legally, he intended to make immediate arrangements to begin 'free coinage.' My grandfather tried to persuade him not to do so, but when he would not be persuaded, he gave him several hundred weight of the ore, which he then had in his possession, and this ore made the first installment of Waite dollars. Waite took into his confidence a smart Yankee, who assumed an Irish character, and who was supposed to be insane. He was known as Billie Johnson. Billie was not infrequently absent for months. His business was to transport the ore to the Ohio River, at a point now known as the Boone Furnace landing, it being taken across the river in a 'dug-out' and concealed in a place agreed upon. Waite was very ingenious, and divided his time between his mint and a perpetual motion machine. The latter showed more ingenuity than his curious and skillful method of striking coin. His machinery, when once set in motion, would run until worn out, if not stopped. Gravity was the motor, and the power could be increased at pleasure. This machine was never brought to public notice, but it served Waite many a good purpose. Science may declare perpetual motion impossible, but those who saw this curious piece of mechanism will doubt the dictum.

"Waite's phenomenal success induced parties in Highland County, whose names I do not care to mention, to increase their finances by the same method, and thousands of dollars were made there. The quality of this ore may well be guessed, when it is remembered that there was not a mile of wagon-road between Highland County and Kinniconnick, and the only means of transportation was the pack mule.

"A man named Sprinkle, of Kentucky, was the next to enter the ring. (I know that some will dispute this and claim that the scene of Sprinkle's operations was in Virginia.) The principal scene of his operations was on Laurel Fork of Kinny, and they were of no mean proportions, either. Sprinkle often crossed the river at Greenup, and his first stopping place on this side was at a house near what is known as Giant Oak Mills, on Pine Creek. On these occasions he was always loaded, but he much oftener made his way to Vanceburg, and many a goodly structure in that vicinity owes its existence to Sprinkle dollars. (Two Sprinkle dollars are now owned in Vanceburg.) The next to take the cue was Shepherd, of Kentucky fame. The scene of his operations was about fifteen miles from Boone Furnace, Ky.

"Shepherd was a regular 'moonshiner,' and had a smelter of no mean proportions concealed in the mountains, which was guarded night and day. He was soon trapped, and was sent to the penitentiary for eight years. The ore worked by him was not very good, and gave him a good deal of trouble to flux it. It is to be found about ten miles beyond Boone Furnace, where my uncle left off prospecting.

"The next to add to the circulating medium was George Wright & Co., of near Haverhill, in this county. Shepherd having served his time in prison, returned to his old haunts and questionable ways. Wright and others, all well-to-do farmers in the vicinity of Haverhill, O., formed an acquaintance with him, and undertook to work the ore on this side the river. Wright was an ingenious mechanic, but the impurities of the ore baffled him. Shepherd came to his relief by smelting the ore in his furnace, and casting it in long strips the exact thickness and width of a half dollar. These bars were taken to a trysting place near Greenup and turned over to Wright. Wright procured a powerful machine from Cincinnati. This machine was working with a lever, and every stroke made a half dollar. But the old proverb—'The wicked are taken in their own craftiness'—was here verified. A slight indiscretion of one of the parties revealed their little scheme. Wright went up for five years, the others for a shorter term.

"Shepherd was indiscreet, and being closely watched, soon found himself the second time in 'limbo,' and went up for a long term, dying before his time expired.

"I have endeavored to give a brief and connected outline of the principal actors upon this curious drama. Many others of lesser note might have been instanced, but to follow the devious wanderings of all would make this too long a newspaper article.

"The question may well be asked, what became of all this spurious coin? The answer is easy:

"Having once passed into circulation, it could not be distinguished from the genuine, because it was silver. After becoming a very little worn, the slight defect of execution could not be noticed; and if any one should receive a Waite or Sprinkle dollar to-day he would be satisfied to know that it was silver without having it tested for the copper alloy. They are all in circulation, and if you should chance to have two dollars in your pocket, one from Waite's and the other from the United States mint, you can not tell 'which is which.'

"This article would seem incomplete without a brief outline of the circumstances that led to the discovery of silver by my ancestors in the territory here named. One who has ever visited Kinny will be surprised at the number of weird traditions related to him by the old settlers, and would find it a hard task to trace the traditions back to their origin. In the year 1776 a small party of men were making their way from the East to the new settlements of Kentucky. On the journey they were attacked by Indians, and one of their number, named McCormick, was taken prisoner. He was taken to the head of Kinny, where the main body of Indians were encamped. He was tied to a stake, and they proceeded to roast him after the manner of their instinct. As the Indians were firing the fagots, three white men approached. The three white men proved to be French missionaries, who interfered and saved McCormick's life. On the day following an Indian brought into camp a specimen of pure silver, which excited the curiosity of these Frenchmen. Upon making inquiry they found that it existed in abundance near the camp. After a careful investigation they decided to work the mine, and one of the men—De Burtte by name—and an Indian started to Fort Pitt for men and material. In due time they returned with sixteen other Frenchmen, and proceeded to build a small smelter, to make charcoal, and to open the mine. Twenty of the Indians remained with the French, and they continued their operations for the space of nearly three years. The Revolution was now in full blast, and the Indians went on the war path. Nearly the entire product of this mine, consisting of silver bars, was concealed near the

32

scene of operations. The above is a condensed statement of De Burtte's story, given in writing thirty-five years later. Andrew Beatty had discovered the old furnace and the old mine, and had prospected the entire country from the head of main Kinny to near the Spheherd mine, and had found many rich deposits of silver before he ever saw De Burtte's statement. Perhaps the richest of these is on Laurel Fork. My father had what he considered some 'lean samples' of this ore assayed, which yielded seventy per cent of silver.

"But this article has increased in length far beyond my expectations, and I am not through. If it should seem to interest any one, I may have more to say hereafter. W. R. BEATTY, SR."

"If any one is curious to locate the old mine worked by the French and Indians, they will proceed up main Kinny until they come to the property owned, in A. D. 1867, by a man named Coleman. About one mile above the Coleman residence, a long, deep hollow intersects Kinny on the right as you face up stream. At the mouth of this hollow (in the fifties) stood a log cabin owned and occupied by a man known as Billy Burriss. The cabin burned down long since. This cabin stood on nearly the exact spot where McCormick was tied to the stake, and also on the spot occupied by the little smelter which was built by the French, and is truly an historic spot. Standing on this spot, with the face up Kinny, the old mine is on the left, a short distance up the hill, and is an object of much interest. It is easily found, and presents a strange appearance. The furnace, when found by my uncle, was compeltely in ruins. All the mining tools and implements used by them were in the furnace, and a small portion of their last heat was chilled in the crucible.

"I know that geologists will and do say that the geological conditions of Southern Ohio and Northern Kentucky preclude the possibility of the precious metals, but since the declaration of these geologists silver has been discovered in Adams County, Ohio, and I speak the words of truth when I say that I know there are rich silver mines in Lewis and Carter Counties; and further, some as rich specimens of gold quartz as I ever saw were found on the dividing ridge between main Kinny and Triplet Creek. I have been in many placer gold mines, and I wish to say with emphasis that the locality here named shows every evidence of free gold. Has there ever been a single panful of dirt washed in all this region?

"W. R. BEATTY."

"MR. SPRINKLE'S GOOD DOLLARS

"'I saw by the papers the other day where three of the famous "Sprinkle" dollars had shown up,' said F. L. Strowbridge, of Peoria, Ill., to a Washington *Times* reporter.

"'Do you know what the "Sprinkle" dollars were? No? Well, Josiah Sprinkle, the man in question, lived in one of the roughest sections of Lewis County, Ky. Washington, the county seat of Mason, was then a thriving town. One day Sprinkle, then an old man, appeared at Washington with a buckskin pouch full of silver dollars of his own make.

"'In every respect they appeared the equal of the national coin. The weight was more than at present, and the quality and the ring were all that could be asked for. He spent them freely and everybody accepted them upon the assurance of Sprinkle that they were all right, except that they were not made by the United States mint. Upon being asked where he got the silver, he replied, "Oh, it do n't matter! There is plenty of it left." The inscriptions on the coins were rudely outlined, and in no wise was an attempt made at imitating the national coin. On one side of the coin was an owl, and on the other a six-pointed star. The edges were smooth. The coins were considerably larger and thicker than the United States coin.. Whenever Sprinkle came to town he spent the dollars of his own make.

"'At one time he volunteered the information that he had a silver mine in the West, but the old man refused to tell any one where it was located. Finally the Government agents heard of the matter and came on to investigate. Sprinkle was arrested and brought into court, but the dollars were proved to be pure silver, without alloy, worth, in fact, a trifle more than one dollar each. After an exciting trial he was acquitted. When the verdict was announced Sprinkle reached down in his pockets and drew out a bag of fifty of the coins and paid his attorney in the presence of the astonished officials. Sprinkle was never afterward bothered, and continued to make the dollars until the time of his death. He died suddenly and carried the secret of his silver mine with him. This was in the early thirties, and it has been twenty years since a Sprinkle dollar has been found.' "

It was on the trail from Vanceburg to the interior settlements, and near Kirk Springs, that the only recorded fight with Indians in Lewis County occurred. Collins' History gives it as follows, on page 300:

"A party of Indians having stolen horses from some of the upper stations, were pursued by a party of whites, who called at Stockton's Station for reinforcements. Ben (a colored man belonging to Major George Stockton), with others, gladly volunteered. The Indians were overtaken at Kirk's Springs, in Lewis County. The whites, dismounting, secured their horses and advanced to the attack. Only eight or ten Indians could be seen, and they retreated rapidly over the mountain. The whites followed, but in descending the mountain, discovered, from an attempt to outflank them, that the retreating Indians were but part of the many remaining behind to decoy them into an ambuscade, prepared at the base of the mountain. Various indications plainly showed that the Indians were greatly superior in number, and the whites were ordered to retreat. Ben was told of the order by a man near him, but was so intently engaged that he did not hear. The man, in a louder tone, warned him of his danger. Ben turned upon him a reproving look, with indescribable grimaces and ludicrous gesticulations, admonishing silence, and springing forward, set off at a furious rate down the mountain. The man, unwilling to leave him, started after, and reached his side in time to see him level his rifle at a huge Indian down the mountain, tiptoe on a log, peering, with outstretched neck, into the thick woods. Ben's rifle cracked, and the Indian, bounding high in air, fell heavily to the earth. A fierce yell answered this act of daring, 'and the Indians (said Ben) skipped from tree to tree, thick as grasshoppers.' Ben, chuckling with huge self-satisfaction, bawled out, 'Take that to 'member Ben, de black white man,' and set off in earnest after his retreating party."

Isaac Carr used (1836) to run a hotel that was situated on the river bank, at Vanceburg, just in front of where the Bireley flouring mill now stands. In one of the carousals at the inn a general fight took place, and Larkin Liles, of Kinny, bit off the lip of Ed. Campbell. He was sentenced by the court to serve one year in the penitentiary for his offense. W. B. Parker, who was sheriff at the time, was to take him to Frankfort. Mr. Liles told him that, as it was now fall, and that his corn needed cutting and his family would need wood for the winter, that he would go home and attend to these matters and then meet him in Vanceburg on a certain day, ready to make the trip to Frankfort. Strange as it may seem now, the sheriff consented to this arrangement, and on the appointed day, true to his promise, Mr. Liles appeared. He then told the sheriff that he would walk through the country to Frankfort, and that he could go round by the stage route and meet him there. This was also agreed to, and Mr. Liles reached the Capital several days in advance of the sheriff. Not being able to find Mr. Parker, Liles reported to the governor, to whom he told the whole story, and also said that he was ready to go to the prison and commence serving out his time. The governor informed him that he had no right to commit him to prison till the officer should arrive with the necessary papers and identify him as the prisoner. He waited till the sheriff arrived, and when he did so and vouched for the correctness of Mr. Liles' story, the governor pardoned him, and he and Mr. Parker came back home together.

Between 1840 and 1845, Brown, Wooster and Company were operating a lot of gang sawmills on Kinny, near the residence of T. B. Harrison, and they built a tram railroad from their mill, up Grassy and over the mountain, and down by Dry Run to Vanceburg. Over this road, with cars drawn by mules, they hauled their lumber to the river. Part of the old timber of the road could still be seen only a few years ago, and perhaps it is still there.

It is said that there was an old trunk in the McKellup family which was one hundred and two years old. It was sent from Wilson's Bottom, March 17, 1896, to Elizabeth Woodworth, Russelville, Brown County, O. There is also an old stew pot in Robert McKellup's possession which twice crossed the Atlantic from England to Virginia, and finally emigrated to Kentucky, about 1800. It is supposed to be about four hundred years old.

Robt. Carter at one time thought the salt water at Vanceburg might still be of some value if it had been superseded for salt making, so he built a vat near the present residence of N. B. Webster, filled it with salt water, and then planted it with oysters. He intended that Chesapeake Bay should be brought right to the door of Vanceburgians; but alas for human expectations, his oysters failed to thrive, and the enterprise had to be abandoned. But he furnished lots of fun for the gossips, and as he was wealthy he did not mind it much. He was only experimenting, anyway.

Ezekiel Stone tells the following story:

"About the year 1800, when all the 'Kinny' country was a vast wilderness, an old hunter by the name of Barker built his cabin on Laurel Creek, where the bear, deer, and other game was plentiful. One day he found it necessary to go for salt at the furnace near Vanceburg. Although it was bitter cold, he fared forth, and nearing his journey's end, he came by a giant poplar tree, on the farm now owned by Jas. Stone, and leaning against the base of the tree was a little white boy, frozen to death. The old hunter thought, of course, the boy belonged to some neighbor. He started out to find his home, and although he looked and inquired among the few settlers, no trace of the boy's home was ever found. The old hunter buried the little fellow at the foot of the great tree, and his origin still remains a mystery."

INDEX OF LEWIS

COUNTY, KENTUCKY

.

A.

ADAIR
Henry, 155
ADAM(S)
--- 76
G. P., 89, 342
James, 279
Jennie, 458
J. Q., 89
T. J., 340
ADKINSON
James, 278
AGNEW
S. A., 340, 480
W. W., 225
AIL(L)S
Family, 37
Benjamin, 37, 247, 262,
274, 283, 314, 328,
331
John, 101, 314
Rebecca, 101
Richard, 273
Samuel, 33
William, 101
ALDRIDGE
Frank, 412
Margaret, 412
ALEXANDER
Ally, 106
ALLEN
J. W., 469
ALLEY
Nancy J., 379
ALMS
House (County), 310
AMES
Ezinah, 274
ANDREWS
L. W., 337
APPERSON
Charles T., 332
APPLEGATE
Horace, 226
Jacob, 310
James, 252
ARCHARD
John, 98
ARMSTRONG
A. J., 340
Henry, 25
John, 204
Sam P., 81
ARNOLD
John, 288
Nancy, 288
Upton, 288
William, 288
ARRNS
Mose, 36
Sarah, 36, 37
ARTHUR(S)
David, 256, 294
David, Jr., 196
AUMILLER
George, 169

B.

BAGBY

BAGBY continued
--- 128
John, 310
Robert, 251, 252, 282,
310
Robert, Jr., 307
T. F., 89, 343
Theodore, 342
William, 310
Willis, 310, 328
BAIL(E)Y
Josh, 252
W. H., 365
BAIRD
L. B., 219, 225
Moses, 251
BALDRIDGE
J. W., 231
BALDWIN
--- 155
D. H., 75
BALL
Harrison, 319
William P., 244, 291
311, 319
W. P., 270
BALLINGER
David, 97
BAND
James, 279
BANE
Baldwin, 92
Clayton, 66, 319
Cleaton, 344
Gabriel, 335
G. H., 340
G. P., 226
Richard, 324
BANNISTER
Marion, 388
BARARD
T. J., 365
BARBER
R. G., 336, 338, 339
BARCLAY
--- 40
James, 137
BARKER
--- 504
BARKLEY
Daniel, 59
Henry C., 197
James, 218, 255
James H., 48, 98, 228
John C., 362
Samuel, 59
Thomas, 59
T. J., 207
William, 47, 49, 59, 255,
290, 291, 305
BARNES
--- 73, 131
BARNETT
--- 73
BARNEY
L., 172
BARRETT
John, 60, 61
Minor, 60, 61
W., 82
BASSETT

BASSETT continued
--- 492
BATE
Fannie, 403
Samuel, 170, 171, 200, 403
Thomas, 200
BATEMAN
John, 178
BAYLES
Benjamin, 88
BEAL
Samuel, 424
BEAN
W. W., 231
BEARD
Pleasant, 276
BEASLEY
Eliza, 377
BEATTY
Aaron, 88
Andrew, 493, 494, 496
W. R., 493, 498, 499
BECKET(T)
Edward, 238
Emily M., 357
Humphrey, 286, 289, 332
Jeremiah, 294
John, 286
Reason, 286, 294, 313
Thomas, 286
William, 286
BEDFORD
--- 82
Ben, 269, 305
Littleberry, 305
Robert, 160, 178
Thomas, 269
BEDINGER
Graham, 101
Henry, 274, 277, 282
Henry C., 317, 322
H. C., 299
BELL
--- 81
H. I., 340
Humphrey, 98, 278
John, 271, 294
BELYEW (See BILYEN)
Abraham, 380
Anna, 38
Betsy, 380
Eli, 45, 380
Harriet, 380
Hiram, 380
Margaret, 380
Nancy, 380
Paul, 380
Samuel, 380
William, 380
BENNETT
N. R., 365
BERRYMAN (BERRIMAN)
E., 82
Ezekiel, 84
Thomas, 269
BERTRAM
--- 22, 209, 211
Adam, 159
M., 342, 464, 465
Marshall, 341
M. M., 89

BERTRAM continued
  T. M., 345
BEVEN(S) (BEVIN(S))
  Family, 58
  Albert R., 391
  Andrew C., 391
  Benjamin D., 391
  Ben R., 391
  Catharine, 391
  Charles A., 391
  Chole, 391
  Cora A., 391, 392
  Elizabeth, 391
  Elizabeth J., 391
  Harry W., 391
  James H., 391
  James T., 391
  John F., 391, 392
  John T., 42
  Lizzie, 391
  L. M., 42
  Lonzo J., 391
  Mary E., 291
  Moses, 258
  Paris C., 391
  Richard B., 391
BIBB
  --- 292
BIDELL
  John, 444
BILDERBACK
  James, 344
  William, 252
BILYEN (BELYEW?)
  Abraham, 269
  Eli, 318
  H. L., 341
  John, 269
  Paul, 269, 318
  Samuel, 318
BIREL(E)Y
  --- 501
  William M., 228
BIVEN(S) (BIVANS)
  Benjamin, 228
  Henry, 296, 319, 330
  James, 269
  James H., 296
  Patrick, 79
BLANKENSHIP
  Sylvestor, 365
  William, 336
BLANTON
  Mary, 431
BLEW
  Abraham, 76
  Paul, 76
BLISS
  Martin, 84
  Stephen, 334
  Stephen V., 332-335
BLOOMFIELD
  Family, 31
BLOUNT
  Andrew, 61
  J. W., 365
BLYEW
  --- 86
BOGGESS
  Araminta P., 414, 416,
    417

BOGGESS continued
  Thomas, 416
BOGGS
  Thomas, 290, 310
BOLINGER
  --- 40
BOLLING
  William K., 353
BONHAM
  Nancy, 430, 432
  Nehemiah, 432
BOONE
  Daniel, 396, 415
BOOTS
  ---, 385
BOVARD
  George W., 71, 72
BOWMAN
  J. T., 341
  Maggie J., 447
  T. M., 342, 465
  William, 67, 345, 447
  Win Parker, 447-449
BOYD
  Archibald, 107, 262, 283,
    288, 290
  D., 128
  D. H., 233, 339, 340
  Edward, 279
  George, 78, 287
  Harriet, 73
  H. G., 365
  James, 73, 249, 278, 297,
    309, 331-334, 362
  J. L., 81, 82
  John, 101, 270, 284, 301
  John L., 318, 319
  Samuel, 262
  William, 265, 269, 363
BRADFORD
  B. F., 237
BRADLEY
  J. B., 6, 64
  John B., 468
  John L., 48
  "BRADLEY'S MILITIA"
  374
BRADY
  --- 492
BRAGG
  Amanda, 293
  Lucy, 274
  Thomas, 255, 262, 293,
    295, 305
BRANHAM
  Benjamin F., 339
  B. F., 201, 225, 341
BRECKINRIDGE
  John, 345
BREWER
  --- 254
  Asabel, 283
  A. W., 366
  Edward, 257, 278
  James B., 264
  John, 260
BRIGHTMAN
  --- 172
  Abner, 28, 322, 331
  D. H., 338
BRITTAIN

BRITTAIN continued
  W., 325
BROOKS
  John, 378
BROWN
  --- 76, 80, 503
  August W., 84
  Elizaneth, 257
  George, 59, 87, 91, 98, 10
  James, 59
  John, 59
  Landen C., 238
  Paris C., 84
  Thomas, 84
BROWNFIELD
  John, 98, 268
BRUCE
  --- 278
  Family, 28
  Aaron B., 376
  Alexander, 28, 153, 260,
    293, 311, 314, 320, 322
    325, 331, 332, 343, 344
    364, 375-378, 380
  Alice, 378
  Andrew J., 376
  Aristides, 376
  Brunette, 379
  Constantine, 327, 375, 37
  Eliza, 379
  Elizabeth, 377
  George W., 28, 160, 283,
    285, 375, 379
  George W., Jr., 235
  George Washington, 303
  G. W., 118, 257, 293
  H. C., 219, 343, 375, 37
  Henry, 377
  Henry C., 28, 125, 204,
    219, 225, 248, 254, 33
    378, 379
  Henry Clay, 376, 377
  Horatio, 261, 264, 329,
    375-377
  Isabel, 375
  John, 254, 261, 262, 343,
    344, 375, 376, 380
  John L., 378, 379
  Mahala, 376
  Margaret, 376
  Minnie, 378
  Nancy, 379
  Patrick H. C., 335
  Patrick H. Clay, 376
  Perry G., 375, 379
  P. H. C., 344
  Polly, 254
  Richard P., 375,
  Robert, 376, 377
  Samuel E., 379
  S. M., 365
  Susan, 379
  T. H. C., 344
  Therese, 376
  Thomas, 327, 376
  Thomas H. C., 379
  Thomas H. Clay, 375, 37
  Thomas J., 178, 225
  Thomas J. M., 378
  T. J., 237
  Washington, 378

BRUCE continued
  William E., 379
BRYANT
  --- 53
  Bailey, 249, 251
  J., 365
BULLETT
  Thomas, 19
BULLOCK
  --- 327, 469
  T. B., 222, 340
  Thomas B., 360
  W. G., 339, 340
  William G., 254
BUNN
  Thomas J., 326
BUNTON
  George Watter, 9
BURCHART
  J. T., 342
BURK
  William, 252
BURNS
  --- 79, 86
  M. H., 85
  W. R., 77
BURRIS(S)
  Family, 32, 38
  A. B., 365
  Abel, 40
  Basil, 31, 310, 323
  Billy, 498
  Elizabeth, 40, 455
  Josiah, 335
  Mathew, 106
  Ruth, 310
  Thomas, 45
BUSBY
  J. T., 365

C.

CADWALADER
  Morgan, 40, 42
CAIN(E)
  --- 230
  Charles, 151
CAINES
  Charles, 152, 153, 301,
    320, 322
  C. J., 301
CALHOUN
  James, 268, 297
CALVERT
  Family, 22
  --- 275
  Ann W., 293
  Dudley, 21, 291, 328,
    337
  Landon (Landen), 22, 25,
    28, 87, 91, 95, 102,
    107, 240
  Lewis, 87, 91
  Stephen, 279
  W. H., 271
CALVIN
  George, 32-34
  John, 84
CAMMING
  --- 83
CAMPBELL

CAMPBELL continued
  --- 25
  Family, 222
  Alexander, 403
  A. R., 89, 342
  Ed(ward), 327, 502
  S. B., 42
  Thomas, 327
  W. H., 86
  William, 26, 293, 328
CANE
  --- 41
CARLISLE
  John G., 418
CARMACK
  --- 24, 25
CARR
  --- 217
  Abraham, 285, 323
  Daniel, 282, 290, 296
  F. M., 113, 117, 161,
    167, 207, 225
  Isaac, 501
  James, 273, 296, 386
  J. K. (Mrs.), 229
  O. D., 86
  William, 106, 363
CARRINGTON
  --- 26, 27
  Daniel J., 281, 294
  Jesse, 293
  Jesse B., 26
  John T., 363
  Nancy, 281
  William, 26, 281
  William E., 22
CARSON
  John, 269
CARTER
  Anna, 386
  James, 284
  J. O., 365
  John, 37, 268, 322
  Robert, 503
  Robert C., 333
  Robert G., 333
  Thomas, 37, 126, 387
  Thomas H., 125
CARTMELL
  --- 85
CASE
  R. B., 336
  Thomas, 490
CATT
  --- 95, 111, 247, 280,
    289
CAX
  Samuel, 279
CEMETERY
  Associations, 218, 219
CHADWICK
  J. L., 128
CHAMBERS
  John, 271
CHANDLER
  Isaac, 78
CHANEY
  Edward, 101
  James, 277
CHAPMAN
  William, 266

CHITWOOD
  John R., 245
CHURCHES
  22, 23, 41, 42, 74-77, 80,
    103, 109, 115, 121, 123,
    126, 127, 195, 228, 237,
    262
CLARK
  --- 125
  E. G., 128
  James, 327
  John A., 323
  P. H., 336
  Simon, 365
  Thomas, 28
  T. M., 365
CLARY
  Joseph, 174
  Richard, 257
  Warner, 257
CLAY
  Elizabeth, 375
CLEM
  John, 261
CLEVELAND
  Grover, 55
COCHRAN
  Robert A., 197
COFIN
  William, 275
COFRIN
  Sallie, 377
COGAN
  Family, 318
  Samuel, 318
COKER
  Martin, 280
COLE
  A. E., 195
  Benjamin, 270, 314, 315
  G. K., 237
  H. K., 125
  James C., 160, 173
COLEMAN
  --- 498
COLLINS
  George W., 332-334
  Thomas, 95
COLVIN
  Jacob, 260, 276
CONDIT
  --- 76
CONLEY
  Isaac, 346
CONNELLY
  Levy, 252
CONRAD
  --- 31
CONWAY
  George, 328, 363
  Richard, 255, 328
COOFER
  A. N., 340
COOLEY
  Charles, 280
COOPER
  Ammon, 340
  Anna, 463
  James, 284, 313, 345, 463
  James H., 332
  Jane, 383

COOPER continued
Julia, 463
Murdoc(k), 92, 265
Spencer, 275
Thomas, 341, 342
W. B., 340
W. T., 444, 445
CORDINGLY
--- 299
Frank, 97
John, 97
William, 96
CORNS
Jonathan, 304
William, 363
COTTINGHAM
Family, 22
James, 290, 335
John, 290
Joseph W., 340, 341,
364, 384
J. W., 340
Mary, 397, 398
Polly, 266
William, 246, 247, 252,
253, 266, 397
COURTHOUSE
(Lewis Co.), 93
COWNE
Augustine, 271
COX(E)
Charles, 277, 279, 290,
307
Edward, 267
Elijah, 37
John, 37, 125, 128, 378
Joseph, 149, 369
Martha, 34
Peter M., 300
Rebecca, 387
S., 365
Samuel, 40, 92, 95, 98,
281, 287, 343
W. H., 91, 343
W. H. (Mrs.), 313
William, 379
CRABBE
J. G., 451
CRAIG
John, 28
CRANE
O. S., 365
CRAWFORD
L. (Mrs.), 233
Susan, 379
Valentine V., 268
CRAXTON
--- 366
CRAYCRAFT
--- 45
CRISWELL
Samuel, 266, 270
CROPPER
--- 24
Solomon, 317
W. B., 341
William, 317
CULBREATH
Nancy, 39
CUMMINGS
(See CUMMINS)

CUMMINS
--- 95
John, 244
Rebecca, 101
Samuel, 101, 252, 263,
272, 274, 312
William, 83
CUPP
Daniel, 323
CURRIN
W. H., 86
CUTCHER
John, 362

D.

DALE
C. S., 128
George W., 341
DARNELL
Levi, 279
DARRAGH
James, 173
Leonidas, 225
W. E., 341
DARROW
J. W., 219
DAVENPORT
R. S., 365
DAVIS
Family, 22
---101, 277
Alexander, 269
Catharine, 292
Christina, 35
David, 36, 305, 327
David W., 271
Elijah T., 92, 95
George M., 480
George N., 92, 95
George W., 221
G. N., 102, 250, 255
James H., 82, 332
J. H., 82
Joseph, 318
Joseph H., 331
Man (Mrs.), 229
Mary, 253
Richard.W., 332, 333
Thomas N., 325
Turner, 35, 36
Walter, 253
DAY
--- 74
W. L., 86
DAZIER
James, 249
"DEAD FALL"
72
DEAN
Abraham, 252
Michael, 25
DE ATLEY (DEATLEY)
A. H., 337
Austin, 297
Austin B., 335
Griffith, 297
DE BWITTE
--- 497, 498
DESHA
--- 287

DEWEY
Oliver, 31
DICKEY
Thomas D., 333
DICKSON
Isaac, 342
James, 268, 303, 332
Lewis, 339
DILLINGER
Solomon, 84
DIMITT
Moses, 288
DIXON
James, 324
DODD
John T., 341
S. I., 340
DODGE
--- 168
DONALDSON
Israel B., 290, 344
DONEHOO
J. M., 128
DONOVAN
John, 244
Joseph, 95
DORCH
William, 252
DORNAN
Phillip, 280
DOUGHERTY
Thomas, 88
DOW
Lorenzo, 77
DOWNEY
--- 313
John, 268
DOYAL
David M., 35
D. M., 91
Edward, 390
Elizabeth, 390
Ezekiel, 318
G. S., 232
John, 91, 305, 324, 320
John A., 390
Michael, 305
Nancy, 390
Nichelson, 390
Rebecca, 390
Samuel, 318, 319
Susan, 390
Thomas, 319
DOXIER
George, 83
DREDDEN
John, 309
John (Mrs.), 309, 312
DRENNAN
D. J., 470
DUDLEY
Austin, 363
DUGAN
W. W., 218
DUKE
Alexander, 264, 273
Basil, 28
James, 327
John R., 81, 332, 336
Thomas A., 153
DUMONT

DUMONT continued
--- 74
DUNBAR
David M., 337
D. M., 205, 338
G. E., 341, 342
George E., 341, 342
DUNNEGAN
T. M., 365
DUNNING
J. W., 365
DUZAN
Peter, 270, 277, 337
DWIAR
Stephen, 269
DYAL
Alexander, 269
David, 269
John, 87, 98, 105,
250, 267, 268
Simon, 269, 291
DYER
Catherine, 436, 437
Family, 31

E.

EADS
Isaac, 323
E(A)SHAM
Family, 22
Arthur, 381
Betty, 381
Charles, 381
Clark, 381
Clay, 381
Crosby, 381
Edward, 381
Elisha, 381
Eliza, 381
Frederick, 381
George, 381
Harriet, 381
John, 317, 381
John Handley, 381
Jonathan, 224, 381
Joshua, 281, 381
Lucretia, 381
Lucy, 381
Margaret, 26
Marion, 381
Martha Jane, 381
Mary, 381
Nancy, 381
Ora, 381
Parma, 381
Peggy, 381
Rebecca, 381
Richard, 381
Robert, 381
Sarah, 381
William, 25, 26, 299,
317, 380, 381
EATON
--- 468, 469
EDWARDS
John S., 363
EIFORT
--- 168
ELIJAH
George F., 324

ELLIOTT
--- 438
ELLIS
Samuel, 198, 210, 215,
336-338
ELSON
Catherine (Davis), 292
Nicholas, 291, 314
Richard, 101
ELY
Seneca W., 171
EMMONS
Rufus, 67, 345
EPSON
Joseph, 76
ESSEX
Thomas, 39, 313
EULITT
Family, 31
EVANS
Anthony, 73
David, 280
Jefferson, 321, 331
Mary, 391
Mary Louise, 357
Milton, 334, 364
Milton, 334, 364
Richard, 280
EVERETT (EVERITT)
--- 317
Artensia, 357
John D., 144, 149, 281
Harrison, 323

F.

FABER
E. G., 365
FAGAN(S) (See FEAGANS)
Francis, 324
Henry, 324
Raleigh, 324
FALKNER
J. H., 365
FALLS
E., 237
FARRIS
Daniel, 56
FARROW
000 229, 275
FATE
--- 76
F(E)AGANS
Buck, 84
Francis, 330
Frank, 77
John, 270
Rolley, 76
FEARIS
Family, 91
David, 337
David W., 197, 204, 336
D. W., 198, 338, 339,
363
George, 87, 91, 92, 95,
98, 107, 240, 244,
255, 259, 285
James, 278, 279
Lewis, 279
FEATHERKILE (FEATHER-
KYLE)

FEATHERKILE (FEATHER-
KYLE) continued
D., 365
George, 55
FEE
John G., 56
FENLEY
John B., 156, 335
FENWICK
David, 101
William, 48, 202
FERRIS
David, 73
FETCH
John L., 66
FETTERS
Charles, 252, 269
Daniel, 279, 302, 319
Harrison, 365
Jacob, 269
J. E., 365
Michael, 269, 279, 319
FIELDS
--- 76
FINK
William, 296
FISHER
Family, 22
N. G., 128
R. H., 118, 340, 341
W. B., 125
FITCH
Benjamin, 392
E. H., 340
F. A., 459
James, 106
J. B., 180, 196, 198, 336-
338, 344
J. J., 338
John L., 344, 392
Joseph, 106
Joshua B., 125, 133, 173
Joshua D., 339, 363
Olive, 392
William, 433
William L., 305
W. L., 339, 462
FLEMING
William P., 88, 102
FLINN
Willoughby, 324, 330
FLORA
--- 117
FORD
G. W., 365
FORMAN
--- 19, 252
John, 280
Samuel Ezekiel, 321
FORT
Christopher, 266
Peggy, 266
Thomas, 305
FOSTER
--- 128
Thomas, 468
FOWLER
John, 67
FOX
George F., 313
FOXWORTHY

FOXWORTHY continued
  Joseph, 328
FOYCE
  A. W., 340
FREEMAN
  A. E., 393
  Daniel, 392
  J. M., 82
  John M., 82
FRIZZELL
  Alexander, 326
  Alfred, 328
  Alfred H., 332
  A. P., 225
  Archibald, 26, 147, 247,
    253, 255, 310, 312,
    330
  Jacob, 280, 285, 331,
    332
  James A., 326
  John, 385
  Joseph, 25
  Margaret, 326
  Polly W., 326
  William, 324
FRUIT
  George, 138
  Jubes, 160
FRY
  Bushrod, 266
  D. F., 77
  Ferdinand, 248, 269, 279,
    319
  Frances, 389
  George, 248, 256, 365
  John, 253, 256, 275,
    284, 306, 307, 311,
    334, 335
  Lewis G., 304, 319
  Richard, 268
  Samuel, 232
  S. V., 77
  Thomas M., 197, 205
  William, 268, 319
  W. M., 89
  W. W., 365
FRYER
  A. W., 339, 340, 342,
    343
FULLER
  Enos P., 63, 64
  Solomon, 257
FULTON
  --- 201
FULTS
  James M., 339
FLUTZ
  Charles H., 460, 463
  John, 460
FUFFE
  James, 305
  Nancy, 305

    G.

GALBREATH
  L. W., 453
GAMES
  T. M., 232
GANET
  Clifton A., 286

GARDNER
  James, 387
  S. D., 221, 235, 236
GARLAND
  --- 375
  Anderson, 293
  Anderson M., 154
  Anderson N., 293
  Cynthia Ann, 293
  James R., 174, 204, 336,
    338, 363
  J. R., 159, 176, 180,
    211, 342
  Nathaniel, 152
  Nathaniel R., 293, 333
  Nat G., 334
  N. R., 155, 337, 339, 344
  Robert B., 293
GARRETT
  James H., 228, 333, 480
  J. H., 232
  Joseph G., 334
GARTH
  David, 274
GATES
  John, 231
GAULT
  David, 270
GAW
  --- 376
GAYLE
  Thomas, 253
GEORGE
  G. W., 77
  William H., 340
  W. N., 260
GIBBONS
  Thomas, 309
GIDDING (GIDDYNS)
  Harvey, 59
  James, 74
  James R., 339
  Louis, 106
  Peter, 106
GILBERT
  Bink, 233
  Elias, 259, 269
  G. H., 340
  John, 269
  Robert, 42
GI(L)LESPIE
  Henry, 263
  J., 365
  Joseph, 292
  Robert, 209
  Thomas, 292, 370
GINN
  --- 431
  G. S., 365
  Isaac, 328, 431
  John, 298
GIVEN(S) (GIVINS)
  Benjamin, 59, 66, 274,
    344
  Joshua, 66, 344
  Moses, 56, 59
CLAS(S)COCK
  N. A., 178
  Numan, 335
  Thomas, 155
GOODING

GOODING continued
  David, 105
GOSSETT
  David Mcakelroy, 259
GONLD
  --- 76
GRAHAM
  A. H., 77
  Elijah, 38, 42
  Elijah (Mrs.), 38
  George, 276, 277
  George G., 316
  James, 268, 327
  Joshua, 319, 327
  Sarah, 153
  William, 101, 255
GRANT
  Jesse R., 41, 79
  Rebecca, 282
  Robert, 306
  U. S., 41, 79
GRAY
  --- 70
  Dexter B., 364
GRAYSON
  Robert H., 251
GREEN
  John, 271
GREENHOW
  Frank, 42
  George, 42
  John, 38
  Richard, 38
GREENLEE
  John, 82, 318, 380
  John M., 363
  William, 82
GREENUP
  Christopher, 88, 92, 251
GREER
  W. D., 73
GRIFFITH
  Harvey, 331
  Hesekiah, 286, 294
GRIGSBY
  B. C., 343
  Isaiah, 67, 218, 221, 339
    341, 345
GRIMES
  --- 41, 79
  Henry, 153
  L. S., 86, 225, 227, 228
GROVER
  Jonathan M., 296
  Thomas, 290, 305
  Thomas M., 290
GRUNDY
  --- 76
GULLETT
  Dyal, 238
GULLY
  W. D., 341
  W. R., 365

    H.

HACKWORTH
  E. W., 341
  John, 339
  John J., 168, 169
  William, 169

HAINES
 James, 279
HALBERT
 --- 27
 Catharine, 395
 Daniel, 274, 291, 293,
  303, 304
 Frances A., 403
 George, 171, 248
 George T., 159, 173, 180,
  225, 336
 G. T., 125, 345
 Harlan R., 403
 Henry, 26, 253, 261,
  268, 282, 295, 307,
  330
 Isaac, 22, 394, 395, 396
 Israel, 252
 John, 255, 266, 274, 285,
  287, 291, 293, 303,
  314, 330
 John Bate, 430
 Lavinia A., 394
 Mary, 125
 Nathan, 291, 293
 Stephen, 266, 279, 280,
  321, 397
 W. C., 125, 132-134,
  160, 161, 204, 208,
  210, 228, 237, 337,
  338, 340, 341, 343,
  345, 426
 W. C., Jr., 219
 William, 171
 William C., 22, 154,
  171, 174, 395-403
 William C., Jr., 403
HALL
 Cornelius, 97
 J. E., 209
 Samuel L., 340
 S. L., 464
HAM
 --- 131
HAMILTON
 G. W., 341
HAMLIN
 Aaron, 226
 Hiram, 365
 John, 248
 William, 294, 309, 321,
  331, 332
HAMMON(D)
 --- 125
 Charles, 125
 John, 237, 271, 294
HAMPTON
 Charity, 391
 James, 300
 John, 331, 391
 John P., 333
 Joseph, 290
 Samuel, 284
 W. K., 230, 341
HAMRICK (HAMRICH)
 --- 195
 Jesse, 248, 282, 289,
  323
 Thomas H., 365
 Thomas M., 364
 W. H., 341

HAMRICK (HAMRICH) continued
 William, 334
 William F., 332
HANCE
 Alice, 26
HANFORD
 H. G., 460
HANNA
 R. C., 345
HANNAH
 David, 91
 Hugh, 87, 91, 95, 252,
  261
 James, 149, 369
 Thomas, 91
 William, 274, 280
HANNING
 Mathew, 312
HARD
 Jesse, 108, 140
HARDEN
 Harriet M., 42
HARDIN
 Ben, 349, 350, 352, 355,
  356, 358
HARDY
 William, 224
HARE
 Jonas, 252
HARGIS
 --- 215, 218
HARMON
 Alfred, 337, 340
 William, 252
HARPER
 Family, 22
 William, 25, 95, 102
HARRISON
 --- 40
 A., 341
 Alexander, 230
 Alfred, 177, 232, 336-
  338, 360
 Elizabeth, 105
 G. H., 340
 Headly, 197, 205
 J. B., 271
 John, 108, 253, 285
 T. B., 55, 178, 219,
  224, 294, 314, 503
 Thomas B., 173, 200,
  201, 204
HARRY
 Family, 256
 Amos, 256
 Evan, 256
 Joshua T., 357
 J. T., 256
HARVEY
 M., 82
 Roland, 42
HATHAWAY
 --- 300
 David, 321
HAWLEY
 James R., 171
HAWTHORNE
 --- 131
HAYDEN
 John, 323
 Jonathan, 285, 310, 323

HAYIMAN
 John, 279
HAYS
 E. R., 340
HAYSHIP
 J. H., 81
 J. M., 82
 John, 318
HEATH
 --- 283
 Jane, 275
 John, 91, 275
 John G., 88, 95
 William, 151, 275, 286, 291,
  294, 309, 312
 Zachariah, 91
HEINISCH
 --- 128
HELOY
 Peter, 279
HENDERSON
 --- 45, 128
 Andrew, 268
 Francis, 269, 289, 303
 G. A., 178
 James,
 Jane, 391
 P. C., 89, 342
 R. C., 360
 Thomas, 67, 335, 336, 342,
  344
 Thompson, 226, 230
 William P., 284
 W. P., 291
 W. R., 89, 342
 W. Rich., 342
HENDRICK
 --- 76
 John, 291
HENDRICKSON
 --- 315
 A. J., 67, 230, 344
 Daniel, 95, 310
 David, 27
 George F., 332
 G. W., 365
 Jack, 341
 John, 305, 324
 John T., 204
 J. P., 84
 Oke, 87, 91, 96, 101, 107
 William, 303, 310
 William R., 336-338
HENNESS
 Benjamin, 325
HENRY
 --- 42
HERBERT
 James, 107
 S. J., 388
 William, 388
HERN
 John, 277
 Milton, 277
HERRIN
 --- 198
 George W., 339, 340
HERRON
 George, 226
HESELTON
 George W., 340

HEVIN
  George W., 230
HICKS
  T. A., 365
HIGGINS
  R. W., 341
HIKE
  --- 128
HILDERBRAND (See
  HILTERBRAND)
HILL
  James, 253
HILLES
  John, 316
HILLHOUSE
  Samuel, 255
HILLIS
  --- 121, 122, 254
  Samuel, 255
  S. G., 36, 221, 227,
    341, 345, 373
  William, 36, 317
HILTERBRAND
  --- 45, 105
  J., 365
HIMES
  Charles, 302, 319
  G. H., 365
  John H., 292
  J. R., 365
  Robert M., 292
  Thomas, 292
  Thomas J., 205
  W. D., 365
  W. E., 365
  W. H., 365
HINER
  James, 160, 173
HINES
  Isaac T., 237
  John, 270
  J. T., 228
  R. R., 339
  Thomas, 270
HINTON
  Thomas, 53
HISEY
  Willis, 339
HOGGINS
  Towsand, 279
HOLBROOK
  S., 154, 337
  Socrates, 133, 152, 321,
    331, 332, 334-336,
    344
HOLDERNESS
  E., 80, 468
HOLLAND
  J. S., 365
  O. H., 196
HOLLE
  S., 333
HOLLENGER
  J. D., 365
HOLTON
  Ben T., 296
HONAKER
  --- 74
HOOBLER
  George, 324
  John, 324

HOOD
  Francis T., 271, 283
  T. J., 354
HOOVER
  Elizabeth, 293
  H., 365
  James, 332
  John, 268, 319
  Peter, 268, 304, 492
  Sarah, 382
HORD
  Francis T., 274, 276
HOUGHTON
  --- 444
  C. B., 235
HOWISON
  John, 140
HUBER
  --- 128
HUDSON
  Joseph, 252
HUFF
  J. P., 469
HUFFMAN
  John, 279
  Joseph, 318
  Richard, 279
HUGHBANK
  James, 286
HUGH(E)S
  Cornelius, 233
  George, 336
  J. N., 77
  T., 365
  Thomas, 279
  W. H., 45
HULL
  F. H., 345
  Frank, 67
  James, 226
  Samuel, 235
  William, 257
  W. R., 221
HUNT
  Abednego, 309, 312
  Armilda Jane, 406, 410
  Joseph, 411
HUNTER
  George T., 231
  John, 318
  Ophelia, 280
HURST
  Harmon, 327
  Lander, 323
HUSTON
  Joseph, 252
HYMES
  John, 248

I.

INFIRMARY
  (County), 117-122
INGRAM
  --- 128
  A. G., 386
  John C., 117, 167, 205,
    219
INGRIM (INGRAM)
  H., 161
  J. C., 160

INGRIM (INGRAM) continued
  John C., 427
  Margaret M., 427
IRELAND
  Samuel, 59
  William, 59
  William C., 334
IRVIN
  John, 38, 81
  Margaret, 38
  Moses, 258
  Olive, 391, 392
  Robert N., 38
  Thomas, 35
  Thomas M., 38, 42
  T. M., 38, 392
IRWIN
  --- 304
  Alexander, 280, 317
  Betsy, 284
  David, 317
  John, 284, 297
  Moses, 284
  Thomas W., 341

J.

JACK
  Rachael, 277
  Robert, 362
JACKSON
  Andrew, 45, 382
  B. F., 42
  James D., 392
  Jesse W., 387
  Thomas, 42
JACOBS
  James, 61
JAMISON
  --- 376
JANUARY
  Peter, 291
  Peter D., 295
JEFFERS
  W. S., 232
JENKINS
  Hesekiah, 155
JOHNSON
  --- 40, 438
  Family, 22
  Billie, 494
  David, 246, 278
  George, 317, 323
  Hannah, 278
  Jack, 71, 72
  James, 287
  John, 153, 279, 283, 307
  John W., 315
  Joseph, 279
  Mary, 397
  Mary Jane, 325
  S. R., 365
JONES
  Family, 32
  B., 365
  E. A., 89, 341, 360
  Emma, 430
  Eugene A., 470, 473
  Fleming, 292
  Pauline, 379
  Rufus N., 430

JONES continued
Sallie (Voiers), 430
Tacie G., 435
W. F., 231
William F., 196
William, 226
W. T., 337
Tanyard, 24
JORDAN (JORDON)
George W., 207
N. F., 73
William, 381

K.

KAHELER
--- 173
KAUFFMAN
H. G., 365
KELLUM
A., 365
G., 365
John, 269
Richard, 318, 330
William, 320
KELLY
Edward, 264
John, 327
William, 252, 316
KENDRICK
--- 261
John, 276, 280, 329
KENARD
(See KENNARD)
KENNARD
Family, 38
James, 319
Mary, 309
William, 95, 309
KENTON
Simon, 390, 396
KENYON
Jonathan, 92, 98, 248
Thomas, 251
KEY
Marshall, 88, 107
KEYSER
John, 379
John W., 339
KIBBY
Samuel, 201
KINDER
William, 196
KING
William, 325
KINNARD
Simon, 269
KIRK
Lewis, 210
Nathaniel, 329
KIRKENDALL
B. G., 45
KISSICK
William, 42
KLINE
John, 379
KNAPP
Joseph H., 274
W. H., 365
KNOX
John, 273

KNOX continued
Margaret, 389
KUBINS
Thomas, 311

L.

LAECH
John, 331
LAIRD
James, 293
John S., 252
LAISH
Jonathan, 268
LANE
Josepy, 266
Samuel, 268
LANG
A. M., 232
J. E., 340
John F., 238
LANTZ
Christian, 279
Christiana, 248
Curtis, 279, 306
Leonard, 279
LATIN
Theophilus, 279
LAUGHLIN
James, 252
LAUNTZ
America, 389
Curtis, 306
LAWSON
William, 37, 42
LAYTON
P. S., 344
LEACH(E)
John, 332
John V., 334
John W., 249, 282, 333-335
J. W., 291, 352
LEE
Annie B., 412
Barton, 149, 310, 369
James, 409
James A., 364
James F., 412
James H., 409
James Harrison, 406, 409-411
James M., 341, 363
J. M., 89, 341-343
Joseph Marion, 406, 412
Lennie B., 412
Louis, 409
Mary E., 412
Nancy J., 412
O. F., 89, 302
R. H. (Mrs.), 229
Richard Wilson, 268
Rosie A., 412
Thomas R., 412
LEITCH
John, 280
LEONARD
--- 287
LEVY
A., 82
LEWIS

LEWIS continued
--- 321
Charles, 108, 140
James, 168
Mary, 249
Merriweather, 16
M. P., 339
Stephen, 292
W. S., 342, 468
County, 15, 88-347
LILES
Henry, 327
Larkin, 306, 329, 502
LIIDLEY
--- 84
Thomas, 78, 82, 362
LINLEY
Isaac, 318
Joseph, 318
Thomas, 318
LISSON
Mary, 389
LITTLE
--- 292
George, 204
LITTLETON
Johnson, 315
LLOYD
William, 309
LOGAN
H. G., 365
John M., 266
Mary, 379
Tobias, 196
W. C., 312
William H., 196
LOONEY
--- 97, 101, 402
David, 254, 258, 301, 302
Peter, 269
LOVEL(L)
John, 78-80, 82, 84, 153, 178, 315, 318, 319
R. B., 80, 86, 178, 211, 214, 215, 315
Robert, 197
Robert B., 338
LOWDER
J. D., 345
LOWERY
Samuel G., 279
LUCAS
Henry, 325
LUMAN
Henry, 322
Jessee, 322
John, 277
LYKINS
D. D., 345
Dyal, 238
George, 465
G. W., 342
Isaac W., 339
J. W., 340, 341
Peter D., 238, 339
LYONS
Joseph, 249
William D., 316

Mc.

MC ANDREW(S)
John P., 174, 196, 209
MC BRIDE
John, 107
MC CALL
--- 385
John, 45, 160
Peter, 45
MC CANDLESS
John, 269
William, 269
MC CANE
John, 45
William, 45
MC CANN
Ailsie, 40
Alexander, 40
Amanda, 40
Arthur, 42
Edward, 39, 40
Edward B., 39, 455
Elizabeth, 39
Ella, 40
James, 39
John, 39, 40, 317, 456
John H., 8, 33, 455, 456
Mary Ann, 40
Nancy, 40
R. H., 45
Thomas, 40
William, 39-41, 268,
280, 281, 317
W. W., 39, 42
MC CARAHAN
John, 233
MC CLAIN
--- 86
E. W., 341
James, 92, 244, 247,
278, 279, 283, 303,
304, 314, 331, 332
John, 269
King D., 84, 269, 317,
326, 330-333
Squire, 257
MC CLUNG
Marion, 154
MC CONE
--- 86
MC CORMICK
--- 497, 498
James, 154, 265, 273,
278, 289, 302, 304,
317
MC CREARY
George, 308
MC DANIEL
--- 31, 267, 368
Alexander, 281
Ambrose, 27, 276, 315
Ambrose D., 31
Celia, 27
J. G., 111
John, 22, 24, 27, 28, 95,
102, 107, 149, 252,
265, 275, 294, 310,
365, 369
John B., 317
Nancy, 27
Sallie, 26
William, 27

MC DANIEL continued
William B., 281
MC DERMOTT
James, 201, 338
MC DOWELL
A. D., 362
J. C., 244
John, 154, 248
John G., 32, 87, 88, 91,
250, 251, 254, 274,
295, 304, 314, 322,
324, 331
MC ELDOWNEY
Family, 32
Robert, 334, 335
Samuel, 224, 337, 339
William, 146, 293, 295,
304, 306
MC ELVAIN
Thomas, 244
MC FARLAND
Edwin F., 235
MC GILL
Marion (Mrs.), 385
MC GINNIS
E. V., 365
MC GOUGIN
Elizabeth, 388
MC ILVAIN(E)
Hugh, 274, 295, 308
Thomas, 95, 98
MC KAY
A. H., 225
A. L., 469
MC KEE
Henry, 158, 339, 340
Samuel, 158, 168
MC KELLEP
Melissa R., 428, 429
MC KELLUP
Robert, 503
S., 388
U. B., 344
Uriah, 66, 320
Uriah B., 334
U. R., 155
MC KENSIE
--- 273
MC KENZIE·
--- 269, 310, 316
Alexander, 105, 324
Alexander S., 105
Anna, 105
Hannah H., 105
John, 269, 324
Sally, 105
Thomas, 105
MC KEY
T. J., 45
MC KINLEY
--- 479
MC KINNEY
Thomas, 268
W. H., 169
William S., 158
MC KINZIE
Alexander, 39, 41
Jane, 39
MC LEAN
John, 171
MC MILLER

MC MILLER continued
James M., 82
MC NEAL
Asa, 61, 62, 332, 335
James, 63, 64
Johnson, 64-64
J. W., 230
MC NUTT
John, 197, 279
Martha, 389
William, 268, 279
MC PIKE
James, 25, 102
MC VANEY
Moses, 37, 42

M.

MACHEN
William B., 343
MACKABOY
William, 330
MACKEY
Thomas, 316
William, 322
MADDOX
Elizabeth, 286
John, 271, 283
MADDUX
Benjamin, 274
John, 274
MAFFETH
J., 365
MAHAN
Thomas, 252
MANLEY
Thomas, 45
MANUEL
Andrew, 326
Samuel, 326
MAPLE
David, 59, 289
George, 255, 256, 262, 29
Melville, 59
MARCUS
M., 128, 131
MARKLAND
Jesse, 178, 337, 338, 340
MARKLIN
Jesse, 76
MARSHAL(L)
--- 292
Alexander K., 101
Charles C., 331, 332
Charles H., 344
E. M., 77
Flora, 456
Humphrey, 235, 456
Stuart, 274
Thomas, 66, 70, 71, 154,
257, 267, 270, 288, 290
305, 314, 325, 343, 344
William, 149, 152
MARTIN
--- 25
Allen, 317
Dudley, 317
Frenchy, 302
H. C., 271
James, 34, 95, 253
Lavinia Virginia, 357

MARTIN continued
Perry, 34
Samuel, 282
Sarah, 34
MATHINY
Jesse, 318
MAVITY
Ephraim P., 364
James S., 468
John, 454
John S., 454
John W., 289
J. S., 469
William Fletcher, 304
MAWK
Peter, 337
Peter C., 337, 339, 340
MAY
Andrew, 399
Charles, 45
John, 265, 392
John S., 356
Thomas, 392
MEADOWS
Marion, 381
Virginia, 381
MEANS
Amos, 228, 232, 237,
269, 324, 330
Andrew, 271
Cooper, 235
George, 244, 262, 287,
290, 329, 331
John, 255, 325, 330, 387
Joseph, 269
Margaret, 387
Nancy, 387
Phoebe, 387
Robert, 154, 269, 312,
322, 331-335, 362,
387
MEFFORD
Family, 22
--- 214
MEGLASSEN
Thomas, 320
MELSON
Family, 22
Fisher, 25
Jesse, 24
Joseph, 25
Spurgin, 25
MENIX
Alex, 323
MEREDITH (MERIDITH)
Mathias, 335
Rebecca, 262
Robert, 154, 262
MERSHAN
Thomas O., 335
METCALF
Thomas, 306
MIDDLETON
Isaac, 155
Lewis, 207
MIERS
Henry, 107
MILES
E. J., 72
MILLER
--- 38, 492

MILLER continued
Elias, 327
Jason, 327
MINER
Jesse, 238
MINERAL SPRINGS
17, 22, 41, 154, 275,
291, 296, 389
MITCHEL(L)
--- 85, 490
Elizabeth, 384
F. A., 464
Hannah, 383
H. I., 464
John, 333, 334, 336
Mathew, 357
T. A., 373
Theresa, 385
Thomas, 152, 244, 251,
253, 273, 275, 312,
331-333, 385
Thomas A., 339-343,
479, 486
Thomas H., 178
Thomas W., 132, 171,
173, 176, 180, 200,
201, 204, 337, 338,
342, 343
T. W., 219
William, 327, 329
MOFFETT
Susanna Belle, 449, 450
MONTEITH
John, 225
MONTGOMERY
John, 256
Joseph M., 332
MOONE
Samuel, 382
MOORE
--- 278
A. F., 225
Andrew, 256
E. L., 256
Elijah, 263
J., 28
James, 289
Jeremiah, 144, 277, 280
Jimmie, 256
John, 225, 318
Joseph, 318
Lewis, 256
M. D., 365
Nicholas, 337
Pres., 197
Tavenor, 78, 258, 305,
318
Thomas, 386
William, 248
W. W., 338
MOOREHOUSE
James, 252
MORGAN
--- 31, 301
D? B., 82, 318
Joseph, 254, 376
Pierpont, 420
MORRIS
John, 318
W. H., 45
MORRISON

MORRISON continued
Henry, 323, 327
Motley M., 304
Robert, 108, 140
MORSE
Nelson, 158
N. G., 201
MORTIMER
John, 292
MORTON
John R., 171
MOSS
George, 326
MOWER (See MOWERY)
David S., 390
Jacob, 172, 235, 335
Jacob P., 205, 387, 389,
390
J. L. P., 390
Samuel D., 390
MOWERY
Jacob, 319
William, 319
MOYLAN
--- 159
MULEER
L. A., 224
MULLINS
A. R., 231
MUMFORD
David, 84
MUNFORD
John, 318
MURPHY
John, 98
William, 98, 270
MYER(S)
--- 254
Eliza,
H. C., 77
Henry, 269
Henry C., 237, 340
Jacob, 255, 258, 269, 284,
318
John, 318
John M., 178, 228, 232
Robert, 269, 318

N.

NASH
James, 259
John, 279
Richard, 279, 332-334
NEAL
Jacob, 271
NELSON
Turner, 36
NEWSPAPERS
(Lewis County), 80, 81, 216,
219, 468
NICHOLLS
William, 290
NOGLE
Peter, 276
NOLAN
Thomas, 173
NOLEN
James, 339
S. A., 365
NORMAN

NORMAN continued
Margaret Alice, 145
NORRIS
Jackson, 160, 232
NORWOOD
James, 59, 60
William, 56, 59, 60,
309, 310
NOWLAND
Stephen, 156
NUTE
Charles, 178

O.

O'DANIEL
Elizabeth, 395
O'DOHERTY
William P., 339
OHARROW
--- 95
"OIL EXCITEMENT"
160, 170, 171
OLDS
Catherine, 257
Daniel, 257
OLIVER
Elias, 283
Thomas, 268
O'NEIL
Daniel, 153
ORCUTT
James, 279
ORMES
Moses, 281, 317
Moses, Jr., 281
ORT
J. T., 128
OSBORN
Champ, 201
OSBURN
Alex., 270, 291
Anderson, 291
John, 319
Madison, 319
Thomas, 322
OVEREND
William, 170
OWENS (OWINS)
Aaron, 247, 310, 345
Alfred, 291
Ellis, 291, 324
Francis M., 334
John, 271
Joshua, 281, 282
R. M., 82, 227
Robert M., 226
Wyatt, 82
Wyatt S., 333
OWINGS
Aaron,
Joshua, 282
OWRY
J. T., 342

P.

PALMER
Barton, 305
PARISH
R. O., 42

PARKER
--- 17, 24, 86
A. H., 225, 228, 237
A. Harvey, 360
Ambrose D., 312
Ambrose Dudley, 385
Anna Maria, 385
Benjamin W., 384
B. W., 232, 239, 309
Charles, 383
Daniel, 389
Edwin, 384
Eliza Preston, 385
Elizabeth, 384, 385
Emma, 385
Fred H., 385
Garland S., 245, 385
Georgia Ann, 384
Granville S., 385
G. Washington, 309
Harriet, 385
Harriet Lucy, 384, 385
Harry, 200, 248, 332, 384
Harry Thomas, 384
Harvey, 231, 383, 384
Jack, 84
James, 383
Jesse, 385
John, 296, 385
John F., 383
John Grant, 384
John T., 176, 336, 337,
366
John Thomas, 113, 117,
161, 167
J. W., 222
J. Win, 221, 226, 228
Leroy P., 334, 335
Leroy Preston, 329
Lizzie, 385
Lucy C., 404
Martha Ellen, 384
Mary Jane, 384
Mason Brown, 385
Melvina Ann, 384
Nancy, 383
Plumer, 385
Priscilla, 385
Rebecca, 385
R. M., 89, 341, 342
Robert, 291, 302, 384,
385
Robert H., 384
Rowland, 326
Rowland T., 23, 111,
244, 262, 296, 314,
323, 326, 329
R. T., 146
Sallie, 385
Seth, 171, 176, 215, 336,
385
S. H., 227, 339
Susan, 385
Thomas, 105, 152, 153,
264, 272, 277, 280,
283, 285, 290, 294,
310, 331, 383, 384,
385
Thomas D., 160, 161,
171, 173, 178, 304
W. B., 151, 152, 244,

PARKER continued
W. B. continued, 259, 262,
295, 302, 308, 320, 329,
340, 344, 509
W. D., 337
William, 332, 365, 383
William B., 263, 328, 343
William M., 339, 389
William S., 156, 282, 329,
331, 333, 337, 338, 385
Winslow, 111, 137, 252, 25
276
W. M., 389
W. S., 211, 316, 327
PARKS
Edward, 318
PASAHAL
John, 318
PATRICK
James A., 196
PATTERSON
--- 380
John, 307, 318
Betsy, 380
PAYNE
Thomas Y., 310
PECKELSIMER
John, 172
PEED
Gabriel, 270, 277
PELL
Henry, 35-37, 326
John, 333-335
John P., 154, 333
William, 200, 316
PENCE
Dyas, 237
PENDLAND
Alex., 196
George, 196
PENROD
R., 365
PERKINS
W. B., 207
PERRY
--- 40, 397
PETERS
Aaron, 279
David, 98
David, Jr., 279
John, 279
William, 278, 279
PETTIT
Robert, 365
PHILLIPPS
John, 244
PHIPPS
William, 84
PHISTER
Elijah, 73
PIERSAL
L. B., 225, 232
PIPER
John, 269, 277, 287, 324
PITTS
--- 101, 269
Isaac, 273
James Lane, 285
Noah, 279
Samuel Campbell, 286
William, 258, 286

PLUMMER
--- 131
A., 365
Abraham, 271
Alexander, 339
Almedia, 458
A. M., 458
Benjamin, 289, 294, 296, 313, 381
Cordelia, 458
H. F., 458
Jennie, 458
Lewis, 209, 214, 338
L. K., 458
Louis P., 457, 458
L. P., 458
Mart, 125
M. L., 458
Nelson, 274, 362
Reuben, 255
Solomon, 289
W. A., 458
William, 125, 457
POE
O. C., 365
POLLETT (POLLITT)
A. D., 67, 226
A. Dud., 339, 345
A. H., 226, 235
Alexander H., 404
B. D., 339-341
James, 317, 322, 404
James S., 336-339
John F., 227
J. S., 338, 342
Louder, 322
Morgan, 74
O. P., 89, 341-343, 464, 465
Orville P., 404
R. C., 447
R. W., 226
Samuel, 128, 326, 362, 441, 442
Thomas, 322
POLLY
David, 265, 304
Elizabeth, 304
POOL
Andrew, 317
Thomas, 40, 41, 280, 281, 317
William, 364
PORTER
Seth, 293
POWELL
David, 290
POWER(S)
--- 131, 295
Dempsey, 335
Henry, 276, 280
Joseph, 231
Joshua, 271, 277, 294, 296, 331-334
W. C., 178
POWLING
John, 24
John O., 275
William O., 291
PRECINCTS
148, 149, 151, 152, 158,.

PRECINCTS continued
160, 169, 170, 172, 195, 237, 263, 264, 298, 488
PRICE
James, 280, 281, 317
Mary, 376
PRIEST
Daniel,
William,
PROCTOR
Larkin J., 84, 333, 350
L. J., 344
PUGH
--- 25, 422
Bessie H., 459
Beulah L., 460
Bruce T., 460
James R., 219
J. R., 125
Mary A., 458
Nellie May, 460
Samuel B., 196, 336, 458
Samuel J., 225, 340
Samuel Johnson, 458-460
S. I., 340
S. J., 125, 128, 339, 342, 362, 468
PURCELL
G. L., 80
John, 196, 251, 305, 329
PURNELL
Mary Wallace, 421
PUTMAN
Daniel K., 306

Q.

QUEEN
Charles, 261
Claude Forest, 42
George (Mrs.), 38
G. L., 42
QUINTANCE
William, 271

R.

RADFORD
John, 137, 244, 248
RAGAN
O. G., 6
RAILROADS
235, 467
RALSTON
Joseph N., 285, 296
RAMSEY
--- 60
RAND
--- 172
Jacob W., 171, 200
J. W., 200
William S., 171
W. S., 370
RANKIN
Family, 32
RAYBORN (RAYBURN)
E. J., 339
Henry, 196
L. N., 89, 340
Robert, 249
William, 196, 322, 327

REA
Family, 318
George, 282, 298, 318
James, 279, 491
Robert, 249, 268, 279, 316, 491, 492
Thomas, 279
Thomas M., 233
T. M., 233
William, 81
READER
G. W., 226
REDDEN
Cole, 315
J. Cole, 386
Joseph D. (?), 224
Thomas, 379
Thomas E., 323
W. F., 196
REDMAN
G., 365
Samuel, 262
REED
Family, 318
D. D., 365
Ezekiel, 318
James, 108, 140, 318
John, 269
W. E., 339, 340
William, 77, 269
William E., 341
REEDER
George W., 363
G. H., 366
REGANSTEIN(ANE) (See REGENSTEIN)
REGENSTEIN
Anna B., 450
Clara, 45
Elizabeth, 453
Ellsworth, 449-454
Ellsworth, Jr., 453
Henry, 299
Henry L., 450
John H., 298, 299, 449
John H., Sr., 449
Maurice E., 450
O. M., 77
Omar, 299
Omar M., 450
REID
John, 269
Joseph B., 243
Walker, 88, 91, 92, 98, 102, 243
REIDINGER
J. H., 77
REIL(E)Y
Samuel, 249, 274
RICE
F. H., 200
RICHARDS
Caleb, 284, 306, 309
James, 268
Robert, 337
RIDDLE
Coleman, 323
RIGDON
Clayborn, 382
Kate, 382
RIGGS

RIGGS continued
  David, 269
  John, 268, 269
  R. A. P., 365
  Samuel, 269
  Sheldon, 318
ROBB
  David, 388
  Joseph, 243, 245, 246,
    251, 266, 287, 289,
    290, 306, 315, 319,
    321, 327, 330-335,
    388
  Robb, 271
  Robert, 95, 98, 137,
    332, 334
  Robert W., 329, 332, 333
  Roch, 85
  William, 262, 337, 338
ROBERTS
  --- 322
  Jack, 98
  Robert, 98
  Woodford, 304
  Woodruff, 282
ROCKEFELLER
  --- 420
ROE
  Edward, 335, 337
  F., 365
ROLF
  L., 127
ROPER
  William, 102
ROULSTON
  John M., 311
ROURK
  Almedia, 458
ROWLAND
  E. C., 341
  George, 72
  George W., 209
  James, 106, 255, 271,
    336
  T. J., 74
  William H., 365
ROWLEY
  Amanda, 386
  Benjamin F., 386
  Charles, 386
  Charlotte S., 386
  Edwin S., 386
  Eliza J., 386
  George W., 386
  Hiram T., 386
  James H., 386
  Millie J., 387
ROWSEY
  J. Louis, 443, 445
ROYSTER
  John, 327
  Levi, 327
  William, 327
RREDDEN
  Joseph D., 224
RUARK
  --- 254
  James, 317, 326, 336
  Jordon, 260, 327
  Joseph, 266
  Martha, 381

RUBY
  William, 365
RUFFNER
  Anges, 311
RUGGLES
  J. M., 384
  John, 220, 282
  Jonathan, 106, 273, 331-
    335
  L. B., 125, 363
  Lewis B., 225
  Moses, 228, 363
  S., 219, 232
  Socrates, 125, 228
  S. T., 365
  Susie (Mrs.), 36
  Thomas, 45, 226, 285
  William B., 335
RUMMANS
  (See RUMMINS)
RUMMINS
  Alex. S., 218
  J. D., 343

        S.

SABINS
  Thomas J., 322
SALISBERRY
  John, 106
SAMPSON
  D., 82
  David, 82
SANDERS
  George, 322
  Thomas, 326
SAULSBERRY
  George, 362
SAUNDERS
  Ivan W., 89
SAVAGE
  Francis Asberry, 325
  James, 96, 325
  James P., 325, 326
  John P., 325
  Pleasant M., 149, 324,
    325, 369
  Polly W., 326
  Sally, 325
  Samuel P., 325
  William P., 325, 328
SCHOOLS
  (Lewis County), 71, 75,
    119, 127-129, 137-139,
    145, 161, 172, 195,
    204-206, 210, 212,
    216, 224, 225, 237
SCHULL
  Levina, 415
SCHIVARTZ
  Henry, 77
SCOTT
  Ed., 252
  Jacob, 252
SEAMAN
  David, 318
  George, 364
SEATLEY
  A. H., 337
SECREST
  Brunette (Mrs.), 297

SECREST continued
  James D., 336
  Joseph D., 339
  O. E., 77
  W. W., 86
SECRET SOCIETIES
  467
SELLARDS
  E. C., 480
  Elias, 379
SETTLEMENTS, TOWNS
  5, 17, 20, 23, 34, 39-41,
    45, 50, 56, 57, 65, 73,
    74, 76-86, 91, 106, 108,
    111-134, 146, 158, 168,
    169, 198-200, 209, 237,
    238
SEXTON
  Daniel, 269, 281
SHAIN
  --- 292
  Ambrose, 365
  David, 252
  Robert, 252
  Thomas, 251, 252, 278, 2
    284, 293
  William, 252
SHARKS
  Jos. A., 342
  William, 340
SHAW
  Alfred, 42
  Allan, 42
  E. A., 42
  Frank, 42
  Frank G., 41, 42
  Green, 42
  Hardin (Mrs.), 357
  Hattie, 434
  R. H., 42
  Richard H., 434
SHELBY
  Isaac, 397
SHENHURST
  A. A., 86
SHEPARD
  (See SHEPHERD)
SHEPHERD (SHEPERD)
  86, 49, 496
  C. B., 82
  Cha(u)ncy B., 77, 78, 30
    331
  Howard, 196
  Robert, 293
SHERDINE
  Andrew, 268, 297
SHORTRIDGE
  Family, 22
  Samuel, 26
SHUMATE
  --- 42
SILVEY
  James, 271, 283, 286, 2
    295
SIMER
  M. V., 365
SIMPSON
  William J., 285-287, 27
    291
  W. J., 261
SINGLETON

SINGLETON continued
  --- 266, 306
  Fred, 331
  Fred R., 247, 251, 274,
    287, 331
  F. R., 206, 320, 343
  James, 276, 312
  James W., 265, 284, 312
SLATER
  John, 275
SLATON
  Jacob, 318
SLOAN
  Thomas, 108
SLOO
  Thomas, 140
SMALLEY
  Andrew, 204
SMALLIN
  Randall, 27
SMITH
  --- 416, 425
  Aquilla, 276, 280
  Balden, 31
  Betsy, 384
  David, 342
  Garret, 244
  Green, 149
  Green H., 271, 284, 295
  G. W., 305
  Henry, 95
  Henry J., 170
  James D., 170
  Joseph D., 318
  Josephine, 379
  Larret G., 253
  Martha W., 379
  Robert, 299
  S., 158
SMULLING
  Curtis, 323
SNIDER
  Sallie, 380
SNYDER
  Jeremiah, 322, 332
SOLDIERS' MONUMENT
  93
SONS OF TEMPERANCE
  81
SPARK(S)
  George, 259
  John, 82, 86
  Joseph, 155, 259, 279,
    363
  Joseph A., 208, 339, 360
  William, 82, 228, 341,
    363
SPAWN
  Michael, 318
SPENCE
  John, 251
  John M. Jr., 196
  Joseph, 265
SPENCER
  Samuel, 327
SPILLMAN
  S., 365
"SPRINKLE DOLLAR"
  495, 496, 499
SPRINKLE
  Josiah, 495, 499, 500

SPURGIN
  --- 260
  Elias, 317
  J., 365
  Lewis, 388
  Mary, 388
  W. D., 365
STAFFORD
  Ralph, 341
  Sophia W., 440
  Sylvester, 440
  William, 172
STAGG(S)
  --- 131, 151
  Family, 31
  Alex., 365
  Frank, 379
  John, 362
  Joseph, 152, 273
  Josiah, 152, 156
STAILEY
  (See STAL(E)Y)
  Christian, 252
  Ernest H.
  H. A., 131, 342
  Jacob, 326
  Susan, 326
STALCUP
  B. C., 34
  Elias, 253
  John, 34, 274, 305
STAMPA
  (See STAMPER)
STAMPER
  Bessie L., 440
  Cinda, 440
  Cora Mae, 440
  George Washington, 435-
    437
  George Washington, Jr.,
    437-440
  George W., Jr., 436
  G. W., 125, 128, 131
  James E., 440
  John, 436
  Joshua, 341, 438
  Julia, 440
  Marie, 440
  Rebecca, 440
  Sallie, 436
  William J., 440
STARKY
  William, 292
STEIN
  A. J., 128, 442, 443
STEPHENSON
  --- 108
  Arthur, 82, 153
  Calvin, 78
  Ed., 305
  Edward, 77, 82, 280,
    288, 305, 307, 318,
    331
  James, 252, 318
  James, Jr., 252
  John, 77, 87, 91, 101,
    105, 249, 257, 262,
    269, 283, 286-288,
    305, 307, 308
  Luther, 78
  Samuel, 78, 82

STEVENSON
  Arthur, 318
  Charles, 318
  Ed., 269
  Edward, 84
  Jack, 84
  James, 318
  John, 86, 269, 318
  John W., 334
  Polly, 84
  Pres. L., 269
  Samuel, 84, 119, 318
STEWART
  James, 364
  W. C., 365
STOCKHOLM
  John, 255, 378
STOCKTON
  George, 501
  John D., 88
STOCKWELL
  Michael, 252
STONE
  Edward, 220
  Ezekiel, 390, 504
  James, 504
  John, 332
  Laural, 220
  Ralph, 379
  Thomas, 31, 89, 390
STOUT
  C. E., 42
  James, 207, 297
  John, 32
  Mary, 325
  Mary Jane, 325
  Obadiah, Jr., 32
  Sally, 325
  Sarah Bell, 297
STRATTON
  --- 292
  Aaron, 31, 88, 91, 95, 98,
    111, 137, 251, 259, 262,
    274, 287, 288, 293, 302,
    322, 330, 331, 343
  Della, 375
  Joel, 259
  Thomas, 490
  Thompson N., 151, 322,
    328-331, 375
STREAMS, RIVERS
  16, 17, 20, 21, 25, 28, 31-
    35, 37-40, 45, 52, 53, 75-
    77, 83, 144, 151, 172, 173,
    237, 254
STRICKLETT(E)
  --- 28, 103
  Benjamin, 128
  Jacob, 34, 35, 330
  James, 34, 42
  James P., 363
  L. C., 338
  Lewis C., 334, 335, 337
  Peter, 105
  Pleasant, 84
  P. M., 384
  T. B., 219
  Thomas, 35, 125
  William, 37, 125
  William G., 35
  William R., 173, 174, 178 .

STRICKLETT(E) continued
W. R., 113, 161
STRODE (STRADE)
John, 314
William, 25
STROWBRIDGE
F. L., 499
STUBBLEFIELD
Beverly, 274
SULLIVAN
Abraham (Mrs.), 386
H. S., 342
John (Mrs.), 386
SUTHERLAIN
--- 367
William, 95
SWAP
George B., 468
SWEARINGEN
--- 23, 290
Alfred, 293
Daniel, 95, 255, 298
James, 248, 293
John, 101, 278
Marmaduke, 279, 293,
297
Mary, 321
Polly, 293
William, 363
W. T., 384
SWEET
Jackson, 197
J. W., 235, 444
SWIM
Anthony, 224
SWINGLE
George, 296, 323
SWITZELIN
George, 279
SYMPSON
William, 490

T.

TACKER
Thomas, 318
TAMNAN
C. A., 341
C. L., 342
TAYLOR
--- 80, 252, 351
A. A., 86
B. G., 153
C. A., 77, 86
Caleb, 271
Charles, 323
F. M., 225, 339
Harrison, 289
H. K., 225
John, 80, 84, 258, 380
Joseph, 249, 269, 281,
303, 326
Nesbit(t), 218, 290, 335,
362, 510
R. D., 82, 178
Richard, 290, 310
Robert D., 333
Thomas, 289
William, 311
William H., 160, 314, 317
William I., 363

TE(A)GAR - (TEAGER)
Adam, 107
Harlan, 49
Jackson, 226
John, 287
TEARIN
John, 365
TECUMSEH
40, 41
THATCHER
Bartholomew, 56
"THE DEADENING"
316
THOMAS
--- 26, 133
Family, 22
Abraham, 168
Abram, 158
Araminta, 422
Bruce Fraser, 422
Catherine, 26
Daniel, 25, 299, 317, 326
Dick, 91
Elijah, 21, 26, 27, 414
Elijah H., 314, 315, 330-
332
Elijah Hart, 416, 417
George, 26, 253, 266,
414, 416
George M., 155, 161, 171,
180, 228, 338, 363, 459
George Morgan, 412-423
G. M., 125, 204, 319,
336, 344, 345
Israel, 26, 248, 302, 416
James, 221, 226
Joanna, 383
John, 291, 315, 320, 332
Lucy, 381
Mary R. Minta, 459
Michael, 414
Plummer, 37, 91, 102,
253, 282
Rowland, 137, 252
Rowland, Jr., 252
Sarah, 26
Sarah E., 384
Solomon, 145, 271, 283,
294
S. Plummer, 88
Susanna, 304
Thomas, 91
Thomas H., 160, 161
Thomas Madison, 217
Walter, 422
William, 422
THOMPSON
Ambrose, 324
Anthony, 252
C. A., 365
J. D., 345
John, 106, 148, 260, 265,
269, 276, 277, 282, 289,
298, 306, 311, 328, 332-
335, 344
Mat(t)hew, 271, 284, 307,
310
Thomas, 284
William, 324
William B., 169
William H., 332

THOROUGHMAN
George W., 430, 432
John L., 42
U. C., 89
Ulysses Cravens, 430-435
Walter Grave, 435
W. C., 342
William, 431
TODD
James M., 160, 335
J. M., 156
TOLL(E)
--- 305
George M., 203
Henry, 77
Henson, 277
James, 59
John, 259, 310, 362
Jose, 298
Joseph, 298, 316
Laban, 304
Matthew, 331
Mat(t)hias, 285, 302, 312,
323, 332
TONCRAY(E)
David, 270
Ezra, 270, 299, 383
James, 226
Joseph, 293
TRABER
W., 228
TRACY
Isaac, 145
Margaret Alice, 145
TRENT
John, 269
TRIPLETTE
William, 19
TRUESDALE
F. M., 233
Jesse, 268, 269, 326
Jonathan, 233
TRUITT
--- 276
George, 282
Jabez, 365
TRUSSELL
Man(d)ley, 218, 337, 338
TUCKER
Ellis, 203
Thomas, 82
TULLY
Charles J.,
Jackson,
J. D., 97
John, 25, 260
John D., 25, 48, 60, 202,
209, 228, 388
John L., 59
J. W., 228
Mary, 26
Thomas J., 57
T. J., 74
William, 323
William J., 363
W. J., 197
TURNPIKES
(Lewis Co.), 178, 196-198
200-210, 213-217, 223-
226, 229-239
TYLER

TYLER continued
John, 70, 71

U.

UNDERWOOD
Jesse, 220

V.

VALLEY
J. K., 444
VANCE
Alexander, 266
Bruce, 77
David, 249
George, 267
John, 77
William, 380
VANCEBURG
Button Factory, 128
Canning Factory, 128
Deposit Bank, 173, 174, 228
Flouring Mill, 174
Hotel Co., 174
VANDEGRAFT
James, 101
VANHORN
Paul, 269
VAN WEST
Abraham, 276
VAN WINKLE
E. L., 172
VAUDEN
P. B., 197
VAUGHN
Eli, 279, 320
John, 279
Thomas, 279
VAWTER
Pascal, 205
VEACH
John, 333
John W., 333, 334
Thomas, 252
VEERS
Edward, 23
VICTOR
Alsea, 280
Samuel B., 276, 280
William B., 280
VINCENT
Charles, 274
VIRGIN
Brice, 318
Matthew, 77
VOIER(S) (VOIRES)
Family, 37
Isaac, 225
John, 305
Patsy, 385
Robert, 95, 253, 336
Robert T., 363
Sallie, 430

W.

WADDELL
John, 333, 334
WADDLE

WADDLE continued
John T., 331, 334
WADE
Elijah, 76
William, 81, 318, 363
WAITE
--- 19
Jonathan, 493-497
"WAITE DOLLAR"
496
WALKER
--- 17
D. M., 460
Hugh, 290
I. I., 480
John, 362
R. T., 365
Thomas J., 309, 312, 338, 339, 362, 344
T. J., 344
William, 137, 270, 276, 291
WALLACE
Edward, 303, 311
WALLINGFORD
Family, 32
B. A., 231
John, 98, 288, 289, 296
Mark, 154, 155
Mary, 382
M. W., 221
Neal, 98
Nicholas, 327
Silas, 323
Thomas G., 334, 335
William R., 365
W. N., 207, 218
WALTERS
H. L., 342
WARD
Joseph, 260
Joseph G., 311
Thompson, 265-270
WARDER
Hiram, 226
H. T., 220, 223
W. T., 220
WARNER
George, 306
WARREN
James, 322
WARRING
Thomas, 108, 140
WASHINGTON
George, 25
WATKINS
Charles, 280
Joseph, 264
William, 78, 95, 152, 255, 275, 302, 305, 310
WATSON
Susan, 380
WAU
--- 492
WAUGH
--- 266
WEATHERS
--- 377
WEAVER
Thomas, 292
WEBB

WEBB continued
--- 131
WEBSTER
J. W., 365
Nathan B., 333, 334
N. B., 160, 173
WILLMAN
Ida, 299
Jeremiah, 233, 299
WELLS
B. T.,
J. M., 225, 237, 340, 342, 445
John G., 171
John S., 425
Matilda, 495
Sallie A., 423, 425
William W., 495
WEST
James, 268, 278, 323
John, 268, 322
Samuel, 197
Staten, 323
T. H., 205
Thomas, 295, 327
WHEADEN
Ishabod, 287
WILEY
James, 269
John, 301
WILL
G. M., 341
WILLIAM
Harry, 290
WILLIAMS
Allen, 318
Benjamin, 322, 382
Cora, 382
James, 382
John, 382
John W., 382
Joseph, 382
Lucinda, 382
Mary, 382
Robert, 382
R. R., 363, 339
Sallie Ann, 382
Samuel, 280
Samuel W., 338, 339
Thomas, 325, 327, 382
Washington, 382
Zachariah, 289, 382
WILLIAMSON
William, 278
WILLIM
Catherine, 388, 421
Ed., 341, 343
Ernest, 388
George, 486
George T., 427-430
Harry, 329, 388, 421, 428
J. C., 234, 340, 464
John P., 171, 173, 388
Sarah, 380
Thomas H., 388, 428, 429
William, 388
W. J., 237
WILSON
--- 23, 101
Family, 22
Andrew, 257, 279, 283, 303, 304

WILSON continued
  Angus V., 336, 337
  A. V., 365
  George, 302, 303, 305, 425
  George F., 423-425
  George McC, 331, 332
  George McCreary, 326
  Hugh, 279
  James, 95
  James G., 232, 452
  James S., 279
  John, 279, 306, 425
  John G., 279
  John Samuel, 425
  Jonathan, 263
  Joseph S., 279
  M. O., 470
  R. D., 297, 340
  Robert D., 425
  Robert Dye, 424-427
  Samuel, 101, 278, 303-396, 425
  Thomas, 197, 254
  Thomas C., 339, 464
  William, 24, 276
  William George, 95, 101
WINDER
  --- 74
WINSOR
  William, 328
WINTER(S)
  --- 74
  James, 245, 249, 255
  S. L., 365
  W. W., 384

WITTY
  J., 365
WOLLEN
  Thurston, 255
WOOD
  Benjamin, 257
  Charles, 77, 269, 297
  Daniel, 268
  F. M., 344
  James, 297
  John, 297
  John (Mrs.), 297
  John T., 84
WOODRUFF
  David, 282
WOODS
  Charles, 286
WOODWORTH
  --- 169
  Elizabeth, 503
  Labun, 158
WOOSTER
  --- 503
WORMALD
  Marian, 453
WORTHINGTON
  William, 255
WRIGHT
  George, 495, 496
  Thomas, 269
  W. H., 340, 341

Y.

YANCY
  A. l., 225

YANCY continued
  William, 270, 292
YAPP
  Thomas, 269
YATES
  Ira, 365
YEAGER
  Samuel, 201
YOUNG
  --- 60
  Alexander, 277, 286, 304
  Bennett H., 346

Z.

ZORNES
  Andrew,
  Martha, 257
  Thomas, 327

www.ingramcontent.com/pod-product-compliance
Lightning Source LLC
Chambersburg PA
CBHW031115020426
42333CB00012B/91